Dedication

To Debbie, Tom, Erin, and Maura, thank you for loving me.

To my mother, Mary Murphy, thank you for being solution-focused
before there was a word for it.

Second Edition

Solution-Focused Counseling in Schools

John J. Murphy
University of Central Arkansas

AMERICAN COUNSELING ASSOCIATION
5999 Stevenson Avenue
Alexandria, VA 22304
www.counseling.org

Second Edition

Solution-Focused Counseling in Schools

10   9   8   7   6   5   4   3   2

American Counseling Association
5999 Stevenson Avenue
Alexandria, VA 22304

Director of Publications
Carolyn C. Baker

Production Manager
Bonny E. Gaston

Copy Editor
Rachel Fending

Editorial Assistant
Catherine A. Brumley

Cover and text design by Bonny E. Gaston.

Library of Congress Cataloging-in-Publication Data

Murphy, John J. (John Joseph), 1955-
    Solution-focused counseling in schools / John J. Murphy. — 2nd ed.
        p. cm.
    Rev. ed. of: Solution-focused counseling in middle and high schools.
    Includes bibliographical references and index.
    ISBN 978-1-55620-247-6 (alk. paper)
        1. Counseling in middle school education—United States—Case studies.
2. Counseling in secondary education—United States—Case studies. 3. Counseling
in education—United States—Case studies. 4. Solution-focused therapy—United
States—Case studies. 5. Problem-solving therapy—United States—Case studies.
I. Murphy, John J. (John Joseph), 1955- Solution-focused counseling in middle and
high schools. II. Title.

    LB1620.5.M83 2007
    373.14--dc22   2007039883

Table of Contents

Preface

This is a book about helping people change school problems in respectful ways that honor their strengths, wisdom, and dignity. Thanks to researchers, we know more than ever about what works in helping people change. *Solution-Focused Counseling in Schools* translates the latest research into practical strategies for resolving problems from preschool through high school. Every strategy is based on an abiding faith in people's resilience and resourcefulness, even in the most difficult circumstances. This is not your typical counseling approach, which is precisely its strength.

The purpose of the book is to illustrate solution-focused counseling in action with a variety of clients and problems. Given that most people learn best through real-life examples, there are many dialogues from actual counseling sessions that I have conducted with students and others. The dialogues are often accompanied by commentary to provide an up-close and personal experience of solution-focused counseling.

Because schools are not set up for counseling, we need to adapt to schools. This may mean conducting counseling sessions whenever and wherever we can—on the playground, in the lunchroom, on the phone with a parent, while walking alongside a student or teacher in the hallway, and so forth. In solution-focused counseling, every contact is viewed as an opportunity for change.

While retaining the practical emphasis and conversational style of the first edition, *Solution-Focused Counseling in Middle and High Schools,* this book includes the following new features:

- A broader focus that covers preschool through high school students
- New examples and dialogues involving different clients and different problems
- Stronger emphasis on the client–counselor relationship, along with practical strategies for building cooperative relationships
- Client-based accountability methods for obtaining feedback on the usefulness of counseling services
- Additional practice exercises at the end of each chapter
- An expanded appendix section with user-friendly handouts, protocols, and other practical tools

This book was written primarily for school counselors, psychologists, social workers, graduate students, and others involved in serving preschool through high school students. Teachers, administrators, and parents have also found this approach to be useful in their work.

For the sake of clarity, the term *client* is used to describe anyone with whom you work to change a school problem, such as a student, parent, or teacher. *Counseling* refers to anything you do with clients to resolve school problems. This includes conducting individual and group sessions with students as well as working with parents and teachers. The term *solution* refers to a noticeable improvement in the problem, not necessarily its total resolution or elimination.

In teaching this approach throughout the world, I have discovered that school practitioners find it appealing for various reasons. For many, the simple and pragmatic emphasis on doing what works is a refreshing change from more cumbersome approaches that are impractical for schools. The positive focus on strengths, goals, and hope is also appealing. Most of us entered this profession to lift people up by helping them help themselves. The client-driven philosophy of solution-focused counseling is very compatible with this goal. The fact that solution-focused counseling accommodates diverse opinions is another attractive feature in an ever-changing and multicultural world. Last but not least, practitioners often report that it is energizing and enjoyable to work with people in this way. These are just a few of the reasons why this approach appeals to helping professionals and holds great promise for schools of the 21st century. But don't take my word for it. Read on, and decide for yourself.

Acknowledgments

A big thanks goes to Steve de Shazer and Insoo Kim Berg for their development of solution-focused therapy. They will be greatly missed, but their ideas live on in this book and many other places. I am also grateful to Barry Duncan, a friend and colleague with whom I have collaborated on several projects over the years. Barry directed my postdoctoral training in family therapy and continues to inspire me by his passion for putting clients first and honoring their ideas and resources.

I am thankful to the University of Central Arkansas for grant funding and to David Skotko, Chair of the Psychology and Counseling Department, for his support of this book. Thanks also go to my colleagues and students in the Psychology and Counseling Department. Many students gave generously of their time to read drafts and provide feedback on versions of the manuscript. A special note of appreciation goes to Chrystal McChristian, Debbie Murphy, April Burling, and Hannah Fielder Fulks for their extensive proofreading assistance. The encouragement and patience of Carolyn Baker, Director of Publications for the American Counseling Association, have been greatly appreciated. I couldn't ask for a better editor. I cannot begin to express my gratitude to my wife, Debbie, who supported me in countless ways during my work on the book. Thanks also go to Tom, Erin, and Maura, who inspire me to reach out to others and try to make a positive difference in the world.

To workshop participants and readers of the original edition, thank you for the feedback over the past several years. Finally, I owe a tremendous debt to the students, parents, and teachers with whom I have been privileged to work. They have been my greatest teachers, and their lessons are woven into every page of this book.

About the Author

John J. Murphy, PhD, is a professor of psychology and counseling at the University of Central Arkansas. He also works as a mental health consultant with Conway (Arkansas) public schools and consults with other school districts and agencies in the United States and overseas. Dr. Murphy taught high school before receiving his doctorate in school psychology from the University of Cincinnati. He completed postdoctoral training in family therapy and has written several books, chapters, and articles on positive approaches with children, adolescents, and school problems. He received the American School Counselor Association's Best Book of the Year award in 1998 for *Solution-Focused Counseling in Middle and High Schools* (American Counseling Association), was named one of the top five school psychologists in the United States by the National Association of School Psychologists, and is featured in the videotape training series *Child Therapy With the Experts* (www.psychotherapy.net). Dr. Murphy is a popular workshop presenter who has trained thousands of helping professionals throughout the world.

To offer feedback on the book or inquire about training, contact Dr. Murphy at the following address:

Dr. John J. Murphy
Department of Psychology and Counseling
University of Central Arkansas
201 Donaghey Avenue
Conway, AR 72035-0001
(501) 450-3193
E-mail: jmurphy@uca.edu
Web site: www.drjohnmurphy.com

PART ONE

Foundations of
Solution-Focused Counseling

CHAPTER 1

Jolene: An Introduction to Solution-Focused Counseling

Force is no remedy.
—John Bright, *On the Irish Troubles*

This chapter introduces solution-focused counseling through an example involving a student named Jolene. After a description of a typical problem-focused approach, solution-focused counseling is presented as a practical way of enlisting Jolene's cooperation and resolving the problem.

Going Nowhere Fast

Jolene, age 16, was referred for counseling because of behavior and academic problems. Most of the problems occurred in Mr. Guinn's science class. Mr. Guinn described Jolene as defiant and unmotivated, adding that she was failing his class for the second time despite having the ability to pass. When confronted about school problems, Jolene would shrug her shoulders and say one or more of the following:

- I don't know.
- It's not my problem.
- Everyone needs to back off and leave me alone.
- Science is stupid.
- Nobody understands.

Jolene reacted in similar ways when lectured by her parents or teachers about the importance of passing grades to her future. Her parents' efforts to reason with her usually ended in a shouting match.

The school counselor was asked by Jolene's parents and teachers to meet with her and "make her understand" what she was doing to herself. They also wanted to know why she refused to work harder and behave better in school. Jolene arrived at the counselor's office, slumped down in the chair, and stared at the floor.

Counseling Session #1: "Getting Through" to Jolene

Counselor: Jolene, I'm trying to help you here, but you have to cooperate. I can't do it for you, your teachers can't do it for you, and your parents can't do it for you. You are the only one who can make things better for yourself, and things will keep getting worse until you decide to do that. Why are you making this so hard for yourself and everybody else?

Jolene: [shrugs her shoulders and slumps lower in the chair] I don't know.

Fifteen minutes later . . .

Counselor: Jolene, we're all trying to help you. If we didn't care about you, we wouldn't be spending this time trying to help you. Do you know what I'm saying?

Jolene: Yep.

Counselor: Well, what are you going to do?

Jolene: [shrugs her shoulders] I don't know.

Counselor: Well, I hope you're going to make a good choice and turn things around for yourself. Your discipline record keeps getting worse, and your grades are not going to look good on your transcript. It's going to get worse unless you do something about it.

Jolene: Can I go now? The bell is about to ring.

Counselor: Yes, you can go. Please think about what I said. I've seen these things get worse and worse for students. The sooner you change, the better. Okay?

Jolene: Yep. [makes a hasty exit]

Going Nowhere Even Faster

Things got worse over the next few weeks as Jolene's discipline file grew thicker. She received several in-school suspensions and was being considered for alternative school. Everyone intensified his or her response to the problem in the following ways:

- Mr. Guinn and several other teachers lectured Jolene about her attitude and performance, frequently sending her out of class to the discipline office.
- Her parents kept asking her why she refused to change. They told the counselor that they had tried everything, and nothing had worked.
- The counselor felt frustrated and helpless because everyone was looking to counseling for the quick fix.
- Jolene refused to acknowledge the problem or the need to change. She continued to feel angry and misunderstood by her teachers, parents, and school counselor.

Counseling Session #2: More of the Same

Jolene met for a second time with the counselor, who emphasized the gravity of the situation and reminded her that she was headed for serious consequences unless she changed quickly.

Counselor: You're digging a big hole for yourself, and it's getting harder to get out of. What's it going to take, Jole.

Jolene: Huh?

Counselor: What's it going to take for you to pull yourself out of this mess?

Jolene: [shrugs her shoulders] I don't know.

Counselor: Do you realize how close you are to a suspension or alternative school?

Jolene: Pretty close.

Counselor: Real close. Are you willing to shape up in Mr. Guinn's class?

Jolene: I guess so.

Jolene left the office, shoulders slumped and head down, and returned to class. The counselor stared at the wall, feeling defeated and wondering how to get through to Jolene.

A Common Scenario in Schools

Jolene's situation is familiar to many students, parents, teachers, and counselors. The people involved in the problem are stuck in a vicious cycle. The harder they try to resolve the problem, the worse it gets. The worse it gets, the harder they try.

Why is it so easy for students, parents, teachers, and counselors to continue doing "more of the same" when it is not working? What can we do to get unstuck or to avoid these cycles in the first place? Is there a better way to approach students and school problems? These questions are addressed throughout the book.

Most helping models focus on the problem. Assessment clarifies the problem's origin, history, and presumed causes; treatment corrects deficiencies and weaknesses. In school counseling, an exclusive focus on the problem implies that there is something wrong or defective about the student. When students do not implement the helper's suggestions, they are considered resistant. This creates two problems—the original one and the student's so-called resistance. As evidenced with Jolene, making repeated attempts to impose our ideas on students is like trying to push a river in a different direction. Besides the fact that it doesn't work, everyone involved becomes more frustrated, fatigued, and hopeless. Solution-focused counseling offers a refreshing and practical alternative.

Solution-Focused Counseling: A Practical Alternative to "More of the Same"

Solution-focused counseling offers great promise as a practical, cooperative approach that shifts the focus from what's wrong to what's working with students. The input and strengths of students are actively sought and applied toward solutions. This positive focus is effective in engaging students' attention and motivation and in resolving problems as quickly as possible.

Solution-focused counseling is based on the notion that we work for the student, not the other way around. Outcomes are enhanced when we conform to students instead of expecting them to conform to us. We can partner with students in setting goals, selecting interventions, and evaluating outcomes. People are much more willing to work toward personally meaningful goals than goals imposed on them by others. As illustrated next, cooperation and solutions are also enhanced by a focus on the student's strengths, resources, and successes.

Jolene Revisited: A Solution-Focused Approach

The following excerpt is from Jolene's first meeting with a different counselor later in the school year. Unlike the previous counselor, who tried to convince Jolene that she needed to change, the new counselor adopts a solution-focused approach involving the following features:

- Asking Jolene what she wants from counseling instead of trying to talk her into a different goal
- Cooperating with Jolene's view of the problem instead of ignoring or challenging it
- Focusing on what's right versus what's wrong with Jolene

Note the difference in Jolene's response to this new approach.

Counselor: I've already talked to your parents and some of your teachers, so I have a pretty good idea of where they're coming from. But I need your help. I need to know what *you* want to see happen with all this school stuff.

Jolene: I'll tell you, but you probably won't believe me.

Counselor: Try me.

Jolene: Okay. I want to get a better grade in science. Nobody believes me, but I do.

Counselor: Why do you want a better grade?

Jolene: I don't want to take this class again for the *third* time. I couldn't handle that.

Counselor: Two times is enough, huh?

Jolene: Really.

Counselor: What kind of grades are you making?

Jolene: Ds and Fs.

Counselor: Are Ds and Fs all right with you, or do you want different grades?

Jolene: What do you mean?

Counselor: Well, everybody's different. I've met some students that are okay with getting Ds and Fs, and others that want As. So I was wondering what kind of grades you would be satisfied with.

Jolene: I'd rather have a C average. It's my second year in this stupid class. I failed last year, and I *have* to pass this year. I couldn't live through another year of this.

Counselor: Have you ever had a C in science for any quarter or grading period last year or this year?

Jolene: Yeah.

Counselor: When?

Jolene: Second quarter. It's been Ds and Fs since then. Mostly Fs.

Counselor: The second quarter of *this* year?

Jolene: Yeah.

Counselor: Just a couple of months ago?

Jolene: Yeah.

Counselor: Wow. What was different about that second quarter when you got the C?

Jolene: I just sat there and did my work, but now there's people around me talking and messing around and all that. And he blames it on me and kicks me out, but he doesn't kick them out. He'll give them a couple minutes after class, and that's as far as it goes.

Counselor: Do you feel like he's picking on you?

Jolene: Yeah.

Counselor: Singling you out and just trying to nail you?

Jolene: Yeah.

Counselor: Okay.

Jolene: He calls my home, too, and tells my stepdad stuff. Then my stepdad yells at me, and I try to tell him it wasn't my fault. He says, "I don't want to hear it," and then I get grounded.

Counselor: So this science class thing is causing you some hassles at school *and* home?

Jolene: Yeah. It's a real bite.

Counselor: Sounds like it. What are some things you've already tried to help improve your grades and get you to your goal of passing the class?

Jolene: Asking more questions.

Counselor: What do you mean?

Jolene: Sometimes I'll ask questions. I'll ask him how to do something and he'll say, "Put your hand down. Wait until later." Then he wonders why we don't turn in our work.

Counselor: So asking questions hasn't worked?

Jolene: No.

Counselor: Okay. What other things have you tried?

Jolene: I've tried sitting in the back and not saying anything.

Counselor: How did that work?

Jolene: What do you mean?

Counselor: Did you get kicked out more or less when you sat in the back, compared to when you sat other places?

Jolene: Less.

Counselor: So it worked out better for you?

Jolene: It worked out better for me because I was farther away from him.

Counselor: Were your grades better or worse when you sat in the back?

Jolene: Probably better, because I paid more attention, and I took the work home to do. Plus, when I'm in the back, I'm not around my friends, and that probably helps. My friends get pretty rowdy sometimes.

Counselor: Okay. Is it possible for you to sit in the back now?

Jolene: I don't know. I guess. He doesn't care where we sit.

The Rest of the Story

The counselor and Jolene continued to discuss how she could do more of the things that helped her get better grades, such as sitting away from her rowdy friends. Several strategies for improving grades were developed, and Jolene implemented most of them. Discipline referrals decreased by about 50% during the remainder of the school year. Although she did not earn a C in science, she improved enough to pass the course and to move on to 11th grade.

Dropping the Rope

When faced with school problems, adults often engage in a tug of war with students. The harder we try to change them or pull them over to our way of thinking, the deeper they dig in and resist. Meanwhile, the tension grows, and the problem gets worse. The best way to avoid these power struggles is to "drop the rope" altogether and work with rather than against students. In Jolene's case, the power struggles with her first counselor were avoided when the second counselor worked with Jolene's perceptions instead of trying to change them. Jolene cooperated because there was nothing to resist. You can't have a tug of war if no one is pulling the other end of the rope.

Summary and Conclusions

Jolene's case offers important hints about what works and does not work in counseling students. As illustrated with the first counselor, we sometimes challenge students' perceptions when they appear irrational or unwise from our perspective. Unfortunately, this usually backfires and makes matters worse.

Instead of trying to force Jolene into changing, the second counselor treated her as a competent collaborator and consultant. Jolene supplied all the necessary material for intervention and was actively involved in developing strategies for improving her science grade. It was no surprise that she followed through on these interventions. After all, it is hard to resist your own ideas! As illustrated throughout this book with a variety of clients (Appendix A), solution-focused counseling treats clients as expert consultants and makes generous use of their input and resources to build solutions to school problems.

Practice Exercises

1. How did the second counselor's approach to Jolene differ from the more typical approach to young people with school problems?
2. Select a small group of elementary or secondary school students who are willing to share their opinions about what works best in adults' efforts to help them. Have them brainstorm a list of "dos and don'ts" that they would recommend to counselors who work with students on school problems.
3. Think of a young person you are currently working with, and list a few ways that you could increase his or her involvement and contributions.
4. In your next counseling session, enlist the student as an expert consultant by asking for his or her ideas about improving things at school. How might these ideas be incorporated into specific school-based interventions?
5. Consider establishing a student advisory group consisting of about five students who agree to meet with you once or twice a month to provide counseling ideas, advice, and other forms of help. Does this strike you as a useful idea? If so, how would you go about doing it?
6. Describe one small step that you are willing to take in your practice as a result of the information in this chapter.

CHAPTER 2

Empirical and Conceptual Foundations

Counselors just don't understand. . . . You have the solutions, for yourself, but
they say "Let's try this and let's try that," and they're not helping.
—Molly, 10-year-old student

It is the client's self-healing capacities and resources that are
responsible for the resolution of problems.
—Bohart & Tallman, 1999, p. xii

The case of Jolene from Chapter 1 highlights some of the practical advantages of solution-focused counseling in schools. This chapter describes its empirical and conceptual foundations by addressing the following areas:

- Core ingredients of effective counseling
- Positive psychology
- Treatment acceptability
- Cultural considerations
- Empowerment
- The sociology of childhood
- Developmental considerations
- A systemic view of schools, students, and school problems

Ingredients of Effective Counseling: The Change Pie

Change is the essence of counseling. Students enter counseling because someone, usually a teacher or parent, desires a change in their school performance or behavior. Our usefulness depends largely on our ability to help people change. Empirical research offers valuable hints for working with people in ways that promote rapid change in school problems.

Let's start with some good news from researchers. Counseling is generally effective for children and adolescents (Kazdin, 2004; Kazdin & Weisz, 2003). This encouraging finding leads to two questions that drive this section and the remainder of the book:

- What makes counseling effective according to the research (core ingredients)?
- What can we do to promote optimal and efficient outcomes on the basis of the research (counseling strategies)?

9

Figure 2.1 draws from decades of research on what works in helping people change in therapy and counseling (Asay & Lambert, 1999; Lambert & Ogles, 2004). The figure includes hundreds of empirical studies with a wide range of clients, settings, problems, and practitioners. On the basis of their comprehensive analyses, Asay and Lambert (1999; Lambert & Ogles, 2004) concluded that effective outcomes result primarily from the operation of four core ingredients, or common factors, of change. These factors, and their percentage of contribution to successful outcomes, are as follows (Asay & Lambert, 1999):

- *Client factors* (accounting for 40% of change)—strengths, interests, values, social supports, and other resources
- *Relationship factors* (accounting for 30% of change)—respect, validation, and collaboration
- *Hope factors* (accounting for 15% of change)—positive expectancy and anticipation of change
- *Model/technique factors* (accounting for 15% of change)—the practitioner's theory and techniques

These core ingredients are called common or nonspecific factors because they are not tied to specific theoretical orientations or counseling models. They are highly interrelated in that the enhancement of one factor strengthens the others. For example, clients may become more optimistic (hope factor) when encouraged to apply their unique strengths and resources toward solutions (client factor). Likewise, a counselor's intervention suggestion (model/technique factor) is more

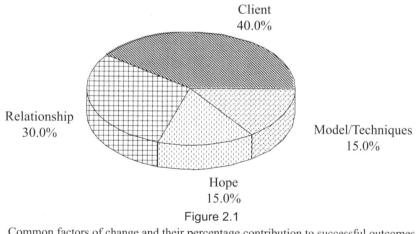

Figure 2.1
Common factors of change and their percentage contribution to successful outcomes
(the "change pie").

Note. Adapted from "The Empirical Case for Common Factors in Therapy: Quantitative Findings," by T. P. Asay and M. J. Lambert, 1999, in *The Heart and Soul of Change: What Works in Therapy,* by M. A. Hubble, B. L. Duncan, and S. D. Miller (Eds.), Washington, DC: American Psychological Association. Copyright 1999 by the American Psychological Association. Adapted with permission.

likely to be accepted and implemented when the client perceives the counselor as caring and respectful (relationship factor).

Every strategy in this book is designed to expedite solutions by empowering the common factors of change. These factors are discussed below in the order of their significance in the counseling process.

Client Factors: The Filling

Common factors of change can be viewed as the essential ingredients of a home-baked pie (Murphy & Duncan, 1997). In the "change pie" metaphor of effective counseling, client factors represent the main ingredient: the filling. Ignoring the strengths and resources of students and others is like baking a pie without the filling.

The term *client factors* refers to naturally occurring assets that students and others bring to counseling, including their strengths, successes, beliefs, values, faith, persistence, hobbies, coping skills, resilience, social supports, potential for change and growth, and changes that are already happening. These are the most powerful of all factors in the counseling process (Bohart, 2006). In their extensive review of research, Tallman and Bohart (1999) concluded that the client's capacity for self-healing is "the most potent common factor in psychotherapy" and "the engine that makes therapy work" (p. 91). Asay and Lambert (1999) reported that client factors account for a substantial 40% contribution to effective outcomes in counseling.

These findings call for a radical change in the way we approach school problems and the people who experience them. Students who are referred for services have often been portrayed as having little to offer toward their own improvement. However, research has made it clear that effective counseling helps people apply their unique resources toward solutions (Asay & Lambert, 1999). As illustrated with Jolene in Chapter 1, solutions emerged when the counselor respected and utilized the client's ideas and previous successes. Outcome research encourages us to view students as resourceful and vital partners in the counseling process. Solution-focused counseling seeks to discover and apply client factors toward school solutions. These factors are there for the asking with every client and every situation.

Relationship Factors: The Crust

Relationship factors are the second most important ingredient in counseling, representing a 30% contribution to change (Asay & Lambert, 1999). The client–practitioner relationship can be defined as the attitudes and feelings that the client and practitioner have toward each other and the ways they are expressed (Gelso & Hayes, 1998). Relationship factors include the client's perception of caring, empathy, respect, collaboration, acceptance, validation, and encouragement from the practitioner. The relationship serves as the crust or container that holds other ingredients together in the change pie.

Of all aspects of the relationship, the therapeutic alliance (hereinafter *alliance*) is the most researched area. *Alliance* refers to the quality and strength of collaboration between the client and counselor. The alliance is typically measured by the relational bond or connection between the client and counselor and their agreement on counseling goals, topics of conversation, and intervention tasks. The impact of the alliance on the success of counseling has been well documented in the research literature (Bachelor & Horvath, 1999; Blatt, Zuroff, Quinlan, & Pilkonis, 1996; Castonguay, Goldfried, Wiser, Raue, & Hayes, 1996; Krupnick et al., 1996; Orlinsky, Rønnestad, & Willutzki, 2004; Wampold, 2001). Although most of this research has involved adults, the powerful role of the alliance has also been demonstrated in many studies of child and adolescent therapy (Karver, Handelsman, Fields, & Bickman, 2006; Shirk & Karver, 2003).

Research has repeatedly shown that the alliance is a reliable predictor of outcomes (Martin, Garske, & Davis, 2000; Shelef, Diamond, Diamond, & Liddle, 2005). After analyzing over 1,000 studies, Orlinsky et al. (2004) concluded that (a) the client's perception of the alliance is the best predictor of counseling outcomes and (b) client participation is the key feature of a strong alliance. *Client participation* refers to the client's engagement, contributions, and collaboration throughout the helping process. Counseling works best when clients are actively involved, when they experience a positive relationship with the counselor, and when counseling addresses what clients see as important.

Relationship factors are the context and foundation of all other ingredients in the change pie. Sturdy relationships support the other ingredients, whereas crumbling relationships jeopardize the very foundation of change and success. Solution-focused counseling enhances relationship factors by (a) inviting clients to take an active role in the change process, (b) monitoring their perceptions of progress and alliance, and (c) adjusting counseling services on the basis of the feedback of clients. The following scenario illustrates the practitioner's attention to client and relationhip factors.

Client and Relationship Factors in Action: Claire. A 15-year-old student named Claire complained of "constant bickering" with her father, stating that these conflicts were affecting her schoolwork. This dialogue occurred early in the first meeting.

Claire: I just started living with my father 2 months ago, and we're trying to learn to live together.
Counselor: That's quite an adjustment.
Claire: He's a bachelor, and he has his ways. I've always lived with my mom. My father and I have two different opinions and we fight a lot.
Counselor: Can you give me an example of a fight?
[The counselor acknowledges Claire's perception and language ("a fight"), which validates her experience and enhances the alliance.]

Claire described a typical fight in the following way: (a) Claire asks her father's permission to go out with friends or to stay out later, (b) her father says no, (c) they argue, and (d) Claire storms out of the room and threatens to move out. Her goals were to fight less, go out more often, and stay out later. Claire believed that her father would let her go out more often and stay out later if they fought less.

Counselor: Tell me about the times you've been successful in going out without fighting with your father or fighting less than usual.

[Asking about previous successes, no matter how small, shifts the focus from the problem to potential solutions. Focusing on Claire's success and competency capitalizes on client and relationship factors by conveying respect for her ideas and contributions. As evidenced next, Claire's response initiated a solution cycle in which one idea led to others. Notice how the counselor "leads from one step behind," allowing Claire to take center stage in developing solutions.]

Claire: Sometimes it's better if I go over to a friend's house and call from there. He usually isn't in the mood for fighting over the phone because he doesn't want them to hear us.

Counselor: So that works pretty well for you?

Claire: Yes.

Counselor: Is there any way you can do that in the future?

Claire: Not every time. Sometimes he won't even let me go over to my friend's house, so I can't call.

Counselor: So you could do that sometimes, but not all the time.

Claire: I guess. Or sometimes, if he's gone, I just leave a note and say that I'm going out.

Counselor: How does that work?

Claire: Okay, until I get back home.

Counselor: Is the fight when you get back home after leaving a note worse, better, or about the same?

Claire: It's better. It's not as bad.

Counselor: It's not as bad?

Claire: No.

Counselor: So, it's better when you use the phone before asking to go out and when you write a note?

Claire: Yes.

Counselor: What else have you tried that seems to work well?

Claire: Cleaning something before I go.

Counselor: Like what?

Claire: Doing the dishes or straightening a room so I can say, "Well, I did this for you, so you should let me go." [smiles]

Counselor: That's a great idea. You've come up with a lot of good ideas here. Are you willing to try any of these out to see how they work?

During the remainder of the meeting, they discussed how Claire could do more of the things that were already working toward her goals. Claire's goals and opinions were accepted and accommodated by the counselor. This conversation enhanced client and relationship factors by exploring Claire's successes and involving her as an active partner in solution building. When asked how the meeting went for her, Claire said, "I had no idea I was doing *anything* that was helping," and added that "there might be some hope for us after all." As discussed next, hope is another potent ingredient of effective counseling.

Hope Factors: The Anticipation

Hope factors are vital to successful change, although their impact is relatively smaller than that of client and relationship factors (Asay & Lambert, 1999). Hope consists of students' expectations about the likelihood of change and confidence in their ability to make important changes and reach their goals. In the pie metaphor, hope factors can be thought of as the positive anticipation of eating the pie.

The well-documented placebo effect attests to the power of hope. The term *placebo* is used in drug research to distinguish those who receive an actual drug (experimental group) from those who receive a sugar pill, or placebo, that mimics the drug but lacks its active ingredients (placebo group). For a drug to be deemed effective, the people who receive it must improve significantly more than those who receive the sugar pill. Placebo participants almost always get better, often reporting as much improvement as those who receive the drug (Khan et al., 2005; Moerman, 2002). Research has confirmed that the expectation of getting better makes it more likely to happen (Frank & Frank, 1991; Snyder & Taylor, 2000).

Another key aspect of hope is self-efficacy, which is the belief in one's ability to resolve problems and reach goals (Bandura, 2006). Self-efficacy helps students cope with frustration and setbacks and maintain improvements once they occur. Solution-focused counseling seeks to enhance people's self-efficacy by acknowledging and amplifying their strengths, successes, and resources. For example, a student who had a bad week might be asked the following questions:

- What would you tell other fourth graders who had a bad week?
- How have you kept things from getting worse?
- How have you handled slips like this in the past?
- How did you manage to hang in there instead of giving up when things got bad this week?

In a series of self-efficacy experiments, Dweck and Leggett (1988; Molden & Dweck, 2006) found that children who linked achievements to their own strengths and actions were likely to sustain their success in the future. These studies encourage us to link school successes to the efforts of students through the following kinds of questions:

- How did you make that happen?
- How did you come up with that idea?
- What did you do differently to get your homework done last night?

Most students who are referred for counseling need a strong dose of hope. Likewise, teachers and parents often feel demoralized by the time they seek our help. Hope is hindered when we focus mainly on the deficiencies of students and their circumstances. The last thing people need is a reminder of what's wrong with them or their life. Hope is enhanced when counseling focuses on possibilities for a better future without denying the pain and frustration of the problem. We can strengthen our own hope, and that of our clients, by (a) viewing people as competent and resourceful, (b) acknowledging both problems and possibilities, (c) focusing on the future, and (d) trusting in the inevitability of change and the potential of the counseling process. Box 2.1 provides an opportunity to reflect on hope from a personal perspective.

Model/Technique Factors: The Topping

Model/technique factors refer to the theory, model, and techniques adopted by the practitioner. Although model/technique factors are important, their 15% contribution to outcomes is modest compared to the collective 85% contribution of client, relationship, and hope factors. Some researchers have reported an even smaller impact of model and technique factors (Wampold, 2001).

Models and methods are like the pie's topping, which is important to the appearance and taste of the pie but does not stand up well on its own. Without the other ingredients to support them, counseling theories and interventions fall flat and are nothing but fluff. In contrast to the medical notion that interventions operate on clients to produce outcomes, counseling research suggests that clients operate on interventions to produce outcomes (Bohart, 2006). The effectiveness of counseling techniques depends largely on the extent to which they accommodate the client's ideas, preferences, resources, feedback, and participation. Research encourages us to hold lightly to theories and techniques and be willing to try something different when they are not working.

Despite marketing claims to the contrary, no single model has proven superior to others in overall effectiveness (Lambert & Ogles, 2004; Wampold, 2006). This well-replicated finding reinforces the importance of adapting our methods to the client instead of squeezing the client into our favorite theories and techniques. Attempting to talk clients into different beliefs or actions is like barging into a house and rearranging the furniture without the owner's permission. As soon as you leave, most people move everything right back where they had it. As illustrated with Jolene in Chapter 1, one of the surest ways to paralyze a potentially good idea is to force it on clients against their will. Jolene's first counselor tried to "rearrange the furniture," with predictably poor results. The second counselor achieved better outcomes by collaborating with Jolene and accommodating her perceptions, goals, and resources.

Box 2.1
What Gave You Hope?

Think of a time you struggled with a problem on your own with little success and then talked to someone who helped you gain a more hopeful or optimistic perspective.

What did the person say or do that was most helpful in improving your outlook?

How might these same elements be applied in conversations with students, parents, teachers, and others with whom you work to resolve school problems?

Summary of Outcome Research: Baking a Pie With All the Ingredients

Research indicates that positive outcomes in counseling result from the operation of four main ingredients or common factors of change: client, relationship, hope, and model/technique factors. Effective counseling involves baking a pie with all of the ingredients by (a) discovering and applying the strengths and resources of students, parents, and teachers (client factors); (b) building cooperative alliances (relationship factors); (c) igniting people's hope for a better future (hope factors); and (d) selecting intervention techniques that fit the client's perceptions and resources (model/technique factors). This book folds these ingredients into an efficient recipe for school-based counseling.

Positive Psychology

All clients need to realize that they have assets.
—Ridley, 2005, p. 103

Given that the client is the most potent force in effective counseling, we need to capitalize on people's strengths and resources in helping them change school problems. Although the counseling profession historically has emphasized wellness and adjustment, psychiatry and psychology have focused on pathology and dysfunction. Consider the growing number of disorders listed in the *Diagnostic and Statistical Manual of Mental Disorders (DSM)*. Whereas the original *DSM* included 66 diagnoses in 1952 (American Psychiatric Association, 1952), the newest version includes 397 disorders (American Psychiatric Association, 2000). This represents a whopping 600% increase, or about one disorder every 2 months for the past 50 years. Are we really becoming that disturbed, or has the fascination with pathology spiraled out of control?

Despite the prevailing emphasis on problems and pathology in the helping professions, a growing number of researchers and clinicians are acknowledging the therapeutic benefits of building on what's right with clients instead of focusing on what's wrong with them (Harris, Thoresen, & Lopez, 2007; Snyder & Lopez, 2007). Attending to strengths and resources is a big part of the current positive psychology movement (Seligman, Rashid, & Parks, 2006). Martin Seligman, a renowned researcher and leader in this movement, has called for a greater emphasis on people's strengths and dignity: "Treatment is not just fixing what is broken, it is nurturing what is best within ourselves" (Seligman, 1998, p. 175). In discussing psychotherapy, Seligman et al. (2006) noted,

> For over 100 years, psychotherapy has been where clients go to talk about their troubles . . . where the focus is nearly always on repairing negatives—symptoms, traumas, wounds, deficits, and disorders. . . . In its emphasis on troubles, psychology . . . has seriously lagged behind in enhancing human positives. . . . Indeed, therapies that attend explicitly to the positives are few and far between. (pp. 774–775)

In the spirit of positive psychology, solution-focused counseling attends explicitly to the rich and varied resources of students, parents, and teachers.

Treatment Acceptability

A treatment that is not used is no treatment at all.
—Witt & Elliott, 1985

Treatment acceptability refers to the degree to which clients accept an intervention strategy (Kazdin, 1980). Research supports the commonsense notion that the higher the acceptability is, the more likely it is that the strategy will be implemented (Mautone, 2005). Unfortunately, counseling is sometimes portrayed as a mechanical process of snapping the right technique (Strategy X) onto the right problem (Problem Y). The growing emphasis on evidence-based treatments has contributed to this cookbook view of counseling, despite an overwhelming number of studies that have failed to show a strong relationship between specific techniques and outcomes (Wampold, 2006). Effective counseling is not an uninhabited landscape of formulas and techniques. It is a relational process involving people. Unlike machine parts or cooking ingredients, people do not automatically yield to the practitioner's influence or favorite intervention recipe.

Students, parents, and teachers may have different beliefs about the problem and solution and varying levels of investment in changing it. Both of these factors influence the type of interventions they will accept and implement (W. R. Miller & Rollnick, 2002). For example, students who view their behavior as "no problem" are less likely to implement a time-consuming intervention than students who view the situation as serious and urgent. Respecting and accommodating the client's position is one of the surest ways to enhance the acceptability of interventions. As discussed next, collaboration and accommodation are also important elements of culturally competent counseling.

Cultural Considerations

Recognizing that each person creates a different model of the world
enables us to cherish rather than judge or fear those differences.
—Lewis & Pucelik, 1982, p. 29

Cultural considerations are crucial to the effectiveness of any counseling approach. In this discussion, *culture* refers to everything that defines and distinguishes a person, including ethnicity, gender, age, sexual orientation, language, values, goals, and life experiences. In discussing culturally competent counseling for minority clients, Ridley (2005) cautioned practitioners against stereotyping by reminding them that "each client is unique . . . and each has a different story to tell" (p. 85). Sue and Sue (2007) similarly warned counselors about overgeneralizing and stereotyping, noting that it is wrong to assume that all persons from the same minority group share the traits that are typically assigned to that group. Cautions about stereotyping also apply to training programs in the helping professions, as evidenced by the following comments of a graduate student:

> What we're mostly talking about in the classroom . . . is stereotypical representations
> of different ethnic groups—"this is a typical Latino, this is a typical Vietnamese

person," but each individual is different, no matter what their race. I think what we should try to develop is a curriculum that exposes people to a new way of thinking, to help them approach all people with an open mindset. (Sleek, 1998, p. 1)

Scholars of culturally competent practices in counseling recommend a highly individualized and collaborative approach to developing goals and interventions to strengthen clients' ownership in the change process (Boyd-Franklin, 2003; Ridley, 2005; Sue & Sue, 2007). Ridley (2005) stressed the importance of a collaborative alliance by noting that minority clients often "enter counseling feeling powerless" and "gain a sense of empowerment and ownership of the counseling process when they participate in their own goal setting" (p. 107). Respecting and accommodating the goals of clients is a hallmark of solution-focused counseling and culturally respectful practice. Accommodating the client's goals does not require us to personally agree with them. Differences between the worldview and values of clients and counselors are inevitable. However, counseling research makes it clear that accommodating the client's frame of reference enhances outcomes. The purpose of solution-focused counseling is to help people change school problems, not to convert them to the counselor's or anyone else's worldview and culture.

The emphasis on strengths and resources in solution-focused counseling is consistent with the literature on culturally competent services to minority clients. As Ridley (2005) noted, "While vigorously looking for psychopathology in . . . minority clients, counselors often miss opportunities to help clients identify their assets and use these assets advantageously" (p. 103). Pederson (2000) recommended that, in discussing counseling with non-Western people, practitioners encourage them to apply their own internal resources and self-corrective mechanisms, because this is a natural aspect of problem solving in non-Western cultures. Boyd-Franklin (2003) similarly advocated a strength-based approach to African American clients, noting that they are often more aware of their problems than their strengths. I have found this to be true for most students who are referred for counseling, regardless of ethnicity and cultural background.

The strategies in this book are responsive to current standards and recommendations for culturally competent practice by (a) treating every client as an individual with a unique frame of reference, (b) collaborating on the goals and content of counseling, (c) tailoring services to clients instead of expecting them to conform to our preferences, and (d) obtaining ongoing feedback from clients on the usefulness of our services and adjusting our approach accordingly. Putting clients first and keeping them in the driver's seat throughout the helping process provides built-in safeguards for culturally sound counseling services.

Empowerment

Cultural respect and collaboration are closely related to the concept of empowerment in schools. In a series of studies on empowerment and helping relationships, Dunst and colleagues (Dempsey & Dunst, 2004; Dunst, Boyd, Trivette, & Hamby, 2002) found that people experienced more empowerment in participatory versus authoritarian relationships. Participatory relationships acknowledge the expertise of clients and invite them to actively participate in constructing solutions. In contrast, authoritarian relationships emphasize the practitioner's expertise, with little attention to client involvement and input.

The prevalence of authoritarian relationships that minimize client contributions has been well documented in the therapy literature (Bohart & Tallman, 1999; Duncan, Miller, & Sparks, 2004). In addition to disempowering clients, authoritarian approaches are incompatible with outcome research (the change pie) and best practices in culturally competent counseling. Research points to the simple fact that the people closest to the problem are also closest to its solution (see Figure 2.2). Solution-focused counseling provides those who are closest to the school problem—students, teachers, and parents—with the empowering opportunity to contribute substantially to solutions.

Research on empowerment (Dempsey & Dunst, 2004; Dunst et al., 2002) suggests the following strategies for working with students on school problems:

- Offer suggestions that fit with students' culture and with their appraisal of the problem
- Encourage students to use natural support networks and personal resources instead of replacing them with professional services

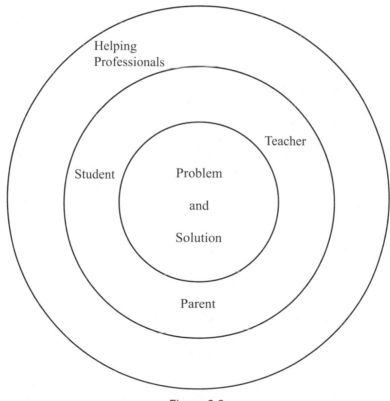

Figure 2.2
Proximity of influence on the problem and solution.

- Treat students as capable partners in the change process
- Convey a sense of joint responsibility for solving problems
- When problems are resolved, give students credit, and help them connect solutions to their own efforts

As discussed next, giving students an active voice in the change process is a clinically and socially significant feature of solution-focused counseling.

The Sociology of Childhood

Sociologists have suggested that children and adolescents in Western countries represent a social minority group because they are typically viewed as impertinent and inferior (Mayall, 1999). This demeaning viewpoint is conveyed in the expression "Children should be seen but not heard." In discussing the sociology of childhood, Mayall (2002) noted that children are often seen as lacking the ability to think for themselves, which leads adults to exert control in ways that stifle children's development of problem-solving skills, responsibility, and self-confidence. Children fall at the lowest level of society's age-graded power structure, rather than being seen as a group with its own culture and its own unique abilities and contributions. Mayall (2002) proposed that children are a socially disadvantaged and disempowered group not only because of their age but also because of their passive position in society as the learner but never the teacher.

Although these considerations pertain to young people in general, they are particularly relevant to students referred for school problems. Many referred students have experienced a history of school difficulties and disappointments. These experiences, coupled with society's disempowering view of young people, can lead students to adopt a hopeless, "what's the use?" position when it comes to improving school performance or other aspects of life.

Solution-focused counseling bolsters students' responsibility and self-confidence by giving them an active voice in developing goals and solutions. Outcomes are enhanced when we treat young people with dignity by helping them help themselves. Another way to convey respect for young people is to accommodate developmental factors that may influence them and their school problems.

Developmental Considerations

This section summarizes key developmental features of childhood and adolescence, along with their practical implications for counseling. Developmental considerations help us tailor our language and style to students of all ages. The following discussion summarizes physical, social, psychological, and intellectual changes across four stages of school-age development: early childhood, middle childhood, early adolescence, and mid-adolescence. This is not an exhaustive description of child and adolescent development, but a brief overview of developmental factors that are important to consider in counseling preschool through high school students. These are general guidelines, not specific predictions or prescriptions about individual students.

Early Childhood (Ages 4–6)

Most children begin their formal education between ages 4 and 6. Some adapt quickly, whereas others have great difficulty adjusting to school expectations and structure. Early childhood is a time of rapid growth in physical, social, psychological, and intellectual development. Although these domains are discussed separately below for clarity purposes, they function in interdependent ways in the child's life. For example, improvement of a 6-year-old's running and throwing skills (physical) can alter the child's self-image (psychological) and peer relationships (social).

Physical. Early childhood is a period of substantial muscle and motor development, which is one reason that many young children have difficulty sitting still for long periods of time. This is also why early childhood classrooms are arranged to permit ample movement; frequent breaks; and physical learning activities, such as printing, drawing, cutting, and playground games.

The following physical activities may help to engage young children's attention and involvement:

- Taking a walk around the school instead of sitting in chairs ("walk talks")
- Allowing students to stand or walk about the office during the interview
- Having students draw a picture of the solution and explain it to you
- Keeping a set of hands-on props in your office, including toys, colored pencils, drawing paper, puppets, modeling clay, and other age-appropriate materials for young children
- Conducting the interview while stacking blocks, rolling dice, assembling legos, or tossing a ball

Social. Social play is a big part of early childhood. Most young children are naturally adventuresome and respond well to counselors who are willing to loosen up a little and play. This may include

- role-playing in which the student assumes the role of teacher and you assume the role of student,
- taking turns talking about what each of you likes the most (and least) about school and why,
- playing a game of basketball or tossing a tennis ball while talking,
- using sentence-completion strategies ("I'm really good at . . .").

Some children are very cautious and quiet at first, and it may be helpful to ease into the conversation instead of beginning with a lot of questions about school. Starting a session by playing a game or taking a short walk helps to break the ice in a way that is familiar and comfortable for many young students.

Psychological. Children at this age begin to develop an identity and to distinguish themselves from others on the basis of gender; physical characteristics; and special interests, such as singing and climbing. They also build greater self-confidence and independence, qualities that fit well with the solution-focused emphasis on active client involvement.

Young children enjoy discussing what they are good at, which can be utilized to develop school interventions based on their strengths and interests. In working with Emma, a preschooler who loved dinosaurs and singing, her teacher asked her to create a short dinosaur song every week and sing it to the class on Friday. This simple intervention improved Emma's class behavior by increasing her sense of belonging and investment in school.

Students in preschool and early primary grades are highly curious, imaginative, and fascinated by the world. They love to experiment and make new discoveries about themselves and their environment. Some preschoolers believe in fictional characters from books, movies, and television. Children's vivid imagination can be utilized in several ways. We can ask how their favorite cartoon character might respond to the current school problem (e.g., "What would Mighty Mouse do?"). We can also invite them to conduct "top secret classroom experiments" in which they behave differently, then secretly observe changes in their teacher's behavior.

Intellectual. Because big words and abstract concepts are difficult for young children to grasp, we should use clear and simple language when meeting with them. It is also helpful to periodically check with them to make sure they are following the conversation. Allowing a parent or teacher to accompany the child can facilitate communication and increase the student's comfort. Regardless of whether parents or teachers attend the session, they can be consulted beforehand for tips on communicating with the child.

Inviting people to envision a better future is a big part of solution-focused counseling. However, the literal quality of intellectual development during early childhood makes it hard for young children to discuss the future in abstract terms. Therefore, we need to be particularly resourceful in communicating with young students about the future. For example, instead of asking, "How will school be different 1 month from now when things start improving?" we can try a more playful and concrete approach: Grabbing a coffee mug and holding it up in front of the child, we might say, "Let's pretend you rubbed this magic cup and a genie popped out and said, 'Michael, you can make three wishes to make school just the way you want it to be.' What would you wish for?" Anything we can do to involve the child in the change process is a step in the right direction. By using clear and simple language, along with the other accommodations noted above, we can conduct meaningful conversations with young students.

Middle Childhood (Ages 7–10)

Students acquire many important skills and abilities during middle childhood, which corresponds to Grades 1 through 5 in elementary school.

Physical. Children develop considerable muscle control throughout elementary school. Small muscle control helps with writing and cutting as well as self-care tasks such as dressing, buttoning, and tying shoes. Large muscle control assists with running, throwing a ball, and lifting heavy objects. Physical delays and difficulties can lead to school-related problems, such as falling behind academically because of slow handwriting or sadness about being excluded from sports and other playground activities.

Puberty begins for a small percentage of children toward the end of middle childhood. Early onset of puberty is usually more difficult for girls, because they may be teased about breast development. This can lead to embarrassment and self-criticism. Puberty can also influence the student–counselor relationship. For example, some children may feel awkward with a counselor of the opposite sex, especially during the early stages of puberty.

Social. Middle childhood is a time of significant social development. Social activities may involve sports, religious institutions, or neighborhood groups. As peer acceptance and popularity become more important, friendships are increasingly selective and exclusive. Peer criticism can be very hurtful for children seen as different or inferior, which may lead them to withdraw or retaliate with aggression.

As children become more adept at social and conversational skills, they can participate more actively in counseling. For example, they are better able to answer socially based questions, such as the following:

- Who do you respect the most in your life, and what would he or she advise you to do about this problem?
- If I asked your friends what they like about you, what would they say?
- How will your parents treat you differently when your grades start improving?

Psychological. Increased social awareness during middle childhood may have detrimental psychological consequences for students who view themselves as inferior to peers. It is not unusual for struggling students to criticize themselves and become frustrated ("My friends are smarter than me. Why should I even try?"). Inviting them to identify successes and competencies encourages a more hopeful outlook.

Elementary-age students typically develop a stronger internal locus of control, which refers to a sense of personal mastery and control in their life. This can be utilized in work with students who express feelings of hopelessness and lack of control. For example, in working with students who say that their teacher picks on them no matter what they do, we can invite them to be especially kind to the teacher for 1 week and to observe changes in the teacher's behavior. This encourages students to take responsibility for the one aspect of life over which they have the greatest control—their actions.

Intellectual. As children progress through middle childhood, they become more skilled at thinking and talking in abstract terms. This enables them to grasp the notion of time and to generalize from one situation to another. The emergence of abstract thinking also assists students in empathizing with others.

These developments are useful in solution-focused counseling because they allow students to take different perspectives and to consider the impact of their behavior on others ("How would you handle this if you were a teacher?"). The increased understanding of time enables students to imagine and describe how their life will be different when things begin to improve:

- How will your teacher treat you differently when you arrive at class on time?
- Who will be the first person to notice when things start getting better?
- How will school be different for you?

Even though elementary-age students develop an increased capacity for abstract thought and language, it is still important to use clear and simple language and to avoid jargon. The use of toys, drawings, or other such strategies can also facilitate communication with students in the middle childhood years.

Early Adolescence (Ages 11–14)

Early adolescence covers ages 11 through 14, although it may begin a bit earlier for girls and later for boys (Schave & Schave, 1989). These ages roughly correspond to the middle school grades, Grades 6 through 8. As you recall this time in your own life, perhaps you can relate to the following comments of eighth-grade students who were asked what advice they would give to their parents:

- If you tell me something and I get the point, don't keep telling me a hundred times.
- Don't treat me like I'm stupid. Just because I'm a kid doesn't mean I'm dumb.
- Don't assume that I'll do bad things and screw up.
- Appreciate me for what I do, and try to understand me and my feelings. (Vernon & Al-Mabuk, 1995, pp. 97–98)

The transition from childhood to adolescence involves dramatic changes, particularly in the psychological area. The development of personal identity and independence is a vital task of adolescence with major implications for counseling. Therefore, psychological development receives considerable attention in the following discussion of early and mid-adolescence.

Physical. As puberty begins and physical maturity unfolds, some students become painfully aware of being more or less mature than their peers. Rapid growth spurts and hormonal changes may detract from the student's physical coordination and attractiveness. These changes can confuse adolescents because they are often accompanied by new sexual feelings, thoughts, questions, and insecurities. Regardless of their maturity rate, most adolescents are critical of their physical appearance.

As with previous stages, the developmental domains of early adolescence are interdependent, in that changes in one domain often influence other areas. For example, physical changes can significantly alter the student's self-image and peer relationships.

Social. Peer influence continues to grow as students want to be like, and liked by, their peers. The strong desire for social acceptance leads some students to feel inferior if they perceive themselves as different from their peers. Early adolescents may feel like everyone is looking at them, especially when they make mistakes and embarrass themselves in public. Striking a balance between fitting in with peers and developing a personal identity is an ongoing challenge of adolescence.

Identifying influential peers and other important people in the student's life can improve our understanding of and empathy with the student. In some cases, these individuals can be included in interventions aimed at improving the student's school behavior. For example, we might encourage the student to invite a favorite relative or friend to a counseling session to provide different perspectives on the problem and solution.

Knowledge of social development is helpful in working not only with students but with parents and teachers as well. Factual information about development may help them understand that some problem behavior is influenced by normal processes of development. For example, when a student's misbehavior is seen as being motivated by a strong desire for peer attention, it normalizes the situation and reduces the likelihood that parents or teachers will view the student as emotionally or behaviorally disturbed. Likewise, parents may feel hurt or angry when their child spends less time with them or questions their authority. Explaining that their son or daughter is displaying a typical developmental transition from childhood to adolescence may help them better understand and cope with these changes.

Psychological. The dramatic physical and hormonal developments of early adolescence, coupled with sexually oriented thoughts and feelings that accompany these changes, may increase the student's anxiety, shame, and self-consciousness. Given the increased importance of physical appearance and social approval, it is no wonder that students' self-esteem varies greatly during adolescence.

Sudden and dramatic mood swings during early adolescence can prompt confusion, anger, and defiant behavior. For students who view mood swings as a sign that they are going crazy (Newman & Newman, 1991), we can validate and normalize their experience by explaining that these changes are scary yet common during this time of life. Early adolescents may engage in magical thinking, which often involves unrealistic perceptions of invincibility. For example, it is not unusual for 14-year-olds to embrace the magical belief that bad things can happen to other people but not to them. This type of thinking may increase risk-taking behavior at school and elsewhere.

It is ironic that the times when struggling students have the greatest need for understanding from adults are the times they may receive it the least. This occurs for two reasons. First, adolescents may not openly discuss their problems for fear that adults will criticize or lecture them. Second, their defiance or other problem behaviors tend to drive adults away instead of bringing them closer. Some adolescents become suspicious and distrustful of adults in general. Listening, which is a big part of solution-focused counseling, is effective in gaining young people's trust and cooperation. Solution-focused counseling is well matched to the psychological tasks and struggles of early adolescence in many other ways. For example, complimenting students on their strengths and resources counteracts the self-criticism and shame that many adolescents experience during the middle school years. In discussing the benefits of strength-oriented approaches, Wolin, Desetta, and Hefner (2000) encouraged practitioners to "look for strengths in even the most troubled young people and encourage them to search for examples of their own competence" (p. 4).

Intellectual. The growing ability to think and speak in abstract terms permits more sophisticated conversations with middle school students. For example, we can ask the following kinds of future-oriented and "what if" questions:

- If this problem vanished in 2 months, how would your life be different in school?
- What do you think would happen if you tried that in class tomorrow?
- How would it change things between you and your parents if you attended school more often?
- What do you think Ms. McCreary would do if you walked into class tomorrow and thanked her for being your teacher?

These questions capitalize on students' development of intellectual skills while inviting them to focus on a better future and on what they are willing to do to improve things at school. In many cases, students have more influence on the school situation than they think. Solution-focused counseling invites middle school students to discover this on their own and to apply it toward solutions to school problems.

Mid-Adolescence (Ages 15–18)

Mid-adolescence corresponds to ages 15 through 18 and Grades 9 through 12. Developmental changes of early adolescence are extended and refined during the high school years.

Physical. Mid-adolescence involves the continuation or completion of physical changes that began in early adolescence. Most girls achieve full breast growth. Boys acquire facial hair, and their voice gets deeper. Concerns about physical appearance become even stronger through the high school years. Perceptions of differences or difficulties in physical development can significantly affect students' psychological and social outlook by influencing how they view themselves and how they are viewed by others.

Social. Peers take on even more importance and influence throughout mid-adolescence. Serious dating and sexual relationships may occur. As adolescents become more aware of sexual feelings, they develop stronger gender identifications. For gay and lesbian students, this period can be very difficult and marked by confusion, anger, and peer rejection.

Whereas friendships during early adolescence are often linked to common connections, such as playing sports or living in the same neighborhood, high school friendships are based more on personal factors, such as values and social compatibility. As a result, friendships usually become more enduring and stable. All of these factors influence students' school performance. For example, friendship troubles can make it difficult for students to focus on classroom instruction and school work.

Psychological. The instability of early adolescence is gradually replaced by more enduring and stable patterns of thinking, feeling, and acting. However, the journey toward increased stability may involve testing out different roles and behaviors. Sexual activity and drug use increase during this time. As students move through high school, they are faced with stressful decisions about future education and career paths. The excitement of increased freedom may be coupled with apprehension and questions such as "What if I make the wrong choice?" or "Is this really what I want to do?"

Increased privileges, such as driving a car and scheduling one's own time, are accompanied by bigger responsibilities. The balance of freedom and responsibility can be a source of major conflict between teenagers and adults. From a parent's or teacher's perspective, it may seem like the student wants more freedom but is unwilling to accept the responsibility that goes with it. From the student's perspective, parents and teachers appear unwilling to provide the freedom that is required for the student to learn how to be responsible.

Of all the issues in adolescence, the quest for independence and personal identity is perhaps the most important one to keep in mind during counseling. In the process of developing a distinct identity separate from parents and friends, adolescents may go to great lengths to protect their autonomy and freedom. Consider the following advice from high school students to their parents:

- Let me make my own mistakes. I have to learn sometime.
- Don't push too hard. If you do, I'll do the opposite.
- Let *me* decide what's best for me. (Vernon & Al-Mabuk, 1995, p. 124)

Although parents typically receive the brunt of their child's struggle for independence, these statements are also relevant to teachers and others who work with high school students. Adolescents resent it when adults question their ability to think for themselves and to be their own person. This is why it is counterproductive to try talking young people out of their opinion and into an opposing viewpoint.

Cooperating with students' frame of reference avoids power struggles and reinforces the notion that they are responsible for their opinions and decisions. The cooperative philosophy of solution-focused counseling is well suited to the adolescent's quest for independence. Listening versus lecturing, asking versus telling, and validating versus criticizing are a few specific ways that we can accommodate students' natural desire for freedom and autonomy. Students are much more likely to cooperate when they have a respected voice in the counseling process.

Intellectual. As their intellect expands, adolescents can engage in increasingly complex discussions. Students' ability to consider different perspectives of the same situation enables them to respond to more abstract and complex questions, such as the following:

- What would your teacher say if I asked her to describe the problem?
- How would you respond if you were the parent in this situation?
- I know how much you respect your grandfather. What would he do about this if he were in your shoes?

Adolescents' ability to visualize and reflect on the future provides additional opportunities to explore what they want and what they are willing to do to obtain it:

- Imagine that it is 2 months from now and things are much better for you at school. How would that feel? What are you willing to do tomorrow to make it happen?
- Who will be the first to notice small improvements in your school work? What will he or she say?
- If this problem suddenly vanished, what would it be like the next few hours at school? How willing are you to try something different to make that happen?

These questions invite adolescents to reflect on the future in ways that accommodate their skills in abstract thinking. Refer to Sigelman and Rider (2003) for additional information on child and adolescent development.

Summary of Developmental Considerations

Developmental factors impact students in a variety of ways from preschool through high school. Although there is considerable variation in the rate and manner in which development unfolds among individual students, basic knowledge of child and adolescent development helps us adapt the counseling process to students of all ages. Accommodating the developmental experiences of students is an important part of establishing cooperative relationships. I urge you to keep these developmental issues in mind throughout the remainder of the book.

A Systemic View of Schools, Students, and School Problems

A system is "an entity made up of interconnected parts, with recognizable relationships that are systematically arranged to serve a perceived purpose" (Parsons & Kahn, 2005, p. 65). Like other social systems, the school is composed of individuals with various needs, goals, and levels of influence, including students, teachers, administrators, parents, and paraprofessionals. Of all these people, students typically have the least amount of power and influence. As Parsons and Kahn (2005) noted,

> It is somewhat ironic that for most school systems . . . the largest population of consumers—those for whom programs are targeted (i.e., the students attending the school)—although [they have] a strong vested interest in the school's successful operation, may have the least influence over the school's operation. (p. 52)

One aspect of school functioning over which students have minimal influence is the process of referring students for counseling and other services. Decisions about who gets referred are typically made by teachers, administrators, and parents with little or no input from the student. The fact that most students are mandated clients who enter counseling at someone else's request has major implications for how we approach them.

Systems theory views school problems as embedded in a social context rather than residing strictly within the student. From this perspective, a referral does not automatically imply that there is something wrong with the student. Some referrals result from a poor fit between the student and the teacher or classroom environment. This explains how the same behavior may be seen as a problem by one teacher and acceptable by another.

The systems perspective does not excuse or deny students' problem behavior or skill limitations but encourages us to be flexible and consider interventions that may involve teachers and parents as well as students. In addition to expanding the scope of counseling to include others, a systems mind-set promotes a more flexible approach to building solutions. This includes exploring the perceptions and actions of key people, utilizing exceptions to the problem, and enlisting the help of influential people in the student's life. As evidenced in this discussion, adopting a systemic view of schools and school problems creates additional solution opportunities.

Summary and Conclusions

This chapter has summarized the empirical and conceptual foundations of solution-focused counseling. Research indicates that successful counseling results primarily from the operation of four core ingredients or common factors of change: client, relationship, hope, and model/technique factors. Solution-focused counseling deliberately seeks to activate these potent ingredients in every contact with clients. The philosophy and methods of solution-focused counseling are also based on research and literature in positive psychology, treatment acceptability, culturally competent counseling, and empowerment. Positive psychology encourages practitioners to build on what's right and what works for people instead of focusing exclusively on problems and deficits. Research on treatment acceptability, culturally competent counseling, and empowerment emphasizes the importance of collaborative relationships, client-driven goals, and client involvement. This approach enhances outcomes by fitting counseling to the client instead of fitting the client to counseling.

Sociologists have suggested that young people represent a legitimate minority group because they are often viewed as inferior and impertinent. Solution-focused counseling bolsters students' dignity and involvement by giving them an active voice in developing goals and contributing to solutions. The chapter has outlined key features of child and adolescent development, along with practical suggestions for accommodating developmental issues in counseling students of all ages. Solution-focused counseling is based on the systemic notion that school problems are embedded in a social system rather than residing strictly within the student. This perspective expands solution opportunities and encourages a flexible approach to school problems and the people who experience them. Chapter 3 presents the therapeutic influences and assumptions of solution-focused counseling in schools.

Practice Exercises

1. List and briefly describe the four common factors or core ingredients of change as identified by outcome research in counseling and therapy.
2. In groups of three or four, discuss your reactions to the research on common factors of change. The following questions can be used to prompt additional reactions and discussion:
   - Were you surprised by any of these findings?
   - What findings are the most and least surprising to you?

- What practical implications do these findings have for working with students, parents, and teachers on school problems?
3. On the basis of their substantial (40%) contribution to counseling outcomes, client factors represent the most powerful ingredient or common factor of successful counseling. List two client factors that most students bring to counseling, and describe how each factor could be applied toward solutions to school problems.
4. Think of a student you are currently working with who is viewed as resistant, unmotivated, or not having much to offer to the counseling process. List some client factors that might be useful in changing the school problem. How could you incorporate one or more of these factors into the counseling process?
5. What are some things that you already do to instill hope in the students, parents, and teachers with whom you work? What are some additional ways that you could encourage hope in your clients?
6. Describe how solution-focused counseling respects the worldview and culture of students, parents, and other clients.
7. Some sociologists have suggested that children represent a social minority group in many Western societies. What impact might this have on young people? What are the practical implications for counseling students about school problems?
8. How can information about child and adolescent development help you in working with students, teachers, parents, and school problems?
9. Brainstorm some flexible methods for working with the following students:
   - a 6-year-old student who is somewhat quiet and withdrawn;
   - an active, adventuresome 10-year-old student who has difficulty sitting still;
   - a strong-willed high school student who says, "I don't want to be here, and you can't make me talk."
10. Discuss the practical advantages of adopting a systems perspective in working with students and school problems.
11. Describe one small step that you are willing to take in your practice as a result of the information in this chapter.

CHAPTER 3

Therapeutic Influences and Assumptions

Nothing is permanent but change.
— Heraclitus

I n addition to the empirical and conceptual foundations in Chapter 2, the strategies in this book borrow largely from three therapeutic approaches: (a) the
work of Milton Erickson, (b) the brief strategic therapy of the Mental Research
Institute (MRI), and (c) the solution-focused therapy of the Brief Family Therapy
Center (BFTC). After discussing each of these influences, the chapter concludes
with five practical assumptions of solution-focused counseling in schools.

The Work of Milton Erickson

You already know what to do, you just don't know that you already know.
—Milton H. Erickson, quoted in Rossi, 1980

Milton Erickson is considered one of the most innovative practitioners in the history
of psychotherapy. Although he died in 1980, his therapeutic methods live on through
continued discussion of his work in books and workshops. Of his many and varied
contributions, the following are particularly relevant to school-based counseling.

One Client at a Time

Erickson was often asked about his general theory of psychopathology and therapy, to which he would reply, "I don't have a 'general theory' because I've never
met a 'general' client." He viewed psychological theories as intriguing but of little
practical use in helping people change. Erickson believed that clients are the best
teachers of what will and will not work in therapy. He customized his approach
to each client instead of squeezing the client into preformed therapy molds and
techniques. Providing services "one client at a time" is a hallmark of Ericksonian
therapy and solution-focused counseling in schools.

Efficiency

Erickson believed that therapeutic solutions can be found quickly and independently of detailed information about the problem. He demonstrated this time and
time again with a range of clients, including those diagnosed with serious psycho-

logical disorders. He spent relatively little time on the problem, focusing instead on the solution. He was a consummate listener and observer, always looking for hints of possibilities and solutions within clients and their circumstances. Regardless of the diagnosis and problem, Erickson believed that every client is inherently wise, resourceful, and capable of changing in meaningful ways. According to Erickson, the quickest and most dignified route to a solution is to build on the client's strengths and resources. Solution-focused counseling adopts the efficient, strength-based focus of Erickson.

Focus on the Future: The Crystal Ball Technique

Erickson was always more interested in where clients wanted to go than where they had already been. In the "crystal ball technique," he invited clients to imagine a problem-free future and describe how they resolved their problem (Erickson, 1954). Clients typically reported ideas and actions that fitted their unique style and circumstances, at which point Erickson would encourage them to implement their own ideas. In addition to shifting the focus from past problems to future possibilities, this strategy often revealed inner resources that clients had forgotten about or discounted. Several years later, Erickson's crystal ball technique was elaborated into the "miracle question" (de Shazer, 1985), a core strategy of solution-focused therapy in which clients are asked to describe what their life would look like after a miracle occurred and their problem vanished.

Emphasis on Small Change

Erickson believed that small changes lead to larger and more meaningful changes. He listened for any sign of change and invited clients to elaborate on it. In summarizing this aspect of Erickson's work, Haley (1973) stated that "he seeks a small change and enlarges upon it. If the change is in a crucial area, what appears small can change the whole system" (p. 35).

The systemic notion that small changes can ripple into larger ones provides hope and encouragement for busy school practitioners, who may have only one or two opportunities to meet with a student. Solution-focused counseling requires ongoing alertness and appreciation of any sign of improvement, regardless of how small it may appear.

Utilization

Erickson's utilization of whatever clients brought to counseling is perhaps the most renowned aspect of his work. He viewed clients as inherently wise, capable, and resilient. Instead of giving clients something they did not already have, he invited them to recognize and apply existing resources toward solutions to their problem. Erickson viewed clients as "stuck" versus "sick" and utilized their hobbies, interests, and strengths in designing creative and individualized interventions. He tailored his words and methods to clients instead of requiring them to conform to his language or favorite techniques. Respecting and utilizing what students, parents, and teachers bring to the change process is a vital part of solution-focused counseling.

Example of Erickson's Approach: The Student Who Refused to Read. Erickson's cooperative and efficient approach is illustrated in the following example involving a 12-year-old student named Paul. Paul was referred to Erickson because he was not reading. When given a first-grade reader, he stumbled through it if he attempted it at all. His parents insisted that he could read and witheld privileges in an attempt to prompt his reading. Despite the loss of privileges and other punishments, Paul held his ground and refused to read.

In his first meeting with Paul, Erickson expressed the view that Paul's parents appeared very stubborn in not accepting that he could not read. Erickson told Paul to "forget about reading" and to think of a fun way for them to spend the therapy hour. When asked about his hobbies, Paul said that he enjoyed fishing and hoped to go on a fishing trip with his father. He told Erickson that his father typically fished in California and Washington but was planning a trip to Alaska in the upcoming year. Erickson pulled out a map and asked for Paul's help in locating the specific towns in which his father fished. As Erickson confused certain towns on the map, Paul corrected him. They spent the next couple sessions "looking at" (not "reading") maps, discussing fishing techniques, and looking up different kinds of fish in the encyclopedia.

Observing Paul's sense of adventure and mischief, Erickson suggested that Paul play a joke on his teachers and parents the next time they observed him attempting to read. Erickson suggested that Paul take the first-grade reader and stumble through it just like he usually did but that he do a little better on the second-grade reader, better yet on the third-grade reader, and so on. Paul thought it was a great idea, implemented it, and displayed no additional reading problems in the future.

Erickson's work with Paul illustrates various aspects of his respectful approach to helping people change. For example, Erickson (a) accepted and accommodated Paul's choice not to read instead of trying to talk him out of it, (b) focused on future solutions versus past problems, (c) identified areas of strength and interest for Paul, and (d) utilized Paul's strengths and interests in developing an individualized intervention. When you consider these features together, it is no wonder that Paul readily accepted and implemented the intervention. Additional examples and descriptions of Erickson's work can be found in Haley (1985) and Short, Erickson, and Klein (2005). Erickson's influence is evident in the following discussion of strategic and solution-focused models of therapy.

MRI: Brief Strategic Therapy

We find that in deliberate intervention into human problems the most
pragmatic approach is not to question why? but what?; that is, what is
being done here and now that serves to perpetuate the problem,
and what can be done here and now to effect a change.
—Watzlawick, Weakland, & Fisch, 1974, p. 86

Influenced by Erickson and convinced that meaningful change can occur rapidly, a group of clinicians and researchers launched the brief therapy project at the MRI in Palo Alto, California (Fisch & Schlanger, 1999; Fisch, Weakland, & Segal, 1982;

Watzlawick et al., 1974). Many innovators in the field of psychotherapy have spent time at the MRI, including John Weakland, Paul Watzlawick, Virginia Satir, Jay Haley, and Steve de Shazer. The MRI group videotaped hundreds of sessions and analyzed therapeutic processes and outcomes with a variety of clients and problems, ranging from children to older adults and from parent–adolescent conflict to schizophrenia. The result was an intriguing theory of how problems are created and resolved.

The Problem Process

As they met with more and more clients and studied the videotapes, the MRI team noticed an intriguing pattern in the way most problems are developed and maintained (Watzlawick et al., 1974). This pattern, which they called the *problem process,* is described below and graphically illustrated in Figure 3.1.

1. An "ordinary difficulty" occurs, such as feelings of sadness or getting in trouble at school (e.g., Jason, a second-grade student, does not complete a couple of math homework assignments one week).

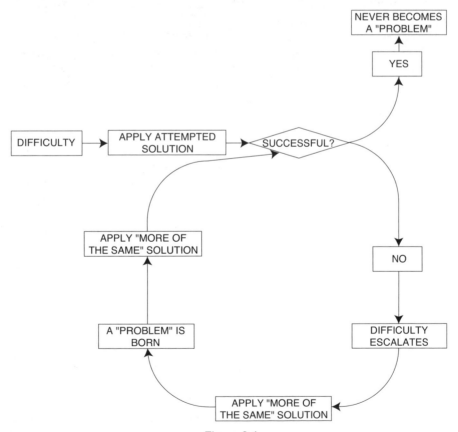

Figure 3.1
The Mental Research Institute problem process.

2. Attempted solutions are applied (e.g., Jason's parents lecture him on the importance of homework completion, and his math teacher reminds him to do homework each day at the end of class).
3. Solution attempts are unsuccessful, the concern escalates, and "more of the same" solutions are applied (e.g., Jason misses two more assignments during the next week, followed by more lectures and reminders).
4. The concern is now viewed as a problem, and solutions are applied even more vigorously, on the basis of the belief that they represent the only sensible thing to do about the problem. The solution has become the problem (e.g., Jason continues to miss homework assignments, while his teacher and parents continue to remind and lecture him).
5. This cycle continues until it is interrupted by someone "doing something different."

The Nine-Dot Problem in Appendix B illustrates how easy it is to get stuck in a vicious cycle of more of the same solution attempts. The notion that solutions can become part of the problem is an important consideration for school practitioners. One of the more common problem patterns involving students is the "responsibility trap." This occurs when well-intentioned adults, usually parents, attempt to resolve a school problem by taking on progressively more responsibility for the problem as the student takes on less (Durrant, 1995). This pattern may persist for weeks or even months despite no major change.

Interrupting Ineffective Solutions by Trying Something Different

Since most problems result from ineffective solution attempts, according to the MRI model, interventions were designed to interrupt existing solutions and promote different responses. Clients were encouraged to "do" and "view" the problem in ways that were opposite or contrary to current solutions.

In working with Jason's situation as described above, the counselor might ask his parents and teacher what they have tried and how it worked. Once people realize that their attempted solutions might be making matters worse, they are more willing to try something different. Jason's parents might be encouraged to apologize for interfering in his school life and explain that school is now his responsibility, not theirs. His teacher could ask him whether he would be willing to serve as her special consultant on various classroom matters. Since both interventions are very different from previous solutions, they have a reasonable chance of resolving the problem on the basis of the MRI model.

Client Position

As noted in Chapter 2, the more acceptable an intervention is to clients, the more likely they are to implement it. Long before researchers acknowledged the important role of treatment acceptability in counseling, the MRI team discovered that the counselor's suggestions were more acceptable when presented with careful attention to the client's frame of reference. The team used the term *client position* to refer to clients' beliefs about the problem and their role in changing it.

It is not surprising that MRI therapists found that clients were more likely to implement interventions that were compatible with their position, as compared to interventions that were not. For example, a teacher who views a student's behavior as manipulative would be more likely to implement an intervention presented with a compatible rationale, such as to regain her control of the class-room, than she would if the same intervention were presented in a way that did not adequately fit her position, such as to support and nurture the child. Likewise, a student who views her teacher as out to get her is less likely to implement an intervention presented as a way to improve the relationship or get closer to the teacher than she would if the intervention were aimed at proving the teacher wrong about her or providing fewer opportunities for the teacher to pick on her. MRI therapists also adapted their suggestions to clients' perceptions of the urgency of the problem and their role in resolving it. For example, ac-tion-oriented interventions that require a lot of time and energy are appropriate for clients who view the problem as urgent and see themselves as part of the solution. These same interventions would not be appropriate for a student who sees the problem as a nagging and overcontrolling teacher and views himself as an innocent bystander.

The concept of client position is one of the most elegant and respectful features of the MRI model. Additional strategies for tailoring counseling services to each client are described in Chapter 4.

Example of Brief Strategic Therapy: Tripping the Responsibility Trap. Joe was a bright and creative third grader referred by his parents and teacher for low grades. Information from Joe's teacher, parents, and school records suggested that he was much more capable than his grades indicated. His low grades resulted primarily from minimal homework completion. Joe's parents were hard-working, conscientious people who were willing to do anything to help their only son. In an effort to get Joe to complete more homework, his parents pleaded with him and offered frequent reminders throughout the evening. These strategies remained in effect for the first couple of months of the school year. This "nagging routine," as aptly labeled by the family, was very upsetting to Joe and his parents. The parents were stuck in a repetitive pattern of ineffective solutions. The more they nagged, the worse it got. They viewed Joe as troubled and saw the problem as a sign of his difficulty adjusting to a new teacher and a new classroom. As caring and con-scientious parents, they were concerned about Joe's irresponsible attitude toward schoolwork and wanted to help him any way they could.

A new and different approach was suggested to Joe's parents on the basis of the rationale that their daily reminders and lectures might be interfering with Joe's opportunity to take personal responsibility for his schoolwork. This rationale ac-commodated their position about Joe's lack of responsibility and their desire to support him any way they could. In an effort to approach things differently, the parents agreed to do the following: (a) meet with Joe and express their confidence in his ability to handle schoolwork and homework on his own, (b) allow Joe and his teacher to work out any difficulties related to school, and (c) go about their business at home without lecturing or even mentioning homework. The parents implemented these suggestions and reported rapid improvements in Joe's homework completion.

By the time students are referred for counseling, many of them have heard the same old song from various adults. When students or others express an unenthusiastic response to our suggestions, it is time to try something different. The wisdom of the MRI team is captured in the practical expression, "If it doesn't work, try something else."

BFTC: Solution-Focused Therapy

Historically psychotherapy has concerned itself with problems
(variously defined) and solutions (seldom defined at all), with the problems
receiving the major share of the effort. In fact, solutions have been looked
at so rarely that solution has become the hidden half of the
"problem/solution" distinction.
—de Shazer, 1988, p. 6

The term *solution-focused therapy* was coined in the 1980s by Steve de Shazer and his colleagues at the BFTC in Milwaukee, Wisconsin (de Shazer, 1985; de Shazer et al., 1986). This approach has enjoyed a growing popularity among practitioners because of its practical emphasis on efficiency, cooperation, solutions, and client strengths. Solution-focused practices have been applied to a variety of clients, problems, and settings, including young children (Berg & Steiner, 2003), chronic psychological problems (Rowan & O'Hanlon, 1999), and schools (Metcalf, 1995; Murphy, 1994).

The BFTC group elaborated on the work of Erickson by partnering with clients to develop goals and build solutions from existing successes and resources. Repeated observations of therapy sessions led them to conclude that (a) the counselor does not need to know a lot about the problem to help the client resolve it and (b) problems are resolved more quickly when counseling focuses primarily on solution-related details and possibilities rather than problem history, presumed causes, and other aspects of the problem.

Skeleton Keys

One of the most fascinating observations of the BFTC was that certain interventions were effective for most clients regardless of their problem. The team called these interventions "skeleton keys" (de Shazer, 1985) and shifted their focus from the lock (problem) to the key (solution). If the counselor's goal is to help clients open the door to solutions, then it is highly inefficient to spend a lot of time studying each lock. It is more efficient to simply insert the keys into the lock. The remainder of this section describes useful skeleton keys in school counseling.

Formula First Session Task

One of the first skeleton keys developed at the BFTC was the "formula first session task," which was presented to clients at the end of the first session in the following way:

> Between now and the next time we meet, I would like you to observe, so you can describe to me next time, what happens in your [pick one: family, life, marriage, relationship] that you want to continue to have happen. (de Shazer, 1985, p. 137)

The BFTC team reported that clients often came to the second session with additional ideas and hope regarding solutions. They were encouraged to do more of whatever they wanted to see continue happening in their life. As the team focused more and more on future solutions versus past problems, they discovered two other useful skeleton keys: the miracle question and exceptions to the problem.

Miracle Question

Inspired by Erickson's crystal ball technique, the miracle question was developed to help clients envision and describe life without the problem: "Suppose that one night, while you were asleep, there was a miracle and this problem was solved. How would you know? What would be different?" (de Shazer, 1988, p. 5). Students enjoy the playfulness of this question, and it helps them define more precisely what they want from counseling (e.g., "I'll get my homework done, and my teachers won't yell at me at school"). The miracle question also helps parents and teachers translate broad goals and expectations (improving the student's independence or attitude) into concrete behavioral descriptions (completing schoolwork with fewer reminders or "answering me when I ask her a question"). In addition to shifting the client's focus from the problem to the solution, these concrete goals serve as practical criteria for evaluating the effectiveness of counseling. As well as helping people develop clear goals, the miracle question boosts hope by focusing on future possibilities.

Exceptions to the Problem

Building on exceptions to the problem is a core intervention in solution-focused therapy. Exceptions, which are times when the problem is absent or less noticeable, represent solutions that are already happening. Counselors invite clients to expand on exceptions by increasing the frequency or settings in which they occur. Encouraging students to describe exceptions helps them to focus on what to do instead of what not to do. Most people prefer to work toward what they want rather than away from what they don't want. Chapter 6 provides strategies and real-life examples of building on exceptions to school problems.

Keeping It Simple

Another aspect of solution-focused therapy that is well suited to the practical realities of school counseling is the notion of "keeping it simple." The BFTC team observed that sometimes all you need is a small change in the client's perceptions or actions to initiate a solution. Solution-focused counselors typically consider simple interventions before suggesting complex, time-consuming strategies. The notion of keeping it simple appeals not only to busy school practitioners but to students, parents, teachers, and other clients.

Example of Solution-Focused Therapy: Growing Solutions From Small Seeds of Success. This example highlights the importance of keeping it simple and building on exceptions to the problem. The parents of a ninth-grade student named Diora asked that I meet with their daughter. Their concerns centered on the increasing arguments between Diora and her mother, most of which occurred shortly after Diora arrived home from school.

Early in our first meeting, I explored exceptions to the problem by asking Diora whether there were any times when she and her mother were able to talk without fighting. After quickly answering "no," Diora corrected herself and recalled that they did not fight at all when they talked about flowers and gardening, a hobby they both enjoyed. We discovered some other common interests and topics that the two of them might be able to talk about without fighting. We referred to these as DDTs, short for doable discussion topics. Diora perked up and became more engaged as we discussed what was working versus not working in her relationship with her mother.

An experiment was suggested in which Diora would (a) initiate a conversation with her mother about flowers or another DDT every day after school and (b) observe and rate how well they got along for the rest of the day. Diora returned the next week and reported that she and her mother still argued about things, but not nearly as often or intensely as they had the week before. No additional concerns were reported that year by Diora or her parents.

The positive, straightfoward approach of the BFTC is well suited to the practical realities of counseling in schools. As illustrated throughout this book, a solution orientation toward what is right and what is working for students and others is applicable to a variety of problems and situations encountered by school practitioners. This orientation drives the major guideline of solution-focused counseling in schools: If it works, do more of it.

As indicated by its title, this book owes much to the therapeutic ideas of de Shazer, Berg, and their colleagues at the BFTC in Milwaukee. Refer to the following sources for additional information on solution-focused therapy: de Shazer et al. (2007), McDonald (2007), Nelson and Thomas (2007), and O'Connell (2005).

Summary of Therapeutic Influences

Table 3.1 summarizes the major contributions of Erickson, the MRI, and the BFTC. Although solution-focused counseling borrows techniques from each of these approaches, it is the client who ultimately determines the acceptability and usefulness of any technique. Research makes it clear that no one method works with every client in every situation. We need to be flexible in selecting and discarding techniques on the basis of the client's response. Regardless of what models or methods a counselor adopts, outcomes are enhanced when counseling is client driven versus technique or practitioner driven. With these points in mind, the following section describes five assumptions of solution-focused counseling for school problems.

Table 3.1

Therapeutic Influences

Therapist/Group	Key Features
Milton H. Erickson	Customized services to each client; used the "crystal ball technique" to encourage clients to focus on the future; encouraged small changes in the problem; viewed clients as stuck vs. sick
Mental Research Institute	Described a common problem process in which attempted solutions become the problem; interrupted ineffective solutions by encouraging clients to "do" and "view" the problem differently; framed interventions to fit the client's position
Brief Family Therapy Center	Emphasized efficiency and "keeping it simple"; focused on future goals vs. past problems; used "skeleton keys" to unlock a wide range of problems; built solutions from exceptions to the problem

Five Working Assumptions of Solution-Focused Counseling in Schools

The following assumptions are derived from the research described in Chapter 2 and the therapeutic influences of Erickson, the MRI, and the BFTC. These pragmatic assumptions guide the entire counseling process.

1. *If It Works, Do More of It. If It Doesn't Work, Do Something Different*

This assumption captures the pragmatic nature of solution-focused counseling. As simple as it sounds, it is not always easy to put into practice. The first part emphasizes the guiding theme of solution-focused therapy: Identify what works for clients, and encourage them to do more of it. Solution-focused counseling favors interventions constructed from what works and what's right with clients, encouraging them to build on their strengths, successes, and other resources. Likewise, practitioners are advised to do more of what works on the basis of student feedback and other measures of progress. The second half of the assumption, based on brief strategic therapy, suggests doing something different when things are not working. Solution-focused counseling encourages practitioners and clients to hold lightly to theories and techniques and be willing to let them go and try something else when they are not working. The value of any technique rests on its practical usefulness in promoting change and moving clients closer to their goals.

In solution-focused counseling, the two primary ways of doing more of what works are building on exceptions (Chapter 6) and client resources (Chapter 7). In regard to doing something different when things are not working, solution-focused counseling draws on numerous strategies for changing the doing (Chapter 8) and changing the viewing (Chapter 9) of the problem.

2. *Every Client Is Unique, Resourceful, and Capable of Changing*

This assumption cautions us against categorizing students and problems on the basis of our previous experiences or favorite theories. Adopting a position of curiosity helps us approach every client from a fresh perspective that honors his or her unique circumstances, goals, and resources. Given that the client is the key ingredient of change, the success of counseling rests largely on the extent to which we respect and utilize "as much of the client as possible," including his or her values, ideas, life experiences, strengths, and feedback on the usefulness of our services.

In the midst of a serious problem, especially one that has occurred for a long time, people often become demoralized and develop a "problem-saturated" story of themselves (White & Epston, 1990). Solution-focused counseling encourages a richer and more hopeful story by inviting students and others to recognize and apply their unique strengths and resources toward meaningful goals. People experiencing school problems are viewed as stuck versus sick, and problems are seen as temporary roadblocks rather than symptoms of pathology. Students are enlisted as valuable consultants and partners in the change process instead of being treated as passive players in an "adults-only" version of counseling. Viewing clients as capable and resourceful does not deny the seriousness or pain of a problem. It does, however, create solution opportunities that might otherwise be overlooked.

3. *Cooperative Relationships Enhance Solutions*

The quality of the client–practitioner alliance is the best predictor of outcomes in counseling (Wampold, 2001). Effective counseling relationships are built on mutual respect and common goals. This includes our accommodation of clients' goals, resources, and feedback and their trust in our commitment and ability to help them reach their goals. Students, parents, and teachers are more likely to implement interventions that emerge from their input and resources as compared to ideas that are imposed on them. Client participation is the pivotal feature of a strong alliance. Counseling works best when clients are actively involved, when they experience a positive relationship with the counselor, and when counseling addresses what clients see as important. In counseling students, we can promote cooperative, change-focused relationships by (a) validating clients' struggles and perceptions; (b) encouraging their active involvement and collaboration; (c) conveying hope in their ability to change; (d) commenting on any positive changes, no matter how small; (e) giving them credit for improvements; (f) focusing on future solutions instead of past problems; and (g) obtaining their feedback and adjusting services accordingly.

4. *No Problem Is Constant*

This assumption acknowledges the ongoing flux of human behavior. Regardless of how constant a problem seems, there are always fluctuations in its rate and intensity. Solution-focused practitioners seek out these fluctuations or exceptions to the problem, explore the conditions under which they occur, and encourage students and others to do more of whatever they have done to bring them about. In addition to providing clues to solutions, discussing exceptions may increase people's self-confidence and hope in the possibility of solutions and in their ability to bring those solutions about.

5. *Big Problems Do Not Always Require Big Solutions*

Solution-focused counseling is based on the practical notion that one small change in any part of the problem system can ripple into larger and more significant changes. This is encouraging to busy practitioners who have neither the time nor the resources to conduct elaborate, time-consuming interventions for every school problem.

As evidenced throughout the chapter, solution-focused counseling differs in several ways from more traditional, problem-focused counseling. These differences are summarized in Table 3.2.

Table 3.2

Comparison of Problem-Focused and Solution-Focused Counseling

Problem-Focused Counseling	*Solution-Focused Counseling*
Focus on weaknesses, deficits, and problems ("problem talk")	Focus on the strengths, resources, and solutions ("solution talk")
Past focused	Future focused
Interview serves assessment and diagnostic functions	Interview serves intervention and solution-building functions
Client is viewed as sick	Client is viewed as stuck
Services are counselor driven: Goals and interventions emerge from the counselor's preferences and model	Services are client driven: Goals and interventions emerge from the client's preferences, theories, and resources
Counselor is the expert and teacher; client follows the counselor's lead	Client is the expert and teacher; counselor follows the client's lead
Intervention failures and client's uncooperativeness indicate that the client is resistant and needs to adapt to the counselor and the intervention approach	Intervention failures and client's uncooperativeness indicate that the counselor and the intervention approach need to be adapted to the client
Assumes a direct relationship between problems and solutions: Solutions emerge from the assessment of problem history, origins, and presumed causes	Assumes no necessary relationship between problems and solutions: Some solutions, like skeleton keys, fit any type of problem regardless of its history, origins, or presumed causes
Solutions are seen as resulting primarily from the counselor's skillful application of counseling models and techniques	Solutions are seen as resulting primarily from a strong alliance and accommodation of the client's ideas, resources, and feedback

Summary and Conclusions

This chapter has described three therapeutic influences of solution-focused counseling. The work of Milton Erickson highlights the importance of approaching counseling one client at a time, utilizing the client's strengths and resources, and inviting clients to envision a better future. Erickson's focus on efficiency and small changes also fits well with the practical realities of school-based counseling. The brief strategic therapy model of the MRI illustrates how attempted solutions can perpetuate the very problem they are intended to resolve. Brief strategic therapy seeks to interrupt ineffective solutions and encourage very different responses to the problem. The MRI model also highlights the importance of accommodating the client's position throughout counseling. The founders of solution-focused therapy at the BFTC discovered that it is more efficient to focus on building solutions rather than eliminating problems. The BFTC used the term *skeleton keys* to refer to interventions that work with most clients regardless of the problem, including the formula first session task, the miracle question, and building on exceptions. The BFTC's emphasis on keeping it simple fits well with the practical realities of school counseling.

The therapeutic wisdom of Erickson, the MRI, and the BFTC was integrated with the empirical research in Chapter 2 to formulate five working assumptions of solution-focused counseling in schools:

- If it works, do more of it. If it doesn't work, do something different.
- Every client is unique, resourceful, and capable of improving.
- Cooperative relationships enhance solutions.
- No problem is constant, and change is inevitable.
- Big problems do not always require big solutions.

Part 2 translates these assumptions into practical strategies for helping students, teachers, and parents change school problems, beginning with strategies for establishing effective relationships in Chapter 4.

Practice Exercises

1. Milton Erickson focused on one client at a time. What are the major advantages and challenges of adopting this perspective in your day-to-day work with students and school problems?
2. Erickson utilized clients' beliefs, attitudes, and skills to develop solutions. Pick a client during the upcoming week and think about how his or her beliefs and talents might be applied toward a solution.
3. What are two elements of the MRI's brief strategic therapy model that are particularly useful in working with students and school problems?
4. Think of a current situation in which people's attempts to resolve the problem appear to be making it worse. What could you suggest to the clients in this case to interrupt their ineffective solution attempts while respecting their beliefs and opinions regarding the problem?

5. Explain the concept of skeleton keys in solution-focused brief therapy. Think about a challenging situation that you are working with, and describe how one of the skeleton keys could be used to promote a solution.
6. During the next week, try out the formula first session task by asking one or two of your clients to make a list of the things in their life that they want to continue happening. Ask them what they have done and are currently doing to make these things happen. For a more personalized experience, make a similar list pertaining to you and your life. Ask yourself what you did to bring these things about and what you can do in the future to sustain them. Observe differences in the way that you and your clients react to focusing on what works instead of what does not work.
7. Discuss three assumptions of solution-focused counseling, with emphasis on how each assumption applies to the everyday challenges of school-based counseling.
8. Describe one small step that you are willing to take in your practice as a result of the information in this chapter.

PART TWO

Tasks and Techniques of Solution-Focused Counseling

CHAPTER 4

Building Cooperative, Change-Focused Relationships

My other counselors never asked me what I wanted to work on.
It's a lot better when you ask a person what they want to do.
—Molly, 10-year-old student

Tell me, I forget. Involve me, I understand.
—Chinese proverb

The quality of the client–counselor relationship as perceived by the client is one of the best predictors of counseling success (Bedi, Davis, & Williams, 2005; Martin et al., 2000). This chapter presents practical strategies for building cooperative, change-focused relationships with students, parents, teachers, and others involved in the counseling process.

Adopting the "Ambassador Mind-Set"

In the beginner's mind, there are many possibilities,
but in the expert's there are few.
—Shunryu Suzuki, *Zen Mind, Beginner's Mind*

One way to promote strong relationships is to approach clients with the attitude of a foreign ambassador entering an unfamiliar country or culture (Murphy, 1997). Good ambassadors adopt the following beliefs and actions, all of which apply to effective counseling:

- Approach people with "a beginner's mind" that conveys humility, curiosity, and a willingness to learn.
- Look, listen, ask, and learn as much as possible before offering suggestions.
- Treat people as experts regarding themselves and their circumstances, and as active contributors to their own solutions.
- Respect people's freedom to accept or reject suggestions and to adapt them to their unique situation.
- Respect diverse opinions, cultural backgrounds, and new ideas.

The ambassador perspective differs from the traditional medical model approach to helping, in which the expert practitioner diagnoses problems and prescribes treatments with minimal input from the client.

The importance of the ambassador perspective was dramatically reinforced at a recent workshop I presented to an international audience. As I described the ambassador perspective, a Native American counselor named Anna described how the "know-it-all" position of helping professionals has gravely impeded their effectiveness with Native Americans: "My people are cautious about sharing their problems with pushy professionals who think they know it all." She made a passionate plea for professional humility, stating that Native Americans deserve to be respected for their unique gifts, traditions, and resources instead of being told what to do by professionals who have not taken the time to adequately understand them. Anna's advice serves as an endorsement of the ambassador mind-set and a useful reminder for those working with people from all cultural backgrounds.

Curiosity

We can convey the ambassador mind-set by being curious and tentative instead of absolute and certain. Anderson and Goolishian (1992) recommended approaching clients from a position of "not knowing." Put yourself in the student's shoes as you read the following scenarios, in which the counselor proposes a different view of the teacher. Pay close attention to the counselor's language (key phrases are italicized in Scenario 2).

> *Scenario 1: The All-Knowing, Absolute, Certain Counselor:* When we met last week, you were saying that your teachers were too strict and they didn't care about you. I've thought about that, along with some other things we discussed. I think you've got your teachers all wrong [statement of certainty]. They actually care a lot about you. It is precisely because they care about you that they take the time and effort to make sure you do your homework and get good grades. [The phrase "it is precisely because" implies absolute truth.] Do you understand?

> *Scenario 2: The Not-Knowing, Curious, Tentative Counselor:* When we met last week, you were saying that your teachers were too strict and they didn't care about you. *I'm wondering* if there could be any other *possible* explanations for what your teachers are doing [statement of curiosity]. *I'm not sure* if this is on target [tentative statement], but I'll let you decide. *Could it be that* one of the reasons your teachers get on your case about turning in homework and getting good grades is because they *might* actually care about you enough to remind you to turn it in, so you can get better grades? *I don't know*, what do you think?

One of the surest ways to ruin a good idea is to force it on people against their will, as illustrated by the counselor in Scenario 1. This counselor disregards the fact that students prefer to form their own opinions of our ideas, which weakens the alliance and sets up a potential power struggle. In contrast to the authoritarian tone of Scenario 1, the counselor in Scenario 2 offers the same idea in a tentative and curious manner. These words convey the ambassador mind-set by putting the student in the driver's seat as the ultimate judge of the counselor's idea. Box 4.1 illustrates the futility of trying to talk people out of their beliefs.

In addition to inviting people to freely accept or reject our ideas, the language of curiosity helps to preserve our credibility when an idea is judged as inaccurate or unhelpful. When clients reject an idea that is presented as a possibility that might work, we can simply move on with our credibility intact. In contrast, presenting our ideas as truths or certainties boxes us into a corner, jeopardizes our credibility, and

---

Box 4.1
George, the Dead Guy: Convincing the Unconvincible

George was referred to a psychiatrist by his wife because he thought he was dead. True to form, George entered the psychiatrist's office and boldly proclaimed that he was dead. The psychiatrist skillfully presented several rational arguments to convince him otherwise, none of which worked to change George's position. The psychiatrist became frustrated and said, "Sir, you seem like a decent fellow. Why don't we talk about what's really bothering you and drop this stuff about being dead. What do you say, George?" George was touched by the doctor's concern but steadfastly maintained that he was dead. Suddenly, a brilliant idea occurred to the psychiatrist, and the following dialogue ensued.

Psychiatrist: George, are you absolutely sure you are dead?
George: Yes.
Psychiatrist: Would you be willing to participate in a scientific experiment to put your belief to the test?
George: Sure.
Psychiatrist: Tell me, George, do dead men bleed?
George: Of course not.
Psychiatrist: Would you allow me to gently prick your finger with a pin to see whether or not you bleed?
George: Sure.

With that, the doctor pricked George's finger, which promptly began to bleed. George looked dejected as he stared at his bleeding finger.

Psychiatrist: You can't escape the facts now, George. You have to admit you were wrong, don't you?
George: [turning to leave the office] Yes, doctor. I was wrong all along. Dead men do bleed.

Note. This story was adapted from *Friedman's Fables,* by E. H. Friedman, 1990, New York: Guilford Press. Copyright 1990 by Guilford Press. Adapted with permission.

limits solution opportunities. The following words and phrases convey a respectful position of curiosity:

- I'm not sure if this makes sense, but . . .
- I don't know, but it sounds like . . .
- Perhaps . . .
- Could it be that . . .
- It seems like . . .
- I'm wondering . . .
- Suppose you tried . . .What do you think might happen then?
- Is it possible that . . . ?

Curiosity is useful throughout the counseling process. For example, the following questions can be used after the client has made positive changes:

- How did you manage to change things so quickly?
- What have you been doing differently?
- I'm curious about how this happened. How did you do this?

The counselor's curiosity about how students and others made improvements encourages them to take credit for such changes and reflect on what they did to bring them about.

I recently asked a 15-year-old student who had been to several counselors for her advice on how helping professionals can work effectively with young people. She replied, "The most important thing is to listen and get to know the person before making any suggestions, and to ask them what they think instead of always telling them what to do." This is sound advice for practitioners who work with students of all ages. Like good ambassadors, the most successful counselors are "shaped into effectiveness" by their clients. In applying the ambassador mind-set with students and others, I often remind myself that I work for them, they don't work for me.

Validation

Effective ambassadors (and counselors) validate their clients by accepting their clients' opinions, respecting their concerns, and assuming that they are doing the best they can under the circumstances. Students, parents, and teachers may be wary of the counselor's judgments for various reasons. They may be embarrassed by the problem or by their inability to resolve it, both of which may create defensiveness during the first session. Validation frees up clients to focus on resolving the problem instead of defending themselves. Once people know that we are not blaming them, they can relax and direct their energies toward solutions. Validation involves

- listening to what clients say and how they say it;
- accepting their perceptions at face value;
- normalizing their concerns and struggles;

- conveying faith in their strengths and resources;
- partnering with them to construct individualized interventions that match their perceptions, goals, and resources;
- acknowledging their desire to make things better and their ability to cope with difficult circumstances.

Validation may involve short responses, such as "yes," "of course," and "sure," or longer statements, such as the following:

- I can see why it's important for you to stand up for yourself on the playground.
- No wonder you're so worried about this. It's a big decision, and you want to make the right one.
- It makes perfect sense to take your time instead of rushing in and trying to fix this all at once.
- With everything you went through last week, it's understandable that you feel like giving up. In fact, I'm wondering how you've managed to hang in there so far without giving up.

Normalizing is a special form of validation that is particularly useful in working with students, teachers, and parents. Consider Elise, an experienced and respected fourth-grade teacher who requested help with Joseph. It was a well-known fact that Elise had the toughest fourth-grade class on the basis of her solid reputation and behavior management skills. Elise was embarrassed as she described how Joseph's behavior bothered her so much and wondered aloud whether she had lost her ability to manage difficult students. She described a specific incident in which she caught Joseph going through her desk and yelled at him, which was not her usual response. Later that week, she got into an argument with his parents when they did not acknowledge the seriousness of Joseph's behavior. Elise cowered as she described these events, as if she was fully expecting to be scolded or criticized by the practitioner. After allowing Elise to describe her concerns and feelings, the practitioner normalized her reactions in the following way:

> Elise, I know you didn't respond to Joseph the way you wanted to, but it's no wonder that you lost it with him and his parents. He has been a thorn in your side all year. You have patiently helped him with his behavior and academics, not to mention all the discussions you've had with his parents. On top of all this, you have a very large class with a lot of tough kids. I'm not surprised that you're frustrated.

Elise was visibly relieved by this validation. With the assurance that she was not "losing it" and that the practitioner was there to support rather than judge her, Elise developed an effective plan for working with Joseph and his parents.

Listening

Listening may be the most underrated skill in the helping professions. Above all, effective counselors are good listeners. Listening in itself validates our interest in clients, their concerns, and their goals. It conveys the respectful notion that, to be useful to clients, we need to learn about who they are and what they want from us. The following example illustrates the importance of listening before giving advice.

Brittany: The Benefits of Listening and "Not Knowing." Several years ago, a high school student named Brittany taught me a valuable lesson about not knowing and listening in counseling with young people. Brittany was referred for counseling by her teachers because of absenteeism and declining grades during the first half of her senior year. Brittany's file referred to a prior sexual abuse experience in which she was molested by her father. Although our counseling goal was to improve grades and school attendance, Brittany's comments regarding sexual abuse are highlighted in the following excerpt from our first meeting.

Brittany: So are you some kind of expert on sexual abuse?

Counselor: No, I'm not an expert. Why do you ask?

Brittany: I saw that book on your shelf [referring to a book on counseling sexually abused children].

Counselor: I see. I have read some things on sexual abuse, but most of what I've learned has come from people like you who have told me about their own experiences and reactions to it. Does that make any sense?

Brittany: Yes. The last psychiatrist I went to babbled on about this and that. Repressed memory, masked depression [laughs]. I'm pretty smart with words, but half the time I didn't know what he was talking about.

Counselor: You mean talking about the sexual abuse?

Brittany: Yes.

Counselor: Did you *want* to talk to him about it?

Brittany: Yes. But *I* wanted to talk about it instead of having him go on and on. He acted like he could read my mind. He would tell me how I felt and what I thought. Give me a break.

Counselor: Well, I promise I can't read your mind, or anybody else's for that matter.

Brittany: [laughs] Thank God.

I met with Brittany four times throughout the remainder of the school year. On the basis of her comments regarding her previous counseling experiences, I listened a lot more than I talked during these sessions. I occasionally asked Brittany what I was doing or not doing that was helping or hindering our work together, and she told me. She accomplished her counseling goal of passing all of her classes and graduating from high school.

Brittany's comments during our last meeting of the year left a lasting impression on me regarding the importance of respecting the student's point of view.

Brittany: Thank you for helping so much this year.

Counselor: You're welcome. What did I do that helped you the most?

Brittany: You listened instead of telling me what to do. Nobody ever listens, but everybody has ideas about what to do, and they're not afraid to tell me. Do this, do that. It's like everybody is an expert on me except me. You didn't do that. You treated me like an adult instead of a weak little kid.

The recommendation to never argue with the client applies to clients of all ages. It is doubtful that Brittany would have accepted any theories regarding sexual abuse until her opinions were heard and validated.

The following guidelines are useful in listening to students, parents, teachers, and others:

- Listen with a beginner's mind, from a position of not knowing.
- Accept the student's comments at face value.
- Listen for any hints of strength, resilience, hope, and other resources.

Listening to students with a nonevaluative beginner's mind can be challenging. Most people do not practice these skills in everyday conversations. When people describe a recent experience in their life ("I bought a new car last week"), we typically respond with an interpretation and evaluation ("Way to go. I'm sure it's great to be driving a new car instead of an old clunker"). In solution-focused counseling, interpretations are generally avoided to keep the conversation firmly anchored to the client's goals, language, and perceptions.

Effective listening also requires alertness to strengths, competencies, hopes, and other resources. As Egan (2007) pointed out,

> if you listen only for problems, you will end up talking mainly about problems. And you will shortchange your clients. Every client has something going for him or her. Your job is to spot clients' resources and help them invest these resources in managing problem situations and opportunities. (p. 86)

Solution-focused counselors are like treasure hunters, continually alert to any and all hints of strength, success, and competency on the part of students and others. Listening speaks volumes about our commitment to clients and our faith in their ability to teach us how to be useful to them.

Asking

Asking the right question may be the most powerful part of thinking.
—Edward De Bono

In addition to listening, good ambassadors ask questions before making a lot of suggestions. Asking questions is an important means of gathering information in all counseling approaches. In solution-focused counseling, questions serve the additional purposes of strengthening the client–counselor alliance and empowering client and hope factors. In this sense, they should be considered *change-focused questions*. Change-focused questions explore what clients deem important (goals, values) and what they bring to the table to help them reach their goals (strengths, resources).

Counseling conversations shape the way clients view themselves, the problem, and the likelihood of solutions. The questions we ask play a big role in shaping the focus and content of a counseling session. In discussing the importance of effective questions, Egan (2007) cautioned against asking too many problem-focused questions:

> Like the rest of us, clients become what they talk about. If you always encourage them to talk about problems, they run the risk of becoming "problem people" . . . so be careful about the questions you ask. They should not keep clients mired in problem talk because problem talk can keep clients immersed in frustration, impotence, and even despair. (p. 244)

In schools, "why" questions are among the most common and damaging forms of problem talk with students. Consider the following questions from the student's perspective:

- Why did you do that?
- Why didn't you just tell the teacher after class instead of yelling it out during class?
- Why do you continue doing things that cause you so much trouble?

The goal of questions in solution-focused counseling is to trigger the key ingredients of change: client, relationship, and hope factors. When viewed in light of these common factors, "why" questions often fall short because they put students and others on the defensive and focus on unchangeable problems of the past versus changeable possibilities of the future.

In contrast to questions that are seen by clients as negative criticism or interrogation, change-focused questions are designed to enhance collaboration and cooperation. The story in Box 4.2 illustrates the benefits of asking versus telling students what to do about their problems.

Box 4.2

Asking Versus Telling: The Question Mark Strategy

A colleague recently told me about a simple strategy he learned from his clinical supervisor in graduate school. Before the counselor entered a session with a client who appeared reluctant to participate in the therapy process, his supervisor grabbed a magic marker and drew a large question mark on the palm of his hand. She told him to glance at it periodically during the session, especially when he was tempted to lecture or preach to the client. She added, "When you feel the urge to tell the client something, ask it instead."

The strategy worked beautifully. Just as he was about to tell the client something ("Maybe you should . . ."), he would spot the question mark and ask instead ("What do you think would be best?"). This simple technique serves as a powerful reminder to ask versus tell in order to enhance the client's involvement.

On the basis of the research-identified ingredients of successful counseling, one of the surest ways to build cooperation and solutions with students is to ask through the following tasks and questions:

- Cast the student as director and the practitioner as facilitator.
  - What do you hope to accomplish in our work together?
  - How will you know that counseling is working the way you want it to?
- Convey acceptance of the student's goals and perspectives.
  - How will things be different at school when your grades start improving?
  - What do you think would help turn things around?
- Encourage students to think of themselves and their school situation in flexible ways that promote hope and empowerment.
  - How did you resist the urge to argue with your teacher?
  - How will your teachers and parents treat you differently when things improve at school?
- Reveal naturally occurring assets in the student's life.
  - What would your friends say if I asked them what they liked most about you?
  - Who do you respect most in life, and what would he or she advise you to do about this?

Of the two overall types of questions, open and closed, open questions are favored in solution-focused counseling because they invite people to expand on their own ideas and perceptions. Closed questions, which can be answered with a "yes" or "no," are useful in gathering certain facts (e.g., "Did you pass your math test?"). However, they should be used sparingly because they keep the practitioner in control and put the student in the passive role of information provider versus active collaborator. Consider how students might respond to the following closed questions as compared to similar open questions.

- *Closed:* Do you care about your grades in school?
- *Open:* How do you view grades?
- *Closed:* I have reviewed your records, and math seems to be your biggest problem. I'd like to talk with you about how you could improve things in math class. Is that okay with you?
- *Open:* What do you think we should talk about today to move you closer to your goal?

Other examples of open questions include the following:

- How will you know whether our meetings are working?
- What do you think needs to happen to improve things?
- What can I do to be more helpful?
- What advice would you give other students who are struggling with this problem?

In addition to keeping the focus of conversation on the student, open questions elicit details about the problem, goals, exceptions, and resources. Consider the following question: "Suppose a miracle happens and the problem vanishes. What would you notice at school tomorrow that would let you know that things were better?" This question elicits concrete details about the student's goal and opens the door to exploring exceptions and other resources related to the goal. Most important, open questions invite students to describe things in their own words and from their own perspective.

Although open questions are favored in solution-focused counseling, closed questions are occasionally used to clarify details. For example, a student who responds to the miracle question by saying, "I won't get in as much trouble at school," might be asked the following closed questions to clarify her response: "Which class do you like the best?" "Do you behave better in some classes than others?" "Which class do you get in the least amount of trouble in?" Unlike other closed questions, which keep the practitioner in control, these questions focus on the student's perceptions and lay the groundwork for additional open questions. For example, if the student reports that she behaves best in science class, we can follow up with open questions such as "How are you different in science class?" and "What is different about your science class from your other classes?"

Change-focused questions serve to gather information, build positive relationships, and activate other potent ingredients of change. The efficiency of addressing multiple purposes in one question is a feature of solution-focused counseling that is particularly appealing to busy school practitioners. As illustrated throughout this chapter, questions often serve as the context for other relationship-building strategies in solution-focused counseling.

Complimenting

The client's hope for a better future is a vital part of successful counseling (Frank & Frank, 1991; Snyder, 2002). Compliments are used throughout solution-focused counseling to boost the hope and energy of students, parents, and teachers as they work toward school solutions.

Compliments are often integrated into questions, such as the following:

- How have you managed to cope so well with this situation so far?
- Some people would have given up on this long ago, but not you. Where do you find the strength to keep going?
- That was a great idea, and it worked for you. How did you come up with it?

In addition to revealing important strengths and resources, these questions compliment people on their resilience, success, and ingenuity.

While complimenting is useful with all clients, its impact may be particularly strong for people who rarely receive positive feedback. Some students have received very few compliments throughout their life, which can diminish hope and result in a "what's the use?" outlook. This makes it hard for them to muster the energy required to work on school problems and to persist in the face of obstacles. Compliments help to reframe students' view of themselves and their circumstances. For example, asking a student who complains of being stressed out and depressed "How have you managed to juggle so many things for so long?" invites a more empowering self-perception.

In a study of the relationship between outcomes and various aspects of solution-focused therapy, the use of compliments correlated strongly with positive outcomes (Linssen & Kerzbeck, 2002). Compliments counteract the demoralization and fatigue that students, teachers, and parents may experience as a result of chronic school problems.

Here are some additional examples of how compliment-based questions and comments can be woven into conversations with students and others:

- I'm impressed that you're willing to put in the effort to be here to improve things at school.
- How have you kept things from getting worse?
- How did you muster up the courage to apologize for being late to class?
- Now that you're an expert on changing school behavior, what advice would you have for other students who are struggling with their behavior at school?
- Wow! That must have been hard to do. How did you do it?
- How did you become such a caring person?
- What have these improvements taught you about yourself?

Some compliments apply to many students. For example, we can compliment most students for attending meetings and trying to improve things. Even in these situations, it is important to customize our comments to the student. For example, we could offer the following compliment to a student who enjoys being with friends and playing guitar:

> I'm impressed that you're here and that you're spending this time to try to make things better. Some students would just blow it off and hang out with their friends instead of talking with someone about it. You could be with your friends or playing guitar, but you're here because you want to change this school thing and you're willing to work to make it happen. That says a lot about you.

Young people quickly figure out when they are being addressed as individuals and when they are not. Like other relationship-building strategies, compliments are uniquely constructed to fit the student and the situation.

Using the Language of Change

Language plays a big role in establishing effective, change-focused counseling relationships. In addition to paying attention to the client's language, counselors can use language in ways that promote hope and solutions. Language and conversation shape our view of reality, which includes perceptions of ourselves, others, problems, and possibilities (Gergen & Gergen, 2003; Shapiro, Friedberg, & Bardenstein, 2006). Given that these perceptions can influence our response to a problem, we need to "make the most of language as an engine of change" (Shapiro et al., 2006, p. 138) in our conversations with students, parents, and teachers.

Solution-focused therapists distinguish between problem talk and solution talk. Problem talk includes detailed and repetitive explorations of the problem and its history, presumed causes, and diagnosis. Berg and de Shazer (1993) stated,

> Our clients have taught us that solutions involve a very different kind of thinking and talking . . . that is . . . outside the problem. It is this talking outside the problem that we call "solution talk." As client and therapist talk more and more about the solution they want to construct together, they come to believe in the truth or reality of what they are talking about. This is the way that language works, naturally. (p. 9)

Solution talk refers to questions, words, and phrases that focus on the client's goals, resources, and possibilities. It is important to allow ample opportunity for people to discuss their concerns and frustrations without becoming stuck in a hopeless cycle of problem talk. In solution-focused counseling, language is deliberately used to invite students and others to embrace empowering and hopeful stories about themselves and their ability to change school problems. We can do this by using the language of empowerment, qualification, and presupposition.

The Language of Empowerment

When asked what they want from us and our services, students, parents, and teachers may initially describe (a) what they do not want or (b) what other people should do differently. In both cases, practitioners can validate their concerns while using the language of empowerment to focus on what they can do to make things better.

Consider the following responses from students, all of which focus on the absence or decrease of undesirable situations in the past:

- I want to be less depressed.
- I don't want to get suspended anymore.
- I want to get in less trouble at school.
- I don't want to fail math again.
- I want to stop worrying so much.

We can validate these responses ("That's understandable") while inviting students to move toward future goals rather than away from past problems:

- If I was watching a videotape of you being less depressed, what would I see?
- What needs to happen for you to get suspended less?
- What will you be doing instead of getting in trouble?
- What can you do to prevent yourself from failing math again?
- What do you want to do instead of worrying so much?

When asked what they want from counseling, clients often describe how other people should change:

- If my parents would stop nagging me about school, maybe I would get better grades.
- Everything would be fine in my class if Jeremy would change his attitude and start doing more work.
- I want my daughter to do what I say instead of sassing me when I ask her to help around the house.

When clients downplay their influence and perceive the solution as external to themselves, we should accept it as their current frame of reference. In discussing the importance of validating the client's perceptions before shifting from an external to an internal focus of conversation, Teyber (2000) stated, "If the therapist does not provide this affirmation first, many clients—especially those who have suffered much invalidation in their lives—will feel that the therapist does not understand or care" (p. 89). In working with students, for example, we can validate their current perceptions while exploring their role in improving the school situation. In the following dialogue with a high school student named Stacy, the counselor validates Stacy's sense of powerlessness and uses the language of empowerment to invite her to consider what she can do to improve things.

Counselor: What needs to happen for things to get better for you at school?
Stacy: They need to get some new teachers here.
Counselor: New teachers?
Stacy: Yeah, teachers who know how to teach. Most of the teachers here don't really teach you anything.
Counselor: Sounds like it's really frustrating for you at school. [validating Stacy's perceptions]
Stacy: It is. It gets old.
Counselor: How does that make things worse for you at school when you feel this way about your teachers? [shifting the focus from the teachers to Stacy]
Stacy: Well, I just don't care. If they're not going to teach me anything, why should I care?
Counselor: That's a good question. Why should you care? Do you care?
Stacy: No. Well, kind of.
Counselor: Kind of?
Stacy: I want to do okay in school. I don't want to be like my brother and flunk out and end up on the streets.
Counselor: Why is it important to you to do okay in school and not flunk out like your brother?

After discussing Stacy's reasons for wanting to succeed at school, which included graduating in order to get a decent job and making her mother proud, the counselor explored what Stacy was willing to do to move closer to her goal of graduating.

Counselor: I can see how this is important to you for many reasons. I also think it's going to take hard work and courage to get where you want to go in school. It's going to be hard to do what you need to do in order to make things better in school and graduate. How willing are you to do what it takes?

Stacy: I'm willing.

Counselor: Even when your teachers do things that you don't like or agree with?

Stacy: Yes.

The remainder of the conversation focused on aspects of the situation that Stacy could influence—her choices and actions—instead of the attitudes and actions of her teachers. Additional questions that use the language of empowerment to enhance hope and invite people to focus on their contribution to solutions include the following:

- Tell me about a day during the last week or so when math class went a little better for you than usual. How did you make that happen? What will it take for you to do more of that?
- Some teachers might have given up long ago. How have you resisted the urge to give up? What will it take for you to keep hanging in there with this student?
- How have you managed to cope with this so far? How can you put those resources to work to improve things between you and your daughter?

Some young people have experienced difficult and disempowering circumstances over which they have had little control. These could include child abuse, an unstable home life, and unsafe neighborhoods. The language of empowerment does not deny these harsh realities but respectfully invites students to focus on changeable and controllable aspects of their life, such as personal values, school-related goals, and behavioral commitments to reach those goals.

The Language of Qualification

Struggling with a difficult problem can be discouraging. It is understandable for students, teachers, and parents to adopt a rather negative and hopeless outlook, as evidenced in all-or-none statements such as the following:

- I've never done well in school, so there's no use in even trying.
- I can't do anything right.
- I've tried everything with this student, and nothing works.
- He'll never change. He's been this way since he was 3 years old.
- My mom and I fight constantly. We just can't get along.

Counselors can validate these experiences while using the language of qualification to invite a more hopeful outlook that allows for the possibility of change.

Check out the following exchanges, in which the counselor's qualifying language is italicized.

Example 1

Student: Ms. Smith [teacher] hates me. She gets on me for everything. It's impossible to please her. I can't do anything right in her class, so I might as well not even try. What's the use?

Counselor: So you and Ms. Smith don't hit it off *most of the time,* and her class has been *really hard* for you. Can you think of a day when things weren't *quite as bad* in her class?

Example 2

Teacher: He never turns in homework, and he misbehaves constantly.

Counselor: Okay. So he's had a *a lot of* trouble with homework and behavior *so far* this year.

These examples show how the language of qualification gently introduces a more hopeful outlook into the conversation without discounting the client's perspective. Like most of the strategies in this chapter, the language of qualification can be integrated into the counselor's questions and comments.

The Language of Presupposition

O'Hanlon and Weiner-Davis (1989) described presupposition as a question or comment that implies something without directly stating it. Presupposition is used by trial lawyers to influence the jury's perception of a witness. Consider the question "Are you still stealing money from the company?" Regardless of the answer, the question implies or presupposes that the person has already stolen money from the company.

The language of presupposition is used in solution-focused counseling to boost hope and encourage people to focus on future possibilities. The italicized words in the following questions are designed to instill hope by conveying the inevitability or presupposition of positive changes in the school problem:

- What *will* be the first small sign that things are getting better?
- What *will* be different at school *when* you start attending class more often?
- How *will* your teachers and parents treat you *when* things start improving?
- How *will* you know *when* things get a little better between you and your daughter?
- Which one of your students *will* be most surprised *when* you start using these new strategies in your classroom?

The counselor's presupposition of change is conveyed by future-oriented words such as *will* and *when.* As illustrated in the following example, the language of presupposition conveys the counselor's faith in the likelihood of change and in people's ability to improve their life.

Andre, a seventh grader referred by the school and court for truancy, met with the school counselor the day after his court appearance. The juvenile court judge recommended increased parental supervision, an evening curfew, and counseling. School disciplinary measures included phone calls to Andre's parents when he was absent, grade penalties, and after-school detention (which he usually skipped). The following dialogue occurred early in the first counseling session.

> *Counselor:* I read all the stuff from the court report. There's a lot going on, huh?
>
> *Andre:* Yeah.
>
> *Counselor:* What would you like to see happen?
>
> *Andre:* I want everybody to back off. They're making it seem like I'm a criminal or something. All I've done is skip school a few times. It's not like I murdered somebody.
>
> *Counselor:* What will be different about your life when people start backing off?
>
> *Andre:* What do you mean?
>
> *Counselor:* How will your parents treat you differently when you start coming to school a little more?
>
> *Andre:* I guess they won't ground me as much or talk to me all the time about skipping school.
>
> *Counselor:* What else will be different when you come to school more often?
>
> *Andre:* I just won't have to get all dressed up to go to court and stand there and listen to all this stuff about the trouble I'm in.

The language of presupposition laid the groundwork for exploring small changes that Andre was willing to make to be treated better at home and school. Although his school attendance did not improve dramatically, he began to attend school more regularly. The people at court and school backed off accordingly. These changes might not have occurred as rapidly, or at all, had the counselor followed suit with the problem-focused emphasis of previous interventions. As illustrated with Andre, the language of presupposition enhances outcomes by inviting clients to focus on future goals and by conveying the counselor's confidence in clients' ability to change.

Accommodating the Client's Theory of Change

The patient, as I finally grasped, insisted—and had a right to insist—that I learn to see things exclusively in his way, and not at all in my way.
—Heinz Kohut, quoted in Stepansky & Goldberg, 1984

As noted in Chapter 2, Erickson adapted his approach to every client, treating one client at a time instead of requiring clients to conform to his preferred methods and interventions: "exploring a patient's individuality to ascertain what life learnings, experiences, and mental skills are available to deal with the problem . . . [and] then utilizing these uniquely personal internal responses to achieve therapeutic goals" (Erickson & Rossi, 1979, p. 1). Taking Erickson's lead, the MRI stressed the importance of selecting and presenting interventions in accordance with the client's "position," which refers to the client's beliefs about the problem and his or her role in resolving it (Fisch et al., 1982). Drawing from decades of empirical research, Frank and Frank (1991) similarly noted that "ideally therapists should select for each patient the therapy that accords, or can be brought to accord, with the patient's personal characteristics and view of the problem" (p. xv). Research supports the benefits of accommodating the client's "theory of change," which refers to the client's unique ideas, experiences, preferences, and expectations related to the problem, the solution, and our role in the change process (Murphy & Duncan, 2007).

Everyone involved with a school problem has a theory about its cause and what will help to resolve it. They also have preferences and ideas about what is helpful to them and what they want (and don't want) from counseling. To be most effective, we need to (a) learn the client's theory of change and (b) tailor the counseling process accordingly. Just as a tailor adjusts a suit to fit the owner, we need to customize counseling services to the client. This includes tailoring the topics and tasks of counseling to each client and being willing to make alterations on the basis of the client's feedback and progress.

The client's theory of change consists of

- ideas and experiences related to the problem (causes and explanations of the problem, what is currently influencing and perpetuating it, prior solution attempts),
- ideas and experiences related to the solution (what will help resolve the problem, prior solution attempts that helped), and
- ideas and preferences regarding our role in the change process (what clients want from counseling and how we figure into that, what we can do to help them reach their goals).

The first step in tailoring counseling services to clients is learning about their theory of change by

- listening for key words and phrases,
- eliciting the client's hunches about the problem and solution,
- exploring prior solutions, and
- determining what the client wants from us and counseling.

These methods are discussed below, along with examples and suggestions for accommodating the client's theory.

Listening for Key Words and Phrases

Listening closely to the client's language often reveals important aspects of his or her theory. I like to take notes to record some of the key words and phrases that clients use to describe the problems, solutions, and related factors. I tell them that taking notes helps me to understand their perspective, and I ask their permission before doing so. I readily share these notes with clients and make copies if they desire. This reduces any mystery or misperceptions about the content and purpose of the notes. Incorporating clients' language into counseling goals, interventions, and conversations conveys the respectful notion that their theories are more important than ours when it comes to resolving school problems.

The following example, involving a 12-year-old student named Clint, illustrates how to accommodate the client's theory by noticing and reflecting key words and phrases in the client's description of the problem (as indicated by italics).

> *Counselor:* Why do you think Mr. Hamilton referred you to me?
>
> *Clint:* He's a *jerk,* that's why. He *gets on me* all the time. He has it out for me. He lectures all the time about stupid stuff, and then he wonders why we flip out and screw around so much in class. Nobody likes him. He *gets on* everybody. He can't teach, so he yells at us instead. He ought to refer himself for counseling. I'm tired of him *getting on me all the time.*
>
> *Counselor:* How does he *get on you?*
>
> *Clint:* He's always asking me questions that he knows I won't be able to answer. He sends me out of class to the principal's office for little stuff. There are some people in there that mess around a lot more than me and never get sent out.
>
> *Counselor:* What else does he do that *gets on you?*
>
> *Clint:* He says bad stuff about me in front of the whole class. Instead of talking to me in the hallway, he does it in front of everybody else. I hate that.
>
> *Counselor:* Have you found anything that you can do in class that make him *get on you less* or be *less of a jerk?*

Integrating clients' language into the conversation conveys our willingess to work within their theory of change to bring about solutions.

Eliciting the Client's Beliefs and Hunches

Solution-focused counseling is based on the assumption that clients not only have all that is necessary to resolve the problem but may have a good idea about how to do it. In addition to encouraging clients' participation and collaboration, eliciting their beliefs and hunches about the problem and solution provides direct access to their theories of change. The following questions can be used with students, parents, and teachers to elicit their ideas about the problem and potential solutions:

- Sometimes people have a hunch about what is causing a problem and what will solve it. What are your hunches?
- What needs to happen to improve things at school?
- What is your theory about how change is going to happen here?
- Everyone has changed something. How does change usually happen in your life?
- What do you and others do to get it started and keep it going?
- If you were working with someone on a similar problem, what would you advise him or her to do about it?

Accommodating clients' beliefs and hunches about the problem and potential solutions is another way to honor their theory of change. People are more likely to engage in conversations and interventions that reflect their ideas about the problem and solutions, as compared to conversations and interventions that ignore or minimize their ideas. Accepting and accommodating the client's ideas and hunches does not require us to personally agree with them. It is simply a more respectful and practical route to solutions than dismissing or minimizing the client's beliefs.

Given that students, teachers, and parents are the ones who are closest to the problem and its solution, it makes sense to respect and utilize their ideas in building solutions. Historically, the wisdom and experience of clients have taken a back seat to the practitioner's chosen model and so-called evidence-based treatments, both of which discount the powerful role of client and relationship factors in the change process (Bohart, 2006; Wampold, 2006). Consider the following conversation with Ms. Brock, a third-grade teacher who sought the counselor's help with a student who frequently disrupted her class. Notice how the counselor ignores Ms. Brock's position and tries to talk her into a different one.

Ms. Brock (teacher): Every time I tell Ariel to do something, she talks back or does something to let me know she doesn't like it. She can be very manipulative with me and the other students.

Counselor: Manipulative is a pretty harsh word. Could it be that she just wants more of your attention or more attention from the students?

Ms. Brock: Have you ever seen her in class?

Counselor: No, I haven't.

Ms. Brock: Come in some time and see what you would call it. She openly defies my instruction and terrorizes other students. Yes, she needs attention all right, but the way she goes about getting it is by being defiant and mean. You really need to observe her in class to understand what I'm saying.

Counselor: Well, I just believe that terms like *manipulative* and *defiant* are not helpful ways to view students because they set up a battle between the teacher and the student.

Ms. Brock: But it *is* a battle. She's battling me for control of the class, and she's winning.

Counselor: I just don't think you're going to be effective with her if you view this as a battle.

Ms. Brock: [becoming more annoyed and angry] Why don't you come into the classroom sometime and see what you would call it.

Ignoring or challenging the client's theory is one of the surest ways to weaken the alliance and create an impasse in counseling. Students, parents, and teachers quickly recognize when their beliefs are being challenged and often respond by digging in and defending their position more strongly. Some clients, like the teacher in the example above, make it clear that they do not appreciate their opinions being discounted by someone who is not standing in their shoes. Others may shut down or talk less to avoid being criticized or challenged. Either way, client involvement and outcomes are seriously jeopardized when the client's theory is not given sufficient attention in the change process.

I now replay the conversation with Ms. Brock, illustrating how it might have gone had the counselor accommodated her ideas instead of challenging them.

Ms. Brock: Every time I tell Ariel to do something, she talks back or does something to let me know she doesn't like it. She can be very manipulative with me and the other students.

Counselor: What does she do that is manipulative?

Ms. Brock: I'll ask the class to do an assignment, and sometimes she'll just say, "I'm not doing it," right out loud so everybody can hear it. Or she'll make fun of other students when they answer a question. If she makes a mistake or something doesn't go her way, she tries to turn it around to make it seem like it's my fault. She openly defies my instruction and terrorizes other students. She can be real defiant and mean. It's like she's battling me for control of the class.

Counselor: Who's winning the battle?

Ms. Brock: At this point, I'd say she is.

Counselor: It must be a huge challenge dealing with this day in and day out.

Ms. Brock: Believe me, it is.

Counselor: A lot of people would have given up after a few weeks of this, but you haven't. How have you managed to hang in there?

Ms. Brock: Good question. I don't know. I guess I consider it a personal challenge to not let her get the best of me. But I'm about at the end of my rope now. That's why I wanted to talk with you.

Counselor: I'm glad you did. It's no wonder that you're frustrated with this situation [validating the client's struggle]. I'm impressed that you haven't given up and that you keep looking for ways to improve the situation [complimenting]. Maybe we can come up with some ideas to help you hang onto the rope and gain more control [accommodating the client's desire to hang on and gain control, which are key components of her theory of change].

As illustrated in this scenario, eliciting and accommodating the client's beliefs and hunches honors his or her theory and strengthens the alliance. Having experienced the counselor's acceptance and validation of her ideas, Ms. Brock could focus exclusively on resolving the problem without the distraction of defending herself and her ideas. As seen shortly, that is exactly what she did.

Exploring Prior Solutions

Exploring prior solutions is another way to clarify the client's theory of change. Conversations about previous solutions can remind people of something that has helped them with the current problem or similar problems. When this happens, we can work with clients to see how previously effective strategies might be modified and adapted for the current situation. These discussions may also highlight ineffective strategies that should be avoided in the future. The following questions are useful in exploring the client's prior solutions and related ideas:

- What have you tried so far? Did it help? How did it help? Why didn't it help?
- Of all the things that you or others have tried, what has worked best? Next best? Worst?
- What have you thought about trying but haven't tried? How might that improve things? What will it take to try this?
- How have you handled similar challenges? How might that help you in this situation?

With respect to Ms. Brock in the previous example, she and the counselor began to explore prior solutions in the following way.

Counselor: What kinds of things have you already tried with Ariel?

Ms. Brock: Oh, let's see. I've talked with her several times one on one to ask her why she acts this way and to explain that it is not acceptable. I've taken away part of her recess, changed her seat, let her earn stickers for good behavior, called her parents, sent her to the principal's office, had her stay after school to help me clean up the room, and even tried in-school suspension for a couple hours one day.

Counselor: Wow, that's a lot. Of all the things you've tried, which ones have worked better than the others, even just a little better?

Ms. Brock: That's a tough question. Well, she loves to play kickball at recess, so I think taking away part of her recess got her attention and worked for a couple of days.

Counselor: Okay. What else helped?

Ms. Brock: Come to think of it, she was a lot better for a day or two after she helped me after school. I did it as a punishment, which was probably a mistake, but she seemed to enjoy helping me when it was just the two of us after school. And we probably got along better during those 30 minutes than we have all year.

Counselor: What do you make of that?

Ms. Brock: I guess she enjoyed the individual attention. Most third graders do, but maybe she craves it even more than the others.

Counselor: That's interesting. So maybe the attention you gave her after school stayed with her for a couple days, almost like a time-release shot of attention. What do you think?

Ms. Brock: [laughs] Maybe so. It's worth a shot.

Counselor: What's worth a shot?

Ms. Brock: Maybe if I give her more of my attention *before* she acts up, she won't act up as much because she already got what she wants.

Counselor: Now that's an interesting theory. How can you test it out?

The counselor and Ms. Brock discussed several attention-giving strategies, all of which complemented her intriguing theory.

Determining What Clients Want From Us and Counseling

In addition to accommodating clients' language, hunches, and prior solutions, determining and honoring what they want from us is vital to effective outcomes. Clients are much more likely to participate with a counselor who is genuinely interested in what they want and willing to adjust services accordingly. Some clients want a sounding board and listener, some want expert advice, and some want to brainstorm and problem solve. Some clients enter counseling eager and willing to try anything to change the school problem. Others reluctantly enter as "mandated clients" who are there at someone else's request. These clients require different approaches from the counselor.

The following questions explore the client's preferences regarding our role and the counseling relationship:

- How do you see me fitting into what you want to happen?
- I want to be useful to you. How can I do that?
- How can I be most helpful right now?
- What role do you see me playing in your goal of [fill in with student's goal, e.g., making friends, improving grades, or graduating]?
- I want to make sure I understand what you want here. Are you looking for suggestions from me about this situation?
- In what ways do you see me and our meetings helping you reach your goals?
- Who has helped you the most with other concerns or problems in your life? What do they do or say that is most helpful?
- Given that you don't see this as a problem and that you were forced into coming here by [your teachers/parents/parole officer], would you like to work on getting out of having to come here?
- How can I help you get your parents and teachers off your case about this school thing?

Identifying and accommodating what clients want from us may be the most important task of all in working with school problems. One reason I say this is because school referrals involve multiple clients, who often may include the student, teachers, parents, and school administrators, each of whom may have different ideas about the problem, the solution, and our role. For example, what do you do when the teacher wants to change the student's classroom behavior, while the student would rather work on making friends? What do you do when the parent views a problem as urgent and the student does not? Another reason this task is so important in school-based practice is because the primary client in school referrals, the student, typically enters counseling at someone else's request. Therefore, some students initially may not want anything from counseling other than to make it go away.

These circumstances can make it challenging to honor what students want from the counseling relationship. The next section describes two situations that school practitioners find particularly challenging, along with suggestions for each situation.

Situation 1: When Students Are Not Interested in Changing the School Problem. Given that students are often pressured into services by someone else, usually a teacher or parent, it is understandable that they may not want to work on changing the school problem when they begin counseling. They may not even acknowledge that a problem exists, or, if they do, they might see it as someone else's problem ("I'm here because my teacher is a jerk. Everything would be fine if my parents would stop pestering me"). Some students may not even know why they were referred, and others may be angry about having to meet with a counselor. Of all the counseling situations, this one seems to be the most difficult and frustrating for school practitioners. As described next, however, there are several useful ways to accommodate clients in this situation.

Responding to Situation 1. The following responses are often useful in situations in which the student enters counseling with little or no interest in changing the school problem. Although this section focuses on students, the ideas and strategies are applicable to similar situations involving parents and other clients.

1. *Acknowledge and validate the student's preferences.* Assume that people think and act in ways that make sense to them on the basis of their circumstances and perceptions. This assumption is reflected in validating comments such as the following:
   - I can see how hard it is for you to have to come in here and meet with me.
   - No wonder you don't want to be here, given that you didn't have a say in the matter.

2. *Be curious and respectful in exploring the student's perceptions.* Approaching students with respect and curiosity conveys our genuine interest in their view of why they were referred to us and reduces the need for them to defend their perceptions.
   - What is your idea about why you were asked to see me?
   - How did you end up here?
   - Whose idea was it for you to come here?
   - What do you think gave him or her that idea?
   - What makes your teacher/parent think you could benefit from counseling?
   - What do you think needs to change in this situation?

3. *Work from the student's perspective to explore potential counseling goals.* Use the student's language and perceptions to explore potential goals that he or she might be willing to work on. The purpose of this is not to trick students into engaging in counseling but to respectfully meet them where they are and explore what they want to change.

- What needs to happen for you to not have to come here anymore?
- What would your teacher/parent say you need to do differently to no longer need counseling?
- What will it take to get your mother and teacher to back off and stop pestering you about this?

4. *Find out what is most important to the student, and explore how school figures into these values.* People of all ages hold "big values" for themselves and their life, including what they want their life to stand for (Murphy, in press). In working with students who are pressured into attending counseling, we can initially push school issues aside and explore the bigger picture of life from the student's perspective. When students accept this invitation, it provides a relevant, student-driven context for exploring connections between their bigger values and the current school situation.
   - Let's forget about school for a minute, because I have a question that is a lot more important than school. In fact, it's so important that I want you to take your time and think about it as long as you need to before answering. The question is, "What do you want your life to stand for?"
   - What is most important to you in your life? Why is that important to you? How does school figure into that?
   - If you could be exactly the person you want to be, describe that person to me. What needs to happen for you to move closer to being that person? How does your school performance or behavior tie into this?

5. *Offer compliments.* Compliment the student for being there, even when he or she chooses not to say much. Look for other opportunities to offer genuine compliments.
   - I'm impressed that you came here today. What made you decide to do that?
   - I know you're not crazy about being here, but I also know that no one handcuffed you and dragged you in here. What gave you the courage to come here today?
   - In a world full of talkers, it's refreshing to meet someone who listens like you do and doesn't feel the need to talk all the time.

6. *Discuss hobbies or other topics of interest to the student.* Discussing high-interest topics not only helps to establish a connection but reveals unique abilities, interests, and other resources that might eventually be applied toward solutions to the school problem.
   - I noticed your Green Day T-shirt. What other musical groups do you like?
   - Your parents told me you're a good basketball player. How long have you been playing basketball? How did you learn to play?

- I can tell you really love sports. I wonder how your knowledge and skills in sports might help you change this school problem and get everyone off your back about it. Any ideas?

7. *Refrain from action-oriented suggestions that require substantial time and effort on the part of the client.* If you recommend any tasks, make sure they are very manageable and compatible with the student's perceptions.
   - Pay attention to the times when you and your teacher get along better, and I'll ask you about it next week.
   - Think about why your teacher might be more concerned about this than you are.
   - Think about what you can do to move closer to the kind of life you want.

8. *Work with teachers, parents, and others to help bring about solutions.* Given that students are the primary clients of school-related services, they should always be given ample opportunity to be included in the counseling process. However, they should not be the only ones involved. School problems occur in a social context or system, and solutions can emerge from any number of people associated with the problem.

One of the biggest mistakes we can make is trying to convince students that they have a problem or that they need to change when they don't think they do. As seen with Jolene and the first counselor in Chapter 1, the harder we push, the more the student digs in and defends his or her position. This is a natural response to being pressured into something against one's will. When students enter counseling uninterested in changing, any attempts to sell them intervention ideas are doomed to failure. In these situations, the practitioner's suggestions are likely to remain just that—the *practitioner's* suggestions—with little or no investment from the person who matters most in the change process.

Unfortunately, students in this situation are often labeled resistant, uncooperative, or unmotivated when they do not implement the counselor's suggestions. These derogatory labels have no place in solution-focused counseling because they compromise the alliance and impede outcomes. It is our job to cooperate with all clients regardless of their preferences and theory of change.

Situation 2: When Clients Acknowledge the Problem but Look to Others to Change It. Students, teachers, or parents may acknowledge the problem and the need to resolve it yet see the solution primarily as someone else's responsibility. Clients may view themselves as innocent bystanders or victims of circumstance who are relatively powerless to change the situation. For example, a teacher or parent may express serious concerns about a student's classroom behavior and ask us to meet with the student to resolve the problem. Students may believe that the primary responsibility for resolving the problem lies with their teacher ("If my teacher would stop pestering me about homework and picking on me in class, I wouldn't get in as much trouble").

It is common practice in the helping professions to confront and challenge clients in this situation (Evans, Hearn, Uhlemann, & Ivey, 2008). This often takes the form of lessons and lectures on the importance of taking responsibility for one's own problems instead of blaming or expecting others to change. As logical as this reasoning may appear to the practitioner, challenging the client's theory of change hinders the alliance and jeopardizes outcomes. Our task is to meet clients where they are by acknowledging their theory and allowing the conversation to unfold from there. In my experience, clients are much more willing to consider how they might contribute to solutions once their views have been heard and respected.

Responding to Situation 2. The following strategies are useful in responding to students, teachers, and parents in Situation 2.

1. *Listen without blaming.* Students, parents, and teachers who are struggling with a school problem appreciate the opportunity to voice their views and frustrations without the threat of criticism from the counselor. For some people, the experience of being heard versus being blamed provides the safety for them to reexamine their role in solutions.
   - This must be very frustrating for you.
   - I'm impressed that you've hung in there and haven't given up on trying to find solutions. How can I help you do that?

2. *Compliment the client for seeking help, acknowledging the problem, and coping with the problem.* Compliments help clients to relax and to realize that the counselor is an advocate. Compliments may also enhance hope by inviting clients to acknowledge their resources, which may be used later to build solutions.
   - I appreciate your willingness to meet with me today. It's one thing to say there's a problem, but it's quite another to make a move toward resolving it.
   - It's impressive that you have the courage to face up to this problem. Some people say facing up to a problem is a big step toward resolving it.
   - The fact that you're talking with me about changing this says a lot about you.
   - How have you managed to cope with this for such a long time?
   - What do you think would be most helpful in changing this?
   - What else might improve things besides [telling your teachers and parents to stop bugging you/getting a new teacher/me talking with the student]?

3. *Invite clients to focus on their role in solutions.* The best way to explain this strategy is through examples. In working with parents who view their child's school behavior as the sole responsibility of the teacher, we can acknowledge their wisdom and experience while inviting them to become more actively involved: "Given that you, as parents, know your child better than anybody else, what suggestions do you have for us in helping her at school?" This question accommodates the parents' position while recruiting their involvement as intervention consultants. We can also expand solution opportunities by using the client's theory as a springboard for new perspectives and actions.

Consider the situation in which a third-grade teacher, after only 2 weeks of a new school year, views the student's problem behavior as a symptom of a serious emotional disorder that requires counseling. To explore a more hopeful and changeable view of Emily (the student) and the problem, we can respectfully explore the teacher's potential role in solutions.

- This sounds like a serious problem that's going to require a comprehensive intervention on several fronts. In addition to your plan of meeting with her parents to explore individual counseling for her, I'm wondering what else can be done at school to give Emily the support she needs. Any ideas?
- It's got to be tough dealing with this day in and day out from the very start of the school year. It would help me to learn what you've already tried and how it has worked. What have you tried? Of all these ideas, which one do you think has the best chance of improving things, even just a little?
- You know Emily and your class better than I ever will. What would you think about stopping here, taking a little time to think about anything that might help Emily and help you, and getting together in a few days to discuss our ideas?
- In reviewing your records, I noticed that you haven't had much trouble in history class compared to your other classes. What are you doing differently in there to make that happen? Are you willing to try that in some of your other classes?

All of these examples respect the positions of clients while inviting them to focus on what they might do to bring about solutions. These strategies gently invite clients to shift from problem talk about circumstances and people over which they have little influence (e.g., a student's emotional disorder or home life) toward solution talk about their own behavior and role in solutions. As noted throughout this chapter, attempting to coerce clients into different beliefs or actions against their will is a futile endeavor. However, respectfully inviting them to consider other options is a useful consideration when their perspectives appear to perpetuate the very problem they wish to resolve.

4. *Assign low-effort tasks.* If tasks are given, clients should be able to perform them without any major adjustments in their daily routine. For this reason, it is useful to give tasks in which the client is asked to reflect on, observe, or predict something related to the problem or solution. These tasks, adapted from de Shazer (1988), can be presented as a way of helping us and clients learn more about the situation before doing anything major to change it.
   - *Reflection task:* "Since you know a lot more about this student and this situation than I do, I'd like to learn what you think would help to make things better. Think about this and we can talk about it next time. I'm not asking you do anything about it unless you choose to. I'm just asking you to give it some thought."
   - *Observation task:* "To help us learn more about this, I'm wondering whether you could observe the things that you and your teachers are already

doing to make things better at school. It's important to learn about this because we don't want to change something that is already working."

- *Prediction task:* "I wonder whether you'd be willing to try an experiment by making a prediction each morning on whether you're going to have a good day or a bad day at school. We can make up a good day/bad day chart for you to write your predictions on. You can write *good day* or *bad day* on the chart every morning. At the end of each day, you can circle it if your prediction was correct and put a line through it if it was incorrect. We can calculate your percentage of hits and misses at the end of each week. How does this sound to you?"

The connection between these tasks and solutions may appear to be somewhat remote. However, they are often effective in engaging the involvement of clients in Situation 2 and in prompting news ways of thinking about and responding to the problem. The following example illustrates various aspects of accommodating the client's theory of change along with other strategies for establishing cooperative, change-focused relationships.

Alia: An Example of Accommodating the Client's Theory of Change

This conversation involves Alia, who was referred by her ninth-grade science teacher (Mr. Davis) because of disruptive classroom behavior. The dialogue picks up at the start of the first meeting.

Alia: This whole thing sucks, and you can't make me talk. He can't either.
Counselor: I definitely can't make you talk, and I won't try. When you say "this whole thing sucks," what do you mean by "whole thing"?
Alia: This counseling. He thinks I'm crazy, and I'm not. If anybody's crazy, it's him.
Counselor: Who?
Alia: Mr. Davis.
Counselor: He's your science teacher, right?
Alia: Yes.
Counselor: Is that who you're talking about when you said *he* can't make you talk either?
Alia: Yes. He's the one who called my parents and said I should see a counselor. So here I am.
Counselor: It sounds like you would not be here if you had a choice. Is that true?
Alia: Definitely.
Counselor: I appreciate you being honest with me. Why do you think Mr. Davis suggested counseling?
Alia: I don't know. I guess you'll have to ask him.
Counselor: I can do that. But you know him pretty well. What do you think he might say if I asked him?

After Alia described several recent conflicts in science class, the counselor began exploring her theory of change.

Counselor: Alia, you've lived with this situation for a long time, and you know a lot more about it than I ever will [casting Alia as an expert on the school situation and approaching her from an ambassador-like position of humility and respect]. How would you explain it [exploring Alia's theory of change]?

Alia: I don't like Mr. Davis, and he doesn't like me. He picks on me. He's done it all year. And I get tired of it. I'm not going to take it. I don't care what he thinks about me.

Counselor: You don't care what he thinks about you [reflecting Alia's exact words].

Alia: [shakes head "no"] I don't care what he thinks. I'm not going to take it from him.

Counselor: What else can you tell me to help me understand?

Alia: He's got this problem getting along with people. He picks on a lot of students, not just me. He's always getting onto people about being lazy and paying attention, things like that.

Counselor: So the cause of this problem you're having in school is that he picks on you [checking for understanding of Alia's theory]?

Alia: That's right. I know I'm the one acting bad. And I end up getting in trouble. But I hate being picked on. My older brother and sister pick on me at home, and then I come here and get the same thing.

Counselor: It's hard when you feel like you're being picked on all the time pretty much wherever you are. So you hate to be picked on, and Mr. Davis picks on you a lot. Is that right?

Alia: Yes.

Counselor: Not a good combination, is it?

Alia: [laughs] No.

Counselor: What has to happen for things to get better?

Alia: He needs to stop picking on me.

Counselor: Okay [accepting Alia's theory at face value]. What have you found to be most helpful in getting him to pick on you less [exploring prior solutions]?

Alia: Nothing, really.

Counselor: Nothing.

Alia: Well, sometimes when I just sit there like a robot and don't say anything, he's okay.

Counselor: Interesting. What does it look like to sit there like a robot?

The following exchange occurred a few minutes after Alia demonstrated sitting quietly and looking at Mr. Davis instead of interrupting him and talking to other students.

Counselor: So doing the robot thing works pretty good and gets him to treat you better?

Alia: Most of the time, but not always. Sometimes he picks on me anyway.

Counselor: Okay. But it works most of the time.

Alia: Yes.

Counselor: I think you're onto something here, Alia. I wonder what would happen if you tried the robot strategy more often next week in science class and paid attention to how Mr. Davis treated you to test your theory and see if he treats you differently. What do you think [expressing curiosity and asking versus telling]?

Alia: [shrugs shoulders] I don't know, I guess I could try it.

Counselor: I wonder if your chances of passing the class will be better, worse, or about the same after this. What do you think [expressing curiosity and asking versus telling]?

Alia: Better, I guess. But I don't know if I'm going to do that. He doesn't deserve it, so why should I be good for him?

Counselor: Actually, I wasn't thinking of him. I was thinking of your goal of passing the class and getting the credit, and wondering whether your robot strategy would move you closer to passing the class [shifting the focus to Alia, her goal, and her theory of change].

Alia: I see what you mean. I think it would help. I don't want to flunk and have to take the class again.

Counselor: I don't blame you.

Alia and the counselor fleshed out the details of the robot intervention, including when to do it and when not to, making sure not to overdo it, and a simple procedure for recording Mr. Davis's behavior in her science notebook. Given that the intervention emerged directly from Alia's theory of change, it should come as no surprise that she implemented it with integrity and commitment. Alia returned the following week, data in hand, and reported that Mr. Davis "was still a jerk" but had treated her better on 4 of the previous 5 school days. Although the relationship between Alia and Mr. Davis was far from perfect, things were moving in the right direction, and she met her goal of passing the class and earning her science credit.

The conversation with Alia illustrates several features of cooperating with the client's theory of change. Phrases and questions such as "You know a lot more about it than I ever will," "How would you explain it?" and "What else can you tell me to help me understand?" conveyed the counselor's interest in Alia's perspective. Like most theories, Alia's included causal attributions and beliefs about the problem ("He doesn't like me") and solution ("He needs to stop picking on me"). Instead of challenging Alia's theory, the counselor accepted it at face value ("Okay") and used it to explore prior successes and to invite her to consider her role in solutions ("What have you found to be most helpful in getting him to pick on you less?"). As illustrated with Alia, theories can also change during the course of counseling or a counseling session. Alia entered the session expecting her teacher to change but gradually shifted her attention toward her own role in bringing about a solution. As shown with Alia, discussing clients' theory of change (a) encourages their participation, (b) validates their input and contributions, and (c) leads to acceptable, client-friendly interventions.

Summary of Accommodating the Client's Theory

This discussion makes it clear that there are as many theories of change as there are clients. Cooperation with these theories occurs one client at a time. Regardless of the circumstances that lead clients to counseling, our task remains the same: (a) to accept and meet clients where they are; (b) to discover what they want to be different and how we might help them reach their goals; and (c) to tailor the counseling process to their unique goals, theories, and feedback.

The point about accepting the client's theory at face value cannot be overstated. There is no such thing as a good or bad theory. We also need to be careful about labeling students or others in negative ways that hinder change, such as calling them resistant, apathetic, or unmotivated. Solution-focused counseling assumes that clients are doing the best they can under the circumstances. This positive mind-set guards us against judging some clients as better than others and encourages us to consider what we can do to cooperate with all clients.

Obtaining Client Feedback on Outcome and Alliance

Shouldn't I be telling you what I think?
—Molly, 10-year-old student

Once we know what clients want from us and from counseling, it is important to obtain their feedback on the usefulness of our services. Function is always more important than form in judging the usefulness of counseling. Clients could care less about counseling models and techniques as long as they are getting what they want from us and our services. In a client-driven approach such as solution-focused counseling, the most respectful and accountable way to monitor the usefulness of our services is to obtain client feedback.

Research has shown that (a) perceptions of clients and practitioners often differ when it comes to evaluating the effectiveness of services (Greenberg, Bornstein, Greenberg, & Fisher, 1992), (b) client perceptions are more accurate in predicting outcome than the perceptions of practitioners (Bachelor & Horvath, 1999; Kazdin, Marciano, & Whitley, 2005; Shirk & Karver, 2003), and (c) the client's early experience of change and connection (alliance) with the counselor are strong predictors of eventual outcomes (Bachelor & Horvath, 1999; Haas, Hill, Lambert, & Morrell, 2002; Lambert et al., 2001). These findings, in conjunction with the empirical link between client involvement and counseling outcomes, urge us to obtain client feedback from the outset of counseling and adjust services accordingly.

Research points to two types of feedback that are particularly important:

- The client's perception of change (feedback on outcome)
- The client's perception of the counselor and the counseling relationship (feedback on alliance)

This section describes practical strategies for obtaining client feedback in both of these areas.

Scaling Questions

Scaling questions serve many purposes in solution-focused counseling, one of which is to evaluate outcomes. Students and others can be asked the following question on a regular basis throughout the counseling process: "On a scale of 1 to 10, with 1 being the worst it can be and 10 the best it can be, how would you rate the school problem/goal during the past week?" This can be asked at every session or via e-mail to provide an ongoing snapshot of progress from the client's perspective. Clients should be explicitly reminded that there are no right or wrong answers and that the purpose is to obtain their perception of progress regardless of what others might say. It is important to invite clients to elaborate on their ratings through follow-up comments and questions:

- Wow, that's two points higher than last week! How would you explain that? What happened? What did you do to make that happen?
- What is different about this week in math class, which you rated 4, and last week, which you rated 6?

Informal scaling questions can also be used to obtain the client's feedback on the alliance: "On a scale of 0 to 10, with 0 being really low and 10 being really high, how would you rate our connection so far?" or "On a scale from 1 to 100, how useful was today's meeting for you?" As with outcome-oriented questions, we can follow up on these questions to further clarify the client's response:

- Okay. So you rated our connection at 7. What can I do differently to make things better next time?
- I'm glad our meeting was useful. I want you to let me know anytime during our work together if there's anything I can do to make sure that these meetings continue to be useful to you. Okay?

Informal scaling questions provide a quick snapshot of clients' perceptions of outcome and alliance. The remainder of this section describes two practical tools for monitoring client feedback in systematic and reliable ways.

Outcome and Session Rating Scales

Numerous studies have shown that obtaining formal client feedback on outcome and alliance can dramatically improve outcomes (Lambert et al., 2001, 2003; S. D. Miller, Duncan, Brown, Sorrell, & Chalk, 2006; Whipple et al., 2003). Although there are several valid measures of client feedback, most were designed for research purposes and are too long and complex for everyday use. In fact, Brown, Dreis, and Nace (1999) found that most practitioners will not use any measure that takes more than 5 minutes to complete, score, and interpret during a counseling session.

In response to the need for practical client-based measures, S. Miller and Duncan (2000; Johnson, Miller, & Duncan, 2000) developed two simple tools for obtaining feedback on outcomes and the alliance in every counseling session—the

Outcome Rating Scale (ORS; S. Miller & Duncan, 2000) and Session Rating Scale (SRS; Johnson et al., 2000). These measures assess research-identified elements of outcome and alliance. Changes in the areas assessed on the ORS—personal distress, interpersonal well-being, social relationships, and overall well-being—are widely considered to be valid indicators of successful outcome (Lambert et al., 1996). The SRS obtains client feedback on key aspects of strong alliances and effective counseling sessions: respect and understanding, relevance of goals and topics, and client–counselor fit.

The ORS and SRS are displayed in Appendix C, along with child versions of each scale for children 12 and under—the Child Outcome Rating Scale (CORS; Duncan, Miller, & Sparks, 2003) and Child Session Rating Scale (CSRS; Duncan, Miller, Sparks, & Johnson, 2003). The child versions use simpler language and smiley and frowny faces to aid the student's understanding. Both scales use a visual analog format of four 10-centimeter lines, with instructions to place a mark on each line. Low estimates fall to the left and high estimates to the right. The four 10-centimeter lines add to a total score of 40. The total score is simply the summation of the marks made by the client to the nearest millimeter on each of the four lines, measured by a centimeter ruler or template. A version of both scales is also available for young children and nonreaders—the Young Child Outcome Rating Scale (Duncan, Miller, Huggins, & Sparks, 2003a) and Young Child Session Rating Scale (Duncan, Miller, Huggins, & Sparks, 2003b). These scales have three faces: smiley, neutral, and frowny, along with a blank face, with the instruction to mark (or draw) the face that best matches the child's experience. All three versions of the ORS and SRS are free for individual use and may be downloaded in many languages from www.talkingcure.com.

Items from the ORS and SRS can be read to clients when appropriate (e.g., with students or others who have difficulty reading the items). When parents and teachers are involved, they should complete the same outcome scale given to the student. For example, if the student completes the CORS, then the parent, teacher, and other involved adults would also complete the CORS. This allows for comparison and exploration of similarities and differences among people's ratings ("Scott, I noticed that you rated School a lot higher than your science teacher did. What do you make of that?"). While it is desirable to administer, score, and discuss the ORS/CORS in the presence of clients, especially in the first couple of meetings, the forms also can be downloaded by clients and completed just prior to each session.

The ORS/CORS and SRS/CSRS have demonstrated adequate reliability and validity (Duncan, Miller, Sparks, Claud, et al., 2003; Duncan, Sparks, Miller, Bohanske, & Claud, in press; S. D. Miller, Duncan, Brown, Sparks, & Claud, 2003) and have resulted in fewer dropouts and significantly higher success rates in several settings (Duncan, Miller, Sparks, Claud, et al., 2003; S. D. Miller et al., 2006). Another important property of these measures is their feasibility. *Feasibility* refers to the quickness and ease with which an instrument can be explained, completed, and interpreted. This is a crucial consideration for school practitioners, many of whom have difficulty finding the time to do counseling in the first place, much less evaluate it in systematic ways. The fact that the ORS and SRS contain only four items and can be administered and interpreted in about 1 minute during a counseling session makes them very practical in the fast-paced world of schools.

In addition to alerting counselors to the type of relationship the student wants, the SRS provides immediate, real-time feedback that allows us to follow up and correct alliance problems right when they occur. For example, when a student rates an SRS item below 9 on the Approach or Method scale, the counselor should follow up by asking for clarification and direction ("What can I do differently to make our next meeting better for you?"). Likewise, the ORS prompts the student and practitioner to discuss options and try something different when things are not improving ("On the basis of your marks [pointing to School scale on the ORS], it looks like things haven't changed much at school the last couple weeks. How willing are you to try something different to make things better at school?"). If ORS scores don't increase after two sessions, we need to openly discuss this with the student, along with options for improving things. The ORS is typically given in the beginning of every session, while the SRS is done toward the end of the session.

Establishing a feedback culture by using the ORS and SRS in every session gives students, teachers, and parents an ongoing and significant voice in the counseling process and conveys our willingness to adjust our approach and services on the basis of their feedback. The two pragmatic guidelines of solution-focused counseling—if it works, do more of it; if it doesn't work, do something different—are very applicable to monitoring outcome and alliance and adjusting services accordingly. The use of quick and simple client-based rating scales allows for immediate adjustments, a major advantage over the more traditional pretreatment–posttreatment strategy of collecting data at the start and end of counseling.

In addition to helping us provide responsive services to individual clients, SRS and ORS scores can be combined across clients to examine trends for individual practitioners, schools, and other agencies for accountability purposes. These client-based measures can also be combined with other evaluation methods on the basis of specific referral concerns and counseling goals, including classroom observations, grades, behavior rating scales, and discipline records. In addition to providing valid indicators of counselor and counseling effectiveness, client-based rating scales enhance the establishment of cooperative, change-focused relationships. Additional details and instructions on the use of the ORS/CORS and SRS/CSRS in schools can be found in Appendix D and in Murphy and Duncan (2007).

Table 4.1 outlines the key strategies for building cooperative, change-focused relationships in solution-focused counseling.

Summary and Conclusions

It is no accident that this is the longest chapter in the book. Despite a compelling and ever-growing body of research on the importance of the alliance in counseling, this topic has not been given adequate attention in the professional literature, graduate course work, and training workshops. When it is mentioned, it is often accompanied by vague terminology *(empathy, warmth, trust),* with little atten-

Table 4.1

Strategies for Building Cooperative, Change-Focused Relationships

Strategy	*Description*
Adopting the ambassador mind-set	Approach clients with humility and respect; look, listen, ask, and learn before offering suggestions; respect diverse opinions and new ideas; express curiosity vs. certainty; listen for hints of strength, resilience, hope, and other change-promoting resources; compliment clients; and use open, change-focused questions
Using the language of change	Use solution talk that invites clients to focus on what they want vs. what they don't want; use the language of empowerment, qualification, and presupposition to boost clients' self-efficacy and hope
Accommodating the client's theory of change	Listen and ask for clients' ideas about the problem and solution; explore prior solutions; determine what clients want from us and counseling; develop interventions in accordance with their theory of change
Obtaining client feedback on outcome and alliance	Use scaling questions to assess clients' perceptions of outcome and alliance; use practical, client-based rating scales to monitor outcome and alliance (Outcome Rating Scale, Session Rating Scale); adjust services on the basis of client feedback

tion to specific relationship-building strategies. This chapter provides practical strategies for nurturing cooperative, change-focused relationships with students, teachers, parents, and others involved in the change process.

Maintaining strong alliances with students and others should be a top priority throughout the helping process. Effective alliances are enhanced when practitioners adopt the mind-set of a foreign ambassador and approach every client from a position of humility, curiosity, and respect. We can convey the ambassador mind-set by listening, asking open-ended questions, complimenting, using change-focused language, accommodating the client's theory of change, and obtaining client feedback on outcome and alliance. Outcomes depend largely on the extent to which clients are involved in determining the goals, tasks, content, and effectiveness of counseling.

Practice Exercises

1. Describe the "ambassador approach" to counseling in your own words. How does this differ from authoritarian approaches? What are the benefits of adopting the ambassador approach in working with students, teachers, parents, and other clients?

2. Select a problem and have your partner interview you from the ambassador perspective for about 5 minutes. Next, have your partner interview you from a more authoritative or expert perspective. Observe the differences in your reactions to these different interviewing strategies. Switch roles, and interview your partner from these two perspectives.

3. Think about a recent conversation in which you shared a personal concern or problem with someone else. Which approach best describes this person's response to you, authoritarian or ambassador-like? How did it work for you? How might things have turned out if he or she had used the other approach? Think about a situation in which someone shared a concern with you, and consider similar questions about your response.

4. Discuss the importance of listening to and validating clients. Practice validating clients by pairing with a partner and assuming the roles of client and counselor. Have the client share a concern or problem, after which the counselor provides a validating statement. Switch roles, and repeat the exercise.

5. Think about an experience in which you received helpful affirmation and validation from another person. How did this person validate you and your experience? How might you incorporate this same strategy in your work with students?

6. Think of a recent situation in which you connected particularly well with a student, parent, or teacher. What did you do to make that happen? Which of these things could you do with other clients in other situations?

7. Practice the following relationship-building strategies in role-plays with a partner, with one person serving as the client and the other person as the counselor. For each skill, the client briefly describes a concern, and the counselor follows up with the strategy. Take turns practicing each strategy by
   - complimenting the client,
   - asking open-ended questions,
   - making suggestions in a curious and tentative (vs. absolute and certain) manner,
   - using the language of empowerment,
   - using the language of qualification,
   - using the language of presupposition.

8. Pick a prior or current situation in which counseling did not work well. Discuss the counseling process through the eyes and experience of the client, using first-person language ("I felt like . . .") to describe why counseling did not work and what the counselor could have done to be more effective. What new ideas has this exercise given you in regard to this client? How can these ideas be applied toward establishing cooperative, change-focused relationships in the future?

9. What are the key features of the client's theory of change, and why is it important to consider the client's theory in school-based counseling?

10. Practice exploring key features of the client's theory of change in role-plays in which one person is the client and the other person is the counselor. As the client describes his or her concern, the counselor can explore the client's ideas

related to the problem and solution, prior solution attempts, and preferences regarding the counselor's role. Switch roles and repeat the exercise.

11. During your next session, obtain feedback from the client using an ORS at the start of the meeting and an SRS at the end. When the session is finished, make a few notes on your reaction and the client's reaction to the measures.

12. Describe one small step that you are willing to take in your practice as a result of the information in this chapter.

CHAPTER 5

Interviewing for Solutions

*So what I'm saying is we have the answers, we just need someone
to help us bring them to the front of our head. It's like they're
locked in an attic or something.*
—Molly, 10-year-old student

The conversations we have with clients influence the way they view themselves, the problem, and potential solutions. Our initial contacts with students, parents, and teachers are especially important in setting a tone of collaboration and hope. This chapter describes the powerful role of interviewing in solution-focused counseling, with emphasis on the first interview.

Unlike traditional interviews, which focus on deficits and diagnosis, solution-focused interviews explore strengths and resources, on the basis of the assumption that it is more efficient to build on what works and what's right with clients than it is to eliminate problems. Information about what people are already doing or capable of doing to resolve school problems is generally more useful than extensive information on problem history.

To make the most of our conversations with students and others, we need to listen carefully and ask useful questions. Questions serve two purposes in solution-focused interviewing: (a) to gather relevant information about the problem and potential solutions and (b) to ignite the core ingredients of the change pie: client, relationship, and hope factors. This chapter outlines the key areas of focus during initial and subsequent interviews, along with useful questions for exploring each area.

Initial interviews are generally aimed at promoting change by clarifying the problem, prior solution attempts, the client's theory of change, goals, exceptions, and other client resources. The extent to which each area is explored varies from client to client, as do the order and manner in which they are explored.

The Problem

Solution-focused counseling does not routinely involve lengthy explorations of problem history or presumed causes unless people indicate a preference for this. However, some basic information about the problem is often helpful in developing solutions and validating the client's struggle. The counselor begins by obtaining a clear description of the problem.

Defining a Changeable Problem

A problem that is described in clear, behavioral terms is more changeable than a vaguely stated problem. For example, it is easier to change the number of times a student starts conversations with peers, attends school, or completes a classroom assignment than it is to change the student's depression, irresponsibility, or attention-deficit/hyperactivity disorder (ADHD).

Our everyday language is full of vague descriptors and labels that mean different things to different people. Students, parents, and teachers often present complaints in vague and abstract ways, as well as including interpretations in their descriptions. For example, a teacher might describe the situation as a motivation or attitude problem. Without additional details, the problem remains unclear and unchangeable. O'Hanlon and Wilk (1987) recommended using "videotalk" to describe the problem (see Box 5.1).

The following requests are useful in helping people define changeable school problems:

- If I videotaped this problem, what would I see and hear?
- Describe a recent example.
- If I were a fly on the wall, what would I see when this was happening?
- Tell me what this looks like.

Box 5.1
Videotalk

The encouragement of "videotalk" (O'Hanlon & Wilk, 1987) is particularly useful when a student, teacher, or parent describes a school problem in terms that are vague ("attention problem") or interpretive ("disrespectful"). We can obtain behavioral definitions by asking people to describe the problem in videotalk as if they were narrating the play-by-play events and actions of a sporting event. Consider the following videotalk descriptions of a student's "attention problem":

- When I ask the class to line up for recess, he just sits there until I remind him a second or third time.
- He never completes his math work sheet.
- He complains when it's time to come into class after recess, and he asks me if he can stay out for a couple more minutes.

These divergent descriptions highlight the importance of obtaining clear definitions of the problem from the client's perspective. The more concretely a problem is described, the easier it is to change. It is easier to increase the number of completed assignments than to correct an attention problem. Encouraging students, teachers, and parents to use videotalk is a practical way to define specific, changeable problems.

Clarifying Related Circumstances

Clarifying the patterns and circumstances of the problem may provide important clues for how to go about changing it.

When? Some problems occur at fairly predictable times, and the following questions are useful in determining such patterns:

- When does this usually occur?
- Is the problem more evident in the morning or afternoon?
- Does the student do this more in some classes than others?
- Have things been better, worse, or about the same during the past week/month?

Where? These questions clarify connections between the problem and specific settings:

- Where does this usually happen?
- Does the problem occur more often in a certain place (classroom, playground, hallway)?
- Are things any better or worse in one place as compared to another?
- Does the problem usually occur during or in between classes?

With Whom? School problems may vary in the presence of different people. The following questions can be used to explore this area:

- Who is usually around when the problem occurs?
- Which teachers report more/less of a problem?
- Does the problem occur more often with one particular teacher/parent?
- Does the problem change depending on who the student is with?

What Happens Right Before and After? Events that precede and follow the problem help in understanding and altering it. This information can be obtained through questions such as the following:

- What happens right before the problem?
- Is the problem more likely to occur during a certain activity (individual seat work, small group activity)?
- What happens right after the problem? Then what?
- How does the teacher/parent usually respond to the problem?
- What does he or she say? What does he or she do?
- How do other students respond?

Information about problem-related circumstances can be used to construct interventions aimed at altering one or more features of the problem pattern. For example, if Miguel's aggressive behavior usually involves a student who sits next to him in class, changing the seating arrangements may improve the situation. If you discover that Liza often misbehaves on arriving at her first period class in the morning, you could suggest that she change the morning routine by walking to her desk and counting backward from 100 to 0 before doing anything else. You might also encourage the teacher to ask for Liza'a help on a few quick chores as soon as she walks into class. Sometimes all it takes is a small change in the problem pattern to build effective solutions.

Solution Attempts

In addition to clarifying the client's theory of change, as discussed in Chapter 4, exploring solution attempts reveals what has (and hasn't) worked in the past. The following questions invite people to reflect on prior solutions and to consider other possible strategies:

- What have you tried so far?
- How did it work?
- Of all the things that you and others have done, what has worked the best? Next best? Worst?
- What have other people suggested doing? Of all these ideas, which one do you think has the best chance of working?
- What have you thought about trying but haven't tried? What will it take to try this?
- How have you handled similar challenges? How might that help you right now?
- You've told me about some things that haven't worked or that made things even worse for you at school. I wonder what you could do that would be really different from anything you've tried so far. What do you think?

For clients with previous counseling experiences, the counselor could ask questions such as the following:

- What did you find to be most helpful/least helpful about counseling the last time?
- What did the counselor do that worked well/not so well with you?
- Of all the things about your previous counselors and counseling experiences, what helped you the most? How did that help you? How did you turn that into something that was helpful to you?
- On the basis of your previous experiences with counseling and counselors, what advice do you have for counselors who work with young people?

Information about how students and others have responded to the problem, and the results of such efforts, provides useful direction for building on what has worked and avoiding what has not worked. In response to one or more of the questions above, many clients have taught me what to do and not do to be effective with them.

The Client's Theory of Change

Don't oppose forces; use them.
—R. Buckminster Fuller

The client's theory of change, discussed at length in Chapter 4, is another important consideration in initial interviews. The manner in which clients discuss problems and solutions reveals important aspects of their theory. In addition to listening for key words and phrases in the client's language, we can ask the following kinds of questions:

- What do you think is causing the problem?
- What do you think will help improve things?
- How does change usually happen in your life?
- How can I be most helpful?
- How is this problem affecting your life?
- How willing are you to do something about this problem?

Clarifying the theory of change allows us to interact with each client in ways that are individualized, respectful, and engaging. Table 5.1 summarizes the tasks of clarifying the problem, problem-related circumstances, solution attempts, and the client's theory of change.

Table 5.1
Clarifying the Problem and Related Features

Task	*Description*	*Useful Questions*
Define the problem	Obtain a specific, behavioral description of the problem	If I recorded the problem on a video camera, what would I see and hear?
		What is the student doing that is "irresponsible"?
Clarify problem-related circumstances	Obtain a clear description of the pattern and context of the problem	When and where does it usually occur?
		Who is around?
		What happens right before/after the problem?
Explore solution attempts	Explore previous solutions and their relative effectiveness	What have you tried so far? How did it work?
		Of all the things you've tried, what has worked best?
Clarify the client's theory of change	Explore the client's ideas about the problem, potential solutions, and the helping process	What do you think is causing the problem?
		What will help to resolve it?
		How can I be most useful?

Goals

A journey of a thousand miles begins with a single step.
—Confucius

Goals are the driving force of effective action. In addition to providing a sense of energy, direction, and hope, goals help people persist in the face of setbacks and obstacles (Snyder, Ilardi, Michael, & Cheavens, 2000). The formulation of effective goals during the first interview keeps counseling on track and provides clear criteria for evaluating its effectiveness.

The process of developing goals is often overlooked in the push for quick solutions. This is especially true in work with students and school problems. In my experience, most counseling failures can be traced to ineffective goals resulting from one or more of the following: (a) failing to explicitly develop and revisit goals throughout the counseling process, (b) invalidating or minimizing the student's goal in deference to the goals of the counselor or other adults (e.g., "I know you want to work on making more friends, but it's more important to bring your grades up"), and (c) placing one's own theories above those of the student (e.g., despite the student's theory that the school problem is caused by peer difficulties, the counselor continues to probe for deeper, intrapsychic causes).

Goal formulation is a cooperative task in which the counselor accepts and works within the goals and perspectives of the client. Developing goals in collaboration with students, parents, and teachers can be a challenging task. However, it is well worth the effort given that the extent to which clients "own" a goal strongly influences the energy they put forth toward reaching it (Locke & Latham, 1990; W. R. Miller & Rollnick, 2002).

Characteristics of Effective Goals

The following considerations and strategies are important to keep in mind when developing goals with students, parents, and teachers. The "5-S guideline" is a practical framework for describing five characteristics of effective goals: significant, specific, small, start based, and self-manageable. Although the discussion and examples focus on students, the five features of useful goals are equally applicable to teachers, parents, and other clients.

Significant. The most important consideration in developing effective goals is to ensure that they are personally relevant and meaningful to the client. We are naturally inclined to strive toward goals that are important and meaningful to us (Frankl, 1959). Likewise, we are not inclined to eagerly pursue a goal that is unimportant to us, regardless of what others say or how important the goal is to them. Check this out for yourself in Box 5.2.

The surest way to develop meaningful goals is to find out what is important to clients and what they are willing to work on. We can do this by asking the following kinds of questions:

- What would you like to work on?
- What do you want to accomplish in counseling?
- What do you think is the most important thing to change in this situation?

Box 5.2
How Important Is It to You?

---

1. Think of a significant goal or project in your life for which you are highly motivated to achieve success.
2. Now think of a less important project that you are involved in.
3. How do your motivation and commitment differ for these two projects or goals? What are some other key differences in your approach to these goals?

Solution-focused counseling promotes meaningful and significant goals by clarifying what clients want from counseling and honoring their goals throughout the helping process.

As discussed in Chapter 4, many students enter counseling at the request of others and may not be interested in developing school-related goals or working toward goals defined by others. Instead of trying to convince them otherwise, it is more productive to acknowledge their position and find something they *are* willing to work on: "I know that counseling wasn't your idea and that you don't want to be here. What needs to happen for you to get out of coming here?" The practice of meeting students where they are to develop meaningful goals is illustrated in the following example.

Mario and the meaningful goal. Mario, a 10th-grade student, was very angry with his teachers and the school principal. He perceived them as unfair and "out to get him" at school. Mario said that the principal and most of his teachers thought he was "a lazy waste." When asked what he wanted to change regarding school, Mario asserted that he would not change in school because he did not care what they thought of him. He added that he was not about to give in to their demands and "control games." For Mario, improving his school behavior represented selling out and giving in to people whom he did not respect.

Instead of challenging Mario's characterization of his teachers and principal, the counselor accepted his position and posed the following question: "What kinds of things might prove them wrong about you?" This question acknowledged Mario's anger and provided an opportunity for him to change in school to prove them wrong. Mario's motivation to prove them wrong was utilized to formulate specific goals regarding his school behavior. These goals were stated in his language and in ways that were personally meaningful to him.

When several people are involved in counseling, it is important to encourage goals that are complementary, even though each goal may be worded differently. In Mario's case, the behaviors required to meet his goals were the same behaviors required to meet the goals of the teachers and the principal. Similarly, parents may define "responsible behavior" in much the same way that a teenager defines "what it will take to gain more car privileges and freedom at home." These examples highlight the importance of accepting and working within the position and language of clients while developing goals. Had Mario been asked to work on the goal of being a better student or not getting into as much trouble, he would not have been as motivated to make the changes that he eventually made in his school behavior.

In addition to respecting and accommodating the client's position, inviting students to consider the connection between their values and school performance is often useful in promoting relevant and significant goals. We can begin exploring this connection by inviting students to "step outside of school" and reflect on what is most important to them in their life:

- Let's forget about school for a minute. If you could be exactly the kind of person you most want to be, what kind of person would that be?
- What do you want your life to stand for?
- Pretend that you are 50 years old and that you have lived every part of your life exactly the way you wanted to and been exactly the person you wanted to be. Now imagine that you are reading a story about yourself and your life at age 50. What are the most important parts of that story?

Once students' "big values" are identified, we can incorporate their words into additional questions that explore the link between their values (in italics in the following examples) and school behavior:

- What are you already doing at school to help yourself become the *loving and caring person* you most want to be? What will it take to do more of that?
- If you were doing just what you needed to do in school to become a more loving and caring person, what would you be doing?
- What are you doing or not doing at school that is blocking you from moving closer to your goal of becoming *a decent husband and father* when you get older?
- If it were possible for you to have a *better life,* would you be willing to take action in order to make that happen?
- If I told you about something you could do at school that might help you become a more *helpful and loving* person, would you be willing to try it?

The discussion of values promotes a student-driven agenda for school-based counseling. These conversations invite students to articulate what is important to them, examine their actions in light of this, and participate in developing attainable goals that move them toward a self-motivated and value-driven life. For example, a high school student who wants to have a loving marriage and successful career can be encouraged to increase school behaviors that support these values, such as studying and paying attention, and to reduce actions that work against them, such as teasing others and skipping class. Likewise, a fourth grader who wants to be a kind person can be encouraged to define and increase kind behaviors at school, such as allowing others to be first in line or volunteering to help a peer with math. Designing goals and interventions aimed at reducing the gap between students' values and actions increases their investment in the change process and makes it more likely that they will maintain behavioral improvements after counseling has ended (A. P. Goldstein & Martens, 2000).

Specific. When asked about counseling goals, clients initially respond with vague phrases, such as becoming less depressed, controlling ADHD, changing their attitude, or being more responsible. These abstract goals are harder to observe and measure than specific goals, such as getting a job, turning in three out of four homework assignments, and arriving at school no later than 8:00. Videotalk is helpful in developing concrete goals. For example, students who want to improve their attitude can be asked, "If we were watching a videotape of you with a better attitude, what would we see you doing differently in school?" The more specific the goal is, the easier it is to notice small changes. Specific goals enhance the likelihood that students and others will notice and acknowledge small improvements when they occur. In the following dialogue, the counselor requests a videotalk description of being a better student to help a middle school student (Andrew) develop a more specific and measurable goal.

Counselor: How will you know when you have become a better student?
Andrew: I don't know. I'll just know.
Counselor: Let's pretend we videotape you tomorrow being a better student, okay?
Andrew: Okay.
Counselor: Now let's pretend we're watching this tape right now. Tell me what we would see if we watched you being a better student. What would you be doing?
Andrew: I'd be answering questions in class and getting better grades.
Counselor: Okay. What else would we see?
Andrew: I'd do my homework on time, and I'd remember to turn it in.

In addition to being easier to notice and measure than vague goals, specific goals are more effective in motivating clients, enhancing hope, and providing a clear direction for counseling. In discussing the relationship between specific goals and hope, Snyder (1995) noted,

There is much to be gained from fashioning very concrete goals. . . . When a concrete goal becomes imaginable, perhaps through the efforts of a counselor, this alone can unleash the person's sense of energy to pursue the goal, as well as the capability to generate pathways. (p. 358)

The following questions invite students and others to describe goals in clear, specific terms:

- What will you do differently when your self-esteem is higher?
- If we videotaped you being less depressed, what would we see you doing?
- You said you wanted to make school better. How will you know when school is better? What specific parts of school do you most want to change?

- If I were watching you on the playground 2 months from now, after things got better, what would you be doing differently?

There is popular expression that says, "If you don't know where you're going, you probably won't get there." We can paraphrase this in positive terms on the basis of the above discussion: "If you know exactly where you're going and what it will look like when you arrive, you probably will get there."

Small. In the context of formulating goals, the word *small* actually means practical, reasonable, and attainable. When asked about goals, clients may express unrealistic hopes and expectations. Some students may fix their gaze on the mountaintop instead of focusing on the first few steps, while others indicate the desire to completely eliminate the problem within a few days. These wishes and expectations must be heard and acknowledged, after which we can ask for a description of one or two small steps in the right direction through the following types of questions:

- What will be the first small sign that things are moving in the right direction?
- [responding to the CORS] Your score on the School scale is 5.4. What will a 5.5 look like?
- If a score of 10 was where you want things to be when we finish counseling and 1 was where things are right now, what would a 2 or 3 look like? What will you be doing differently when you get to 2? How would your teacher be able to tell you were at a 2 instead of 1?
- They say that every big journey involves a lot of little steps. What are one or two small steps that you're willing to take next week to get you closer to your final goal of passing science class this semester?

Small goals build hope by allowing people to experience many successes throughout counseling and to notice subtle yet important improvements. Confucius noted that "a journey of a thousand miles begins with a single step." This adage emphasizes the importance of viewing big visions and goals as a series of small steps. In the following example, the counselor acknowledges a ninth-grade student's long-term goal of raising her math grade from an F to a B while encouraging her to focus her attention and energy on the first few steps toward that goal.

Counselor: You said you wanted to raise your math grade from where it is now, which is an F, to a B by the end of the semester.
Kristy: Right. I just have to work hard and not mess around as much.
Counselor: Okay. The semester is over in about 6 weeks, right?
Kristy: Right.
Counselor: When do you want to start working on this?
Kristy: Right away. I don't have a whole lot of time to make this happen.
Counselor: Okay. It's good that you realize this, because some people set big goals and wait until it's too late to work on them.

Kristy: I know. I've done that before.

Counselor: Me too. What's different about this time for you?

Kristy: I don't know. I guess it's that I'm older and I know I have to do it. Nobody's going to do it for me.

Counselor: That makes sense. What are one or two *small things* you could do *during the next 2 or 3 days* to help you get *a little closer* to your goal of getting a B by the end of the semester? [The italicized words and phrases in this question invite the student to direct her attention and efforts toward small but important initial steps toward the larger, long-term goal.]

Kristy: Well, for one thing, I could turn in homework. That would help because we get grades just for turning it in.

Counselor: I see. So turning in more homework will bring your grade up some. What do you need to do differently to turn in more homework?

The following example illustrates the benefits of small counseling goals and the notion that big problems do not always require big solutions.

Keeping it simple. Gary, a fifth-grade student, was referred by his mother, Brenda, for peer problems and classroom misbehavior. Early in the first meeting, the counselor encouraged Brenda to think small by asking, "What will be the first small sign that things are getting better for Gary at school?" She replied that he would start attending more carefully to his hygiene.

Gary agreed to an experiment in which he would comb his hair and keep his shirt tucked in at school for 1 whole week and observe any changes in the way he was treated by his peers and teachers. He reported that his teachers treated him about the same but that his classmates were "a little nicer" than usual. Gary continued the experiment the next week and observed that his teachers began treating him better. Disciplinary infractions decreased by about 50% during the following month. This example illustrates how one small goal and the changes resulting from it can lead to larger and more significant changes in a school problem.

Start Based. When asked what they want, clients often tell you what they don't want. It is understandable that someone who has dealt with a school problem every day for several weeks or months would express a desire to reduce or eliminate it. However, it is generally more effective to develop goals that describe the start or presence of something desirable versus the end or absence of something undesirable. As de Shazer (1991) pointed out, "Getting rid of something is difficult; the absence of something is hard to know. . . . It is, of course, much easier to know that something different is present" (p. 110).

In addition to being more noticeable, goals that are worded in positive, start-based language (e.g., "to fix my lunch and arrive at school on time") are usually more motivating than goals worded in negative terms (e.g., "to be less depressed"). Consider how difficult it is to observe the absence of depression, anxiety, irresponsibility, laziness, immaturity, or oppositional defiant disorder. What does nondepression or non-ADHD look like? How will you know when it happens?

Start-based goals focus people's attention on moving toward what they want (solutions) rather than away from what they don't want (problems). When students state goals in negative terms, as the absence of undesired behavior (e.g., "to quit messing around in class"), we can ask "instead of" questions, such as, "What will you be doing in class instead of messing around?" By shifting students' attention from what they do not want to what they do want, these questions promote start-based goals, such as "I would be paying attention and doing my work."

Self-Manageable. When asked what needs to happen to improve things at school, clients sometimes state what other people should do instead of what they could do differently. Here are some examples from students:

- I need a different teacher.
- People need to leave me alone and quit bugging me.
- My parents get on my case no matter what I do, so I figure, "Why should I even try?"
- Other students are always messing around in class, so I just join in. If they stopped, I would stop.

Other-focused statements direct attention toward people and circumstances over which students have little control. This impedes solutions by holding others responsible and casting students in a passive and powerless role. We can acknowledge students' perceptions while inviting them to consider what they can do to improve things at school. Teyber (2000) referred to this as shifting from an external focus to an internal focus to encourage clients to view themselves as active and influential change agents. In the following exchange with a high school student (Sharon), the practitioner affirms Sharon's perceptions of her teachers, then invites her to consider a self-manageable goal that focuses on what she can do to improve things at school.

Sharon: My teachers nag me constantly. I can't do anything right, according to them.
Practitioner: That must be hard for you [affirming Sharon's perception]. What do you do when they nag you [shifting the focus from the teachers to Sharon]?
Sharon: I try to ignore them.
Practitioner: How do you do that? What does that look like [obtaining a videotalk description]?
Sharon: Well, I just look the other way and pretend they're not even talking to me.
Practitioner: And then what do they do?
Sharon: That's when they really get on me, because they say I am being disrespectful or that I don't seem to care about anything.
Practitioner: Is that an accurate description of you [shifting the focus back to Sharon]?
Sharon: No. I don't want to fail.
Practitioner: Wow. That's important that you don't want to fail. That's a very important goal. Would you be willing to try an experiment in one of your classes to see how much power or influence you have in your relationships

with your teachers [keeping the focus on Sharon and introducing the playful element of an experiment]?

Sharon: [laughs] Maybe.

Practitioner: [laughs] I guess you want to hear it first before deciding, right? I'm wondering what would happen if you did something very different the next time one of your teachers says something to you and closely observed their response to see if anything different happens. How does that sound?

Sharon: Okay, I guess.

Practitioner: Well, it could be interesting. Who knows what you'll find out? But the only way to find out is to try it. It might help you get closer to your goal of passing. What do you think?

Sharon: I can try it.

Practitioner: That's brave of you, Sharon. I can tell that it's important to you to pass your classes, and I'm impressed that you're willing to try something different to make that happen [complimenting and reinforcing Sharon's willingness to accept responsibility and take action].

During the remainder of the interview, the practitioner and Sharon discussed specific experiments to assess the impact of her actions on her goal of passing. In addition to promoting self-manageable goals, these conversations increase the student's personal responsibility for and ownership of goals and solutions.

Additional questions that invite students and others to consider self-manageable goals include the following:

- How willing are you to try something really different to change things?
- What are you willing to do to change this situation?
- You said you wanted your parents and teachers to stop bugging you all the time about school. What have you found helpful in getting them to bug you less about school?

Summary of Effective Goals

Useful goals honor the 5-S guideline by being significant, specific, small, start based, and self-manageable. As illustrated above, there are many practical ways to encourage such goals while respecting the client's perceptions of the problem and solutions. Table 5.2 summarizes the characteristics of effective goals.

The next section illustrates two versatile strategies for developing effective goals in collaboration with students and others: scaling and the miracle question. Although these strategies serve many purposes in solution-focused counseling, they are described here because they are particularly useful in formulating goals.

Scaling

Scaling was discussed in Chapter 4 as a strategy for obtaining ongoing client feedback on the progress and outcomes of counseling. Scaling can also be used in initial interviews to help students and others develop effective goals, as illustrated in the following examples:

Table 5.2
Characteristics of Effective Goals

Characteristic	Description	Useful Questions
Significant	Relevant and important to the client	What do you want to work on? What can you do at school to move closer to being a decent and caring person?
Specific	Clear, concrete, observable; described in videotalk	If I videotaped you being less depressed, what would I see? What will you be doing differently when you have higher self-esteem?
Small	Realistic and attainable	What will be the first small sign that things are getting better? You said that school was a 3 on a 10-point scale. What will a 3.5 or 4 look like?
Start based	The presence or start of something desirable	What will you be doing instead of being depressed? What should the student be doing in your class instead of goofing off?
Self-manageable	Within the client's control	How can you get your teachers to be nicer to you? How willing are you to try something different to make things better?

- "On a scale from 0 to 10, with 10 being the very best that things could be and 0 being the very worst, where would you rate things in your science class right now? What would the next highest number look like?"
- "If a score of 10 is where you want things to be when we finish counseling and 1 is where things are right now, what will be different when it moves up to 2? How will your teachers and parents be able to tell that you moved up?"
- "If I videotaped you after you moved up 1 point from where you are now, what would I see?"
- Show the child five wooden blocks and say, "I want to know how things are going in school right now." While arranging five blocks in a row or tower on the table, say, "This [pointing to the stack or row of five blocks] means things are really great, just the way you want them to be at school, and this [pointing to one block] means things are really bad at school. Use those blocks to show me how things are going for you at school right now. Okay, what can you do at school to give yourself another block?" Any available

objects can be used for this purpose, including pencils, beads, buttons, paper clips, and plastic chips.

- Draw a vertical line on a piece of paper and say, "If this bottom part shows where you would be if you got into trouble all the time at school and this top part shows where you would be if things were perfect at school and you never got in trouble, show me where you are right now." After the child points to (or marks) a spot on the line, the practitioner can point to (or mark) a spot just above where the child pointed and say, "Tell me what would help you move a little higher on the line, to about here." A horizontal line can be used in the same manner.

Scaling questions can be tailored to the client's age, cognitive and language abilities, and interests. In work with younger students, the scale can be represented by a row of blocks or buttons, a piece of string, a series of smiley and frowny faces, a row of tiles on the floor or wall, or a line on a piece of paper. Students can point to or otherwise indicate their present spot on the scale as well as describe what the next higher spot will look like. If the client is a football enthusiast, the scale can be presented as a football field broken into 10 segments, ranging from farthest away to nearest to the goal. Other examples include

- a baseball field, with first base as the starting point on the scale and home plate as the final goal;
- a stepladder, ranging from the lowest to the highest steps;
- pictures of items relating to the student's special interests or hobbies arranged in a row (musical instruments, cars, animals, etc.);
- a picture of a blank thermometer that can be marked from the lowest to the highest point.

The ORS (S. Miller & Duncan, 2000) is another method of scaling that is helpful in developing initial counseling goals. As discussed in Chapter 4, the ORS is used to obtain clients' perceptions of how they are doing to identify key concerns and to monitor their progress throughout counseling. Once clients identify their most pressing concerns, we can inquire about small steps toward solutions:

- Your score on the Social scale is 4.6. What will a 4.8 or 5 look like?
- I can see that you're very concerned about your son's school behavior on the basis of your 2.5 mark on the School scale. Tell me what needs to happen for this mark to go up to about here [pointing to a spot slightly above the parent's mark on the School scale].
- You rated the Family scale at a 5.5. What could you do to bring this up to about a 6? What will it take to make that happen?

The following examples illustrate how various scaling strategies can be incorporated into goal-related conversations with students of all ages. The first excerpt involves a 12-year-old student named Christina.

Counselor: On a scale of 1 to 10, where 10 is the best things can be and 1 is where things are right now, what will you be doing differently when things get to a 2 or 3?

Christina: I'll be getting more of my math homework done. I won't be arguing with my teacher all the time. I'll feel better about school. I'll like school more.

Counselor: If I videotaped you feeling better about school and liking it more, what kinds of things would I see on the tape?

Christina: I'd be smiling more and having a good time. I'd be joking around with some teachers.

Counselor: Tell me about a time or a class where you have a little better time or joke around more with the teacher.

In the next example, the counselor uses blocks to invite David, a 6-year-old student, to describe what needs to happen for him to move up to the next block.

Counselor: [arranges eight wooden blocks in a row on the table] I want to know how things are going in school right now. We can use these blocks to talk about this, okay?

David: Okay.

Counselor: This [pointing to the eighth block, at the end of the row] means things are really great and just the way you want them to be at school, and this [pointing to the first block] means things are really bad at school. Now you point to a block to show me how things are going for you at school right now.

David: [points to the first block in the row]

Counselor: Does that mean things are going pretty bad for you here at school?

David: [nods "yes"]

Counselor: Okay. Thank you for telling me that. That helps me understand. David, I really want to know what school will look like when things get to be about here [pointing to second and third blocks]. What's going to be different at school?

David: My teacher will like me, and I won't be so bad.

Counselor: Do you want that to happen?

David: [nods "yes"]

Counselor: Why is it important to you for the teacher to like you and for you to be better in school?

David: It's good that way. My teacher will like me, and I won't be so bad.

Counselor: Okay. So how would your teacher know that you went from here [pointing to the first block in the row] to here [pointing to second block]?

David: I would be nice to her.

Counselor: How would you do that?

David: I would do what she tells me.

Counselor: Okay. What else would you be doing when you're here [pointing to second block]?

David: I'd be writing my letters or coloring when she tells us to.

Scaling strategies encourage clients to describe reasonable goals from their frame of reference. Regardless of the type of scale used or where the student's initial rating falls on the scale, asking what the next higher number would look like paves the way for discussing small, specific steps toward desired outcomes. Many students respond more favorably to scaling questions as compared to direct questions about their goals. For people who prefer numbers and visual forms of communication, scaling offers a respectful and appropriate means of developing goals.

The Miracle Question

The miracle question was developed by de Shazer (1988) to obtain a description of life without the problem: "Suppose you were to go home tonight, and while you were asleep, a miracle happened and this problem was solved. How will you know the miracle happened? What will be different?" (p. 5). The miracle question clarifies clients' goals and encourages them to focus on future possibilities versus past problems. Variations of the question include the following:

- Suppose that there is a miracle tonight and this school problem is solved. How would you be able to tell? What would be different at school? What would your teacher notice that's different?
- If this problem completely vanished right here and now, what would you do differently when you returned to class?
- If someone waved a magic wand and made this problem disappear, how would you be able to tell things were different?
- What would be different about you/this student/your son after the miracle?
- Let's pretend that you had a dream tonight, while you were sleeping, and this problem was solved during your dream. How was the problem solved? Who helped solve it? Describe how your life would be different at school after the dream.
- Imagine that there are two movies about your life. Movie 1 is about your life with this problem, and Movie 2 is about your life without the problem. I already know a lot about Movie 1. Tell me what Movie 2 would look like. Who would be in it? What would they be doing? What would you be doing differently in Movie 2?
- Pretend that you are flying in a space ship to a planet called Futureland, where you can live your life without this problem. Describe what your life is like at school in Futureland.

As shown above, there are many ways to ask the miracle question, on the basis of the student's age, abilities, and interests. In addition to asking about a miracle, practitioners can use any number of metaphors for the same purpose. Students can be asked to describe what school is like for them after a magic genie has granted them full freedom from the problem. A crystal ball, problem-vanishing dust, and other such metaphors can be used to engage young children in describing their vision of life without the problem.

We can encourage detailed descriptions of the miracle by asking clients, "What else?" following their initial response. This places clients in the driver's seat by inviting them to address the question as thoroughly as they wish. As illustrated in the following conversation with a fifth grader named Daniel, inviting students to elaborate on their initial response to the miracle question yields a more detailed description of their goals.

Counselor: Suppose that one night while you were sleeping, a miracle occurred all at once and this problem was completely solved. The problem vanishes just like that [counselor snaps fingers]. How would you know the miracle had occurred? What would be different about your life at school and home?

Daniel: I'd stop getting in trouble in school.

Counselor: What else?

Daniel: My grades would be better. I'm close to flunking a couple classes now, so I wouldn't be flunking any of my classes.

Counselor: Okay. What else would be different after this miracle?

Daniel: Oh, I know. My parents wouldn't hassle me about school. They nag me all the time about little stuff. They're always asking me questions about school and everything, prying into my business. So they'd be a lot nicer to me after this miracle. That would be a major miracle.

Counselor: What else?

Daniel: My teacher and I get into fights all the time. So we wouldn't do that if this problem vanished.

Counselor: What else?

Daniel: That's it.

Counselor: Okay.

To flesh out goals even further on the basis of the 5-S guideline, the counselor could invite Daniel to reflect on the significance of these desired changes by helping him connect school performance to bigger goals and values in his life:

Counselor: It sounds like it's important to you to do well in school.

Daniel: Yeah, I'd like to do better.

Counselor: You mentioned staying out of trouble, getting decent grades, and getting along better with your teachers and parents. This sounds like someone who wants school to be better. Why is school important to you?

Daniel: Well, you have to do good enough in school to get a decent job.

Counselor: Why is it important for you to get a decent job?

Daniel: Because you can't have a family or anything without a decent job.

As illustrated next, we can also follow up the miracle question by addressing the other characteristics of effective goals—specific, small, start based, and self-manageable.

Counselor: Daniel, you mentioned that you would stop getting in trouble in school after the miracle.

Daniel: [nods "yes"]

Counselor: What would you be doing instead of getting in trouble? [This instead-of question invites Daniel to think about the presence or start of what he wants instead of the absence of what he does not want.]

Daniel: Paying attention to my teachers and doing my work.

Counselor: If I videotaped you paying attention to the teachers, what would I see you doing differently? [Asking for a videotalk description encourages specific goals.]

Daniel: I'd be sitting at my desk looking at the teacher instead of looking at my friends or out the window.

Counselor: Okay. What else would I see?

Daniel: I guess I'd be taking notes or answering questions, stuff like that.

Counselor: Of all these things, which one would you be most willing to work on first and try to make some small changes on within the next few days? [This question respects Daniel's input and invites him to focus on small changes that are within his control.]

Daniel: I guess taking notes, because it would help me on tests and help get my grades up some.

Counselor: That sounds good. You also said that you wanted your parents to stop nagging you about school and to be nicer to you.

Daniel: Right. I know they mean well, but they're always on my case.

Counselor: I'm wondering if there's anything you could do differently to change things so they nagged you less? [This question paves the way for self-manageable goals by inviting Daniel to focus on what he could do to improve the situation with his parents.]

In this condensed version of the meeting with Daniel, the miracle question created a client-directed context for developing practical goals in accordance with the 5-S guideline. As illustrated with Daniel, clients often mention many aspects of life that would be different after the miracle. In an effort to select starting points and initial goals for counseling, we can ask clients (a) what piece of the miracle they want to work on first or (b) what piece of the miracle is most attainable at the present time.

I have found that people of all ages generally respond well to the miracle question and welcome the opportunity to focus on a better future. However, nothing works all the time with every client. When clients do not respond to the miracle question or otherwise indicate a preference for something different, we should honor their wishes and move on to other goal development strategies.

Final Comment on Goals

The collaborative development of clear goals from the outset of counseling is crucial to success. Effective goals keep counseling on track and focused. As the expression goes, "If you don't know where you're going, you probably won't get there."

Exceptions and Other Client Resources

I didn't know I was doing anything right.
—Robert, 8-year-old student

Client factors, which are the most potent ingredient in successful counseling, include strengths, successes, and a host of other resources that clients bring to the change process. Effective outcomes rest largely on the extent to which these assets are recognized and applied toward solutions. This section presents strategies for discovering and exploring successes and other resources of students, parents, and teachers.

Exceptions to the Problem

The search for exceptions to the problem is a key strategy in interviewing for solutions. *Exceptions,* referring to times in which the problem is absent or less noticeable, serve as the foundation for interventions aimed at increasing what is already working for clients. Exceptions can be viewed as solutions that are already happening, although not as intensely or often as desired.

Even in bleak situations when people initially report that nothing is working and there is never a good time, there are always times when things are a little better than usual. The stress and strain of serious problems can blind us to small but important fluctuations in problem intensity or frequency. de Shazer (1991) observed that "times when the complaint is absent are dismissed as trivial by the client or even remain completely unseen, hidden from the client's view" (p. 58). These powerful building blocks of change may go unnoticed unless we listen and ask for them in our initial interviews with students, parents, and teachers.

Listening for Exceptions. Clients often provide clues to exceptions through the words and phrases they use to describe the problem:

- I'm failing *almost* all my classes.
- I hate everything about school *except* recess and computer time.
- He *usually* acts up right after coming into my class.
- We *hardly ever* talk without arguing.

The italicized words in these statements provide important clues to exceptions. For example, the student's use of the word *almost* in the first example provides the opportunity to ask about a class that the student is passing.

Asking for Exceptions. Another way to discover exceptions is to ask for them with questions and requests, such as the following:

- When is the problem absent or less noticeable?
- Which class do you get in the least amount of trouble in?
- What is your best class?
- When have things been just a little better during the past week?
- Tell me about a time during the last few days when you did a little better in math class—not perfect, but just a little bit better than usual.

- Tell me about a time when you and the student had a conversation without arguing.
- When do you and your daughter get along best?
- [As follow-up to the miracle question] What parts of the miracle are already happening, if only just a little?
- [As follow-up to a scaling question] Tell me about a time during the past month when things were higher than a 3.

Exception-finding questions can often be woven into conversations about the problem and goals. For example, after discussing when and where the problem typically occurs, we can ask about the times and settings in which the problem is least noticeable. Scaling and miracle questions also provide opportunities to discover exceptions. For example, when clients describe what a higher number would look like on their scale (e.g., "I'd smile more and enjoy school"), we can ask about a recent day or situation in which they smiled a bit more often or were a little calmer than usual. We can also follow up on the client's response to the miracle question by asking about small pieces of the miracle that are already happening, even just a little.

Asking about precounseling and between-sessions changes is another way to discover exceptions. Many clients experience positive changes in the problem prior to the first counseling session. In one study, these pretreatment or precounseling changes were reported by 66% of the clients at a community services agency who were asked whether they had noticed any improvements in the presenting problem between the time they scheduled their appointment and their first session (Weiner-Davis, de Shazer, & Gingerich, 1987). Although this percentage has ranged from about 25% to 50% in other studies (Lawson, 1994; Ness & Murphy, 2001), precounseling changes are important exceptions that may be overlooked unless we ask the following kinds of questions in the first session:

- Sometimes people notice that things improve a little after they decide to get some help. What have you noticed?
- Has anything changed for the better since you knew that we were going to be meeting?
- Some people notice that things get a little better right before they start counseling. What have you noticed?
- Has anything changed for the better since your mother/teacher told you that we would be meeting?

Between-sessions changes can be explored and encouraged in the following ways:

- What's better since we last met?
- Has anything changed since we last talked?
- When have things been just a little better during the past week?
- Tell me about something good that happened at school in the last few days.
- Between now and the next time we meet, pay attention to the things the student does in your class that make things better.

- Between now and our next meeting, pay attention to the things that are happening at school that you want to continue happening.

Clarifying the Details of Exceptions. Once an exception is discovered, we can clarify related details with the same kinds of questions used to clarify problem-related circumstances. For example, a student who misbehaves in every class except science can be asked the following questions:

- What is different about your science class from your other classes? What else?
- What is different about your science teacher from your other teachers? What else?
- How do you manage to behave so well in science class?
- How do you resist the urge to mess around?
- What is different about your approach to science class compared to other classes?
- Where do you sit in science class?
- How would you rate your interest in science as compared to other subjects?

Questions for teachers and parents might include the following:

- What was different about last Tuesday, when Jeremy behaved better in your class?
- What do you do or say differently?
- Does Jeremy behave better on certain days of the week? During certain times or situations in your class?
- What is different about the times when you and your son get along better?
- Who is around when things seem to go more smoothly at home?

Chapter 6 presents additional strategies and examples of utilizing exceptions to resolve school problems.

Other Client Resources

In addition to exceptions, clients offer a variety of other resources that may contribute to solutions. These resources include special interests and talents, resilience, coping skills, ideas about solutions, and heroes and influential people in the student's life, to name just a few. These resources can be applied toward school solutions in any number of ways, depending on the student and circumstances. For example, in working with a student who has great respect for a grandparent, we could ask the grandparent to discuss the school situation with the student or to attend a problem-solving meeting at school. We can also ask students for their ideas on resolving the problem and integrate these ideas into school-based interventions. Resource-based conversations enhance the student's involvement in counseling because they address important elements of his or her life. This section describes interviewing methods for exploring various client resources.

Special Interests and Talents. Given that most students enter counseling at the request of others, we need to find out what they are interested in and incorporate these interests into the conversation when possible. The student's unique talents, hobbies, and interests can be explored with the following kinds of questions:

- What do you like doing outside of school?
- What excites you more than anything else in life?
- How would your family or friends finish this sentence about you: "Thomas is really good at . . ."?
- If we could talk about anything here, what would you want to talk about?
- Do you have a hobby? What is it about your hobby that makes it fun and worthwhile for you?
- If you could have any job you wanted now or when you get older, what would it be? What is it about that job that you like the most? What can you do at school right now to have a better chance to get that kind of job?

Conversations about special interests and talents sustain the student's attention and reveal potentially useful solution opportunities. For example, in working with a student who wants to become a professional musician, we might explore similarities between mastering difficult school material and learning a new piece of music for the first time.

Heroes and Influential People. Students typically have heroes and influential people in their life who may serve as useful resources in resolving school problems. This category can include relatives, friends, neighbors, athletes, musicians, actors, or even cartoon characters and other fictional heroes from books or movies. The common element of these resources is their ability to impact the student by way of modeling, advice, social and emotional support, and other forms of influence and assistance.

Regardless of whether they are real or fictional, influential people and heroes can be employed in creative ways to encourage different responses to the problem. The following questions are helpful in identifying key figures in the student's life and exploring the nature of their influence:

- Of all the people in your life, whom do you respect the most? Why do you respect him or her?
- Who believes in you more than anyone else? What does he or she see in you that others may not see?
- Who do you get along with best at school?
- Of all the people at school, who helps you when you have a problem? What does he or she do that's most helpful? How do you go about getting that person's help?
- What other people or groups might help you with this (neighbor, community agency, soccer coach, church group, etc.)?
- Who are your heroes? What do you admire most about them?
- What do you have in common with [hero's name]?

We can incorporate heroes and influential people into interventions in various ways, such as inviting them to participate in counseling sessions, calling them on the phone during the interview, obtaining their advice on the situation directly or through the student, and having the student contact them to discuss the problem and potential solutions. The following questions explore potential links between these resources and solutions:

- What would [hero/influential person] do in this situation? What do you think would happen if you did that?
- What do you think [hero/influential person] would advise you to do about this problem? What do you think about that advice?
- If your grandmother were sitting in this chair [pointing to an empty chair in the office] right now, what would she tell you to do? What would she do if she were in your shoes? Would you be willing to try something like that?
- If you followed his or her advice, would that make things better for you at school? [If yes] What part of that advice are you willing to try next week?

Resilience and Coping. Early in my career, I spent 13 years in a school district in one of the most economically disadvantaged communities in the United States. Among the many things I learned from the students and families in this community, two lessons about resilience stand out: (a) People are capable of remarkable persistence and accomplishments under extremely difficult circumstances and (b) people who are struggling with a serious problem are doing something to cope with it and prevent it from getting even worse. Without minimizing the pain and strain of the problem, I began approaching students and others from a resilience perspective that included questions such as the following:

- How have you kept things from getting worse?
- Why haven't you given up? How have you managed to hang in there instead of giving up?
- A problem like this would knock some people flat on their back, but not you. How would you explain that?
- How do you resist the urge to [drop out of school/mess around more in class/give up when the work gets hard/punch people who tease you]?
- Where do you find the strength and courage to cope with this day in and day out?
- How have you managed to keep your sanity and hope in the midst of your son's school problems?
- I can't imagine how stressful this has been for you all year, but here you are continuing to try and make things better for this student. That takes a special person. How do you do that?
- No one wants to have problems, but they seem to be a part of life, and some people say that they learn from their problems. What about you? Has this problem made you stronger or wiser in any way?
- Have you ever had a problem in your life that ended up making you stronger? How did that happen?

These questions convey our confidence in people's ability to cope, persist, and succeed under very difficult circumstances. Research has verified the resilient, adaptive abilities displayed by people of all ages when faced with serious challenges (Luthar, 2003; Simon, Murphy, & Smith, 2005). As illustrated next, these resources are there for the asking in school-based counseling.

Rosa: Why Haven't You Given Up? Rosa, a 17-year-old high school student, was referred for counseling early in her senior year. She was failing two subjects, and her school attendance was erratic. Rosa's teacher said that Rosa was capable of earning higher grades but did not apply herself or take school seriously.

Rosa discussed several difficulties in her life during the first session. She did not remember her father, who moved away when she was an infant. She had moved back and forth between her mother's and uncle's house eight different times during her school career, with each relocation involving a change in schools. Throughout much of her childhood, Rosa felt that nobody wanted her because she was "a financial burden." Both households were investigated by social services because of neglect and abuse charges.

At the time of the interview, Rosa was working 35 or more hours a week at a local restaurant to support herself and her mother. She often worked the late shift, from midnight to morning, arriving at school directly from her job. The following conversation occurred at the start of the second meeting.

> *Counselor:* I've thought a lot about our meeting last week, and I have a question for you. With all the hardships you've had to deal with in your life, how have you resisted the temptation to give up on school altogether and just quit?
>
> *Rosa:* Why would I want to give up? I've got all of the wonderful experiences ahead of me that I'm going to have in my senior year. I've got all of the wonderful things I'm going to learn in college. Why would I give up? If I give up, then I'm going to be flipping burgers the rest of my life. I want to make something better for myself. If I ever plan to have children, I would like to have some money built up in the bank for them to go to college.
>
> *Counselor:* Sounds like you have a lot to look forward to.
>
> *Rosa:* Definitely.
>
> *Counselor:* And that helps to keep you going, to keep you hanging in there in school when things get tough, huh?
>
> *Rosa:* If it were 2 or 3 years ago, I might have given up. You know, I practically did give up.
>
> *Counselor:* What's different about you now compared to then?

She proceeded to describe differences between the "old Rosa" and "new Rosa." Various aspects of her resilience approach to life were incorporated into practical interventions for improving school attendance and grades. Perhaps one reason that Rosa readily participated in this conversation is because it was so different from previous discussions with her teacher ("Why do you insist on not doing your school work when you have the skills to do it? A high school diploma is essential if you want to get a decent job"). Like many students referred for school problems, Rosa was surprised and pleased by the opportunity to discuss and build on what she was doing right. This allowed her the space to develop her own conclusions and goals regarding the importance of school and graduation. Despite continued difficulties at home and school, Rosa passed her classes and graduated in May.

Clients as Consultants. The wisdom of the people closest to the problem and solution is perhaps the most underrated client factor of all. Clients are the ones who directly experience the problem, are responsible for implementing interventions, and are in the best position to judge the effectiveness of counseling. As such, their ideas and opinions should be actively sought and respected.

Students who are referred for services are rarely asked for their opinion on resolving school problems. As a result, they may begin to see themselves as passive participants in an adults-only version of school intervention. One of the most respectful ways to encourage the active involvement of students is to enlist them as consultants. I usually approach this by explaining that my job is to help others with struggles similar to theirs and asking them for insights and advice based on their experience. As illustrated below, this strategy can be presented in playful ways and is applicable to students of all ages:

- I appreciate your willingness to help other students and me by sharing what you've learned about paying attention and improving your grades. What would you say to other third graders who ask what they can do to pay attention better and get better grades?
- What can I say to a student who says, "Why should I pay attention in school when I can have more fun goofing off and messing around?"
- Pretend you are the teacher and you're teaching a class called How to Stand Up to School Problems Instead of Letting Them Push You Around. What would you teach the students in this class?
- If you were the counselor, how would you help a student who is struggling with this same kind of problem?
- What do you think would help turn this thing around in school?
- [For students with prior counseling experiences] What was most helpful about your previous counselor and counseling experience? What was least helpful?

In all my years of using this strategy, no one has ever refused to share his or her advice and wisdom with others. Everyone appreciates being asked for his or her opinion on important topics. Even when clients are unable to come up with a lot of ideas or advice, the question itself enhances the alliance by conveying respect for their opinions and experiences.

I have been amazed at how often students can provide the essential material for successful interventions if only they are asked. Many opportunities are missed when students are viewed merely as "keepers of the problem," with little or nothing to offer toward solutions. Enlisting clients as consultants gives them an ongoing voice in the solution-building process.

Summary of Exceptions and Other Client Resources

The success of counseling rests largely on the extent to which clients and their resources are included in the change process. Exploring exceptions and other client resources lays the groundwork for positive interventions that build on naturally occurring events and assets in the lives of students, parents, and teachers. Berg (1991) offered the following rationale for identifying and building on what works naturally for clients rather than telling them what to do or teaching brand-new behaviors:

> It is always better for the client to come up with her own solutions rather than being told what to do. When it is her own idea, she is more likely to be committed to successful solutions. In addition, if a solution is generated from within the client's existing resources, it fits naturally with her way of doing things and it is easier to do more of. Furthermore, when the solution is more congruent with her lifestyle than any newly learned behavior, she is less likely to relapse. (p. 64)

The interviewing strategies in this chapter are applicable to a wide range of clients, problems, and circumstances. These tools, like any others, should be adapted to fit your unique style, work setting, and clients.

Summary and Conclusions

This chapter provides strategies of interviewing for solutions, including practical questions for exploring the problem and circumstances surrounding it, solution attempts, the client's theory of change, goals, exceptions to the problem, and other client resources. Clients are encouraged to use videotalk because a clear and observable problem is more changeable than a vague, abstract problem. Clarifying the circumstances surrounding a problem, such as what typically occurs right before and after the problem, may provide clues for resolving it. Exploring solution attempts may reveal previously successful strategies that can be adapted and applied to the problem, as well as helping counselors and clients avoid "more of the same" ineffective strategies. Clarifying the client's theory of change allows counselors to structure their comments, questions, and suggestions in cooperative ways that accommodate the client's views of the problem, solution, and counseling relationship.

The formulation of effective goals is central to solution-focused counseling. Effective goals are significant, specific, small, start based, and self-manageable. Clear goals keep counseling on track and assist in evaluating its effectiveness. The most distinctive feature of solution-focused counseling is its emphasis on exceptions and other naturally occurring resources that all clients bring to the counseling process. The search for exceptions and other resources is guided by the practical notion that it is easier to build on what is already working for clients, if only just a little, than it is to eliminate problems or teach brand-new behaviors. The theme of building on what works is continued in the next two chapters, which describe practical methods and examples of building on exceptions (Chapter 6) and other client resources (Chapter 7).

Practice Exercises

1. With a partner in the role of student, parent, or teacher, experiment with the questions listed below to open the first interview. Note any differences in the responses you get to each of these questions. Ask your partner about any differences in his or her reaction to these questions.
   - What is the problem?
   - What do you want to see happen as a result of counseling?
   - What is the student doing or not doing that you see as the problem?
   - What do you hope to accomplish with counseling?
2. Think of a current concern or problem in your life, and complete the following tasks: (a) Define the problem using videotalk, (b) clarify related circumstances (when, where, and with whom it typically occurs and what happens right before and after it occurs), (c) consider what you have already tried and how it has worked, and (d) clarify your theory about the problem and solution. Use this information to develop a practical plan for changing the problem.
3. Select two of your current counseling clients and ask yourself whether the counseling goals meet the 5-S guidelines of being significant, specific, small, start based, and self-manageable. If not, how might these goals be altered to make them more effective?
4. Think of a situation or problem in your life that you would like to change. What will be the first small sign that things are getting a little better? To practice scaling, rate the problem from 1 to 10, with 1 being as bad as it can be and 10 being as good as it can be. What would the next higher number look like? Be specific in describing what you and others will be doing when things start getting better. What effect did this scaling task have on you? How did it affect your hope regarding future improvement?
5. Select a current problem in your life, and describe what would be different if a miracle occurred and the problem suddenly vanished. How could you or others tell that the miracle had occurred? Be thorough and specific in your description of life after the miracle. Of all those things that would be different, which ones are already happening, if only just a little? What needs to happen to increase or sustain these exceptions or better times? What are you willing to do to make this happen?
6. Explore exceptions in your next session by asking the client questions such as "When does the problem let up or disappear altogether?" and "When doesn't the problem happen?" Once an exception is discovered, explore related details, and encourage the client to increase the exception.
7. Think about a specific situation or challenge in your life that was so difficult that you wondered whether you would survive it—but you did. Somehow

you managed to get through it and keep walking. How did you do that? What resources, within yourself and elsewhere, helped you make it through this situation? How might these same resources be applied to a present challenge or goal in your life? Consider using this same sequence of questions with students and others to acknowledge their resilience and invite them to apply their resources to the present school problem.

8. Describe one small step that you are willing to take in your practice as a result of the information in this chapter.

Building on Exceptions

A Sufi man was walking along the road when he spotted his friend Mulla searching for something under the streetlamp outside his house. When the man asked what he was doing, Mulla said that he was looking for his lost keys. The man got on his hands and knees and joined Mulla in the search. After several minutes, the man asked, "Where exactly did you drop them?" "Way over there," replied Mulla, pointing to a field across the road. "Then why, might I ask, are you looking here?" "Because the light's so much better here," Mulla said.
—Adapted from Shah, *The Exploits of the Incomparable Mulla Nasrudin*

In the field of mental health, the *health* part has traditionally taken a back seat to the search for client pathology and its treatment. Outcome research increasingly suggests that solutions may be more plentiful on the less familiar road of client strengths and resources. Even though "the light may be better" in the familiar area of client deficits and weaknesses, finding the keys or solutions is always more important than looking under the light.

Solution-focused counseling seeks to discover and utilize what works for clients in building solutions to school problems. One of the most effective ways to do this is to build on exceptions to the problem. An *exception* refers to a specific event or situation in which the problem does not occur or occurs less often or intensely than usual.

Building on exceptions has been a big part of solution-focused brief therapy for many years (Berg, 1991; de Shazer, 1985) and offers much promise as a strategy for resolving school problems. Utilizing exceptions is based on the practical idea that it is much easier to increase existing successes than it is to eliminate problems or teach brand-new behaviors. This chapter describes and illustrates a five-step strategy for building on exceptions (Murphy, 1994).

The 5-E Method of Building on Exceptions

*If I focus on a problem, the problem increases,
if I focus on the answer, the answer increases.*
—Alcoholics Anonymous, *Alcoholics Anonymous Comes of Age*

Building on exceptions can be broken into five steps: eliciting, elaborating, expanding, evaluating, and empowering. Eliciting and elaborating were addressed in Chapter 5 and are discussed only briefly below in the description of the entire five-step process.

Step 1: Eliciting

Given that most people overlook small fluctuations in the problem, it is important to listen for any hints of exceptions in the client's comments. It is also helpful to ask questions, assign tasks, use exception-oriented forms and rating scales, and review school records.

Exception-finding questions include the following:

- When is the problem absent or less noticeable during the school day?
- Can you think of a time when the student did a little better this week?
- Of all your classes, which one is the most tolerable?

If no exceptions are identified when we ask direct questions, we can assign exception-finding tasks, such as the following:

- Between now and next week, make a list of the things [in your life/at school/ in math class] that you would like to see continue.
- Pay attention to the times you are able to resist the urge to [hit someone when you're angry/skip school when you're tired] so that you can tell me about them the next time we meet.
- Observe when the problem doesn't happen, and pay attention to how you are able to make that happen.

Rating scales and surveys can also be completed by students, parents, and teachers to elicit exceptions. Most rating scales focus exclusively on problems, with little or no attention to the client's strengths or successes. For example, a teacher or parent might be asked to rate the student on the extent to which he or she demonstrates hyperactivity, aggression, anxiety, and so on. These scales can reveal hints of exceptions when reviewed with an eye toward items scored as less problematic than others.

Counselors can elicit exceptions more directly by using solution-focused instruments specifically designed to identify strengths, resources, and successes. The Solution Identification Scale, displayed in Appendix E, is a checklist developed by Kral (1988) to reveal positive attributes and behaviors of students. Although the scale was originally designed to be completed by teachers and parents, students can also complete it on their own or with assistance. Similarly, the Behavior and Emotional Rating Scale—2 (Epstein, 2004) is a marketed strength-based scale that seeks to identify children's personal, social, affective, and academic strengths.

Appendix E also includes the Quick Survey, an informal questionnaire that I use with teachers to elicit exceptions. The solution-focused nature of the survey encourages teachers to pay attention to exceptions and related circumstances. The survey can be customized to any student and situation and can be adapted for parents to gather information about exceptions outside the school setting.

Unlike other rating scales and surveys, these instruments do not have to be scored in the traditional sense for peer comparison purposes. Instead, they can be used to help counselors and clients devise positive interventions based on strengths and exceptions.

Exceptions can also be discovered in school records. For example, reviewing academic and discipline records with an eye toward the positive can reveal the following exceptions in students' school performance:

- Fewer behavior problems in the morning versus afternoon or in one particular class compared to others
- Better grades in math than other subjects
- More consistent school attendance on Mondays and Tuesdays

Step 2: Elaborating

Once identified, an exception can be further explored and elaborated through questions about related features and circumstances. Chapter 5 provided numerous questions for elaborating on exceptions, such as "What is different about [those times/that class/or whatever the exception is]?" and "How did you approach things differently?" These details lay the groundwork for exception-based interventions in Step 3.

Step 3: Expanding

Expanding is the heart of the 5-E process, in which students, teachers, or parents are encouraged to expand the exception to other situations or to a greater frequency.

Expanding Exceptions to Other Situations. As an example of expanding exceptions to other situations, consider the fourth-grade student who behaves better in science class than other classes. On discovering that science is the only class in which the student sits close to the teacher's desk, the counselor can arrange for a similar seating assignment in one or more of the other classes. As simple as this sounds, improvements in school problems often result from expanding what works in one situation to another, then another, and so on.

Expanding Exceptions to a Greater Frequency. In addition to expanding exceptions to other situations, people can be encouraged to "do the exception" more frequently. Ted, a sixth-grade science teacher, requested help in managing the behavior of his entire class. When asked about times when things went a little more smoothly in class, he reported fewer behavior problems (the exception) during small-group exercises and experiments (the exception context). We discussed how he might increase these activities while meeting course objectives. When I saw Ted 3 weeks later, he commented that things had been much better since he began doing some kind of special activity almost every day. He also added his own touch to the intervention in two major ways. First, he decided to schedule group activities and experiments during the last half of the class because students' behavior was typically worse during this time. Second, he offered certain special activities as rewards contingent on acceptable classroom behavior during the entire week. In solution-focused counseling, people are encouraged to adapt interventions to fit their unique style and circumstances, just as Ted did. Ted's example illustrates the simple yet effective strategy of urging people to do more of what is already working for them.

The last two steps of the 5-E method—evaluating and empowering—apply to changes in general, not just those resulting from exception-based interventions.

Step 4: Evaluating

Evaluating outcomes in solution-focused counseling is based primarily on the client's perceptions and judgments of goal attainment. Many of the evaluation strategies from the literature were designed for research purposes and are too cumbersome and time consuming for everyday use by busy school practitioners. The following discussion describes methods that are practical and compatible with a solution-focused approach to counseling.

Scaling Techniques. Scaling questions are very useful in evaluating the effectiveness of counseling. Students and others can be asked the following question on a regular basis throughout the counseling process: "On a scale of 1 to 10, with 1 being the worst it can be and 10 the best, how have things been going with this problem/goal during the past week?" As noted in Chapter 5, scaling questions can be easily adapted to any problem, goal, or client.

Paper-and-Pencil Methods. Paper-and-pencil methods can also be used to evaluate the effectiveness of counseling. The ORS was introduced in Chapter 4 as a method of establishing goals at the beginning of counseling. The ORS also serves as an ongoing snapshot of the client's perception of change in key areas of life throughout the counseling process. Appendix D provides additional information and examples of how the ORS can be used to evaluate outcomes and adjust services accordingly.

Other kinds of rating scales can also be used to evaluate outcomes. For example, a parent and teacher could fill out a behavior rating scale on a student before and after counseling, and the counselor could compare the two sets of ratings to assess perceived changes in the student's behavior. Although marketed rating scales can be used for this purpose, most are designed for wide-scale use and may include items that are irrelevant to the particular problem, goal, and student with whom we are working. To avoid this, we can design individualized rating scales that are worded to the specific client, circumstances, and goals of counseling. Exhibit 6.1 provides one such example involving a sixth grader named Jerry, with a goal of improving classroom behavior and assignment completion. The scale took 10 minutes to develop and 5 minutes to complete. Jerry's teachers completed the scale every Friday for 2 months. This provided an ongoing snapshot of Jerry's behavior and assignment completion and allowed for timely adjustments in counseling services based on their feedback.

The importance of adjusting services in response to client feedback cannot be overstated. We have all had the disempowering experience of being asked for our opinion, taking the time to provide it, and watching things continue exactly as they had before we were asked for our feedback. We can avoid this mistake by valuing and accommodating the feedback of students, parents, and teachers throughout the helping process.

Exhibit 6.1
Individually Developed Teacher Rating Scale for Evaluating Progress

Student: <u>Jerry S</u>   Teacher/Class: <u>Ms. McCreary/Science</u>   Date: <u>3/15/2007</u>

1. On a scale of 1 to 10, with 1 being "the worst it can be" and 10 being "the best it can be," rate Jerry's behavior in your class during the past week: _____

2. As compared to when the referral was made in late January, Jerry's current behavior in your class is:

   _____ better   _____ worse   _____ about the same

   If better, what is he doing differently now that makes it better?

   Other comments?

3. As compared to when the referral was made, Jerry's completion of in-class assignments during the past week was:

   _____ better   _____ worse   _____ about the same

   If better, what is he doing differently now that makes it better?

   Other comments?

4. As compared to when the referral was made, Jerry's completion of homework assignments for your class during the past week was:

   _____ better   _____ worse   _____ about the same

   If better, what is he doing differently now that makes it better?

   Other comments?

5. Please list the things that Jerry is *already doing* to improve his behavior and assignment completion in your class (other than what is listed above).

6. Please list the things that Jerry *could do* differently to improve his behavior and assignment completion in your class.

7. Add any *other comments or questions* that would help me better understand the situation from your perspective.

Thank You For Your Cooperation.

Permanent Products. Examination of permanent products, such as report cards and discipline records, is another practical way of evaluating the effectiveness of our services. For example, comparison of report cards and discipline records before, during, and following counseling can be used to evaluate the student's goal of improving grades and reducing after-school detention. Additional permanent products include classroom work samples, weekly behavior cards, homework assignments, midterm progress reports, teachers' grade books, and students' cumulative files.

Single-Case Evaluation Designs. Single-case evaluation designs (Barlow, Hayes, & Nelson, 1999) can be used in conjunction with the methods above to evaluate progress. The most practical of these designs is the AB design, where *A* is the preintervention/baseline phase and *B* is the intervention phase. For example, a teacher and/or student might rate and graph the student's daily classroom behavior for a week or so before counseling (the A phase) and for several weeks following it (the B phase). One major advantage of this kind of evaluation is that it provides repeated measures of progress. Frequent and repeated measures are more useful than one or two occasional measures because they provide a more comprehensive picture of the change process and allow for timely adjustments in services. Additional applications of single-case designs in counseling can be found in Barlow et al. (1999).

Step 5: Empowering

When improvements occur at any time in the counseling process, regardless of how small, emphasis shifts toward empowering and maintaining them. This section describes practical strategies for empowering positive changes and helping clients maintain them.

Collaborating. Collaborating with clients throughout counseling promotes their ownership and maintenance of desired changes. One way to do this is by offering suggestions and ideas instead of telling people what to do (e.g., "What do you think would make things better?" "What would you think about asking your teacher what you could do to raise your grade?"). Clients who perceive themselves as active partners in the change process are more likely to take ownership of improvements and continue applying interventions on their own after counseling formally ends.

Giving Clients Credit. It is important that clients view desired changes as resulting from something they did and can repeat in the future. The following statements and questions invite clients to take credit for positive changes and reflect on what they did to bring them about:

- Wait a second. I've got to know how you did that. How did you do it?
- That's very impressive. How did you know to do that?
- What is it about you that helped you make this happen?
- What does this say about you, the kind of person you are, that you took control and made these changes?
- How did you decide that now was the time for action?
- What are you doing differently now to make it through math class for a whole week without getting kicked out?
- How did you manage to get your daughter to school on time for the past 3 days?
- What does this tell you about yourself? What do you think this tells your parents and teachers about you?

Clarifying the Impact of Change. Clarifying the personal and ecological impact of change helps students and others maintain improvements. Questions that explore old you/new you and before/after distinctions are useful in clarifying the impact of improvements on people's perceptions of themselves and their circumstances:

- How is the new you different from the old you?
- What effect have these changes had on your confidence and your view of yourself?
- What does this say about you and the kind of person you are, that you took control of the situation and made these improvements?
- How do your parents and teachers treat you differently now that you have made these changes?
- Since you began asking him fewer questions about school, have you noticed any other positive changes or differences in the way you and your son get along?
- I know that Monique's classroom behavior has improved since you began meeting individually with her for a few minutes on Friday afternoons. Have you noticed any other benefits of these Friday meetings?

Exploring Future Plans. Exploring the client's future intentions and plans also helps to keep the ball rolling following improvements. Asking students, parents, and teachers how they intend to maintain desired changes helps them clarify their plans for sustaining improvements and conveys our confidence in their ability to do so:

- Do you plan to continue these changes in the way you act at school? Why is it important for you to do this?
- What can you do to continue the progress you have made with this student in your math class?
- How are you going to stick with this plan in the future?

Preparing for Relapse. Although people are pleased and relieved by desired changes, they may also fear that the improvements will not last. This is a fairly common reaction, especially when the problem has been a big part of the person's life for a long time. Counselors can empathize with clients' apprehension by suggesting that occasional slips and relapses are a normal part of the change process. Important changes usually do not proceed in a steady manner whereby each day is progressively better than the last. It is more like two steps forward, one step back, three more forward, two back, and so forth. Clients who are adequately prepared for this process are likely to respond in effective ways when slips occur. Without such preparation, they may exaggerate the significance of a relapse and respond to it in unproductive ways. For example, parents and teachers who are not adequately prepared for relapses may revert to the same ineffective strategies that contributed to the original problem. Likewise, students may become discouraged after a difficult day and think, "I'm right back where I started. Why should I keep trying to make things better?" The following questions and comments help clients prepare for the bumps, slips, and feelings that often occur along the road to change:

- Most important changes don't happen in a straight line but are more like up a few steps, back a little, up a little more, back a little, and so forth. What will you do if you have a bad day or notice yourself acting like you used to in class?
- What will you do if your grades start slipping a little in math class?
- What will you do the next time your son does not get up for school?
- How will you handle it if this new classroom management plan stops working as well as it has been?

Asking Clients for Advice. Another way to empower desired changes is to ask clients what advice they would give others who wish to make similar changes. Asking clients for their advice encourages them to reflect on what they did to improve things. Enlisting clients as consultants conveys our respect for their wisdom and contributions, which may enhance their confidence in maintaining desired changes. Questions along these lines include the following:

- What would you say to other first graders who want to pay attention better in class?
- What should I say to a student who says, "Why should I pay attention in school when I can have more fun goofing off and messing around?"
- If you were a counselor, what would you tell students/teachers/parents who are struggling with the same kind of problem that you changed?
- What advice do you have for other students/teachers/parents?

In addition to asking clients for suggestions, we can invite them to write out their success stories for us and others to consult in the future:

- Would you be willing to write a story about how you made these changes?
- Since my job is to help other students/parents make changes like the ones you have recently made, I would really appreciate you taking a few minutes to list some suggestions that I can share with others based on your experience and success with this problem.
- Could you e-mail me a list of suggestions on what other students can do at school and at home to improve their grades?
- Maybe we could work together on a little book called *Michael's Tips* that would tell the story about how you made these changes and offer tips for other students who want to do what you have done.

A book titled *Student Victories Over School Problems* can be assembled every year and maintained at the school for access by students, teachers, parents, and other interested parties. In addition to showcasing stories of success and courage, the act of writing requires students to reflect on their accomplishments and clarify how they brought those changes about.

Another way to empower improvements is to have students work directly with others in tutoring or teaching roles. I recently worked with a fifth-grade student named Terrence, who made steady behavioral improvements during the second semester of the year. At the end of the year, I asked whether he was willing to partner with me in planning and delivering a fall speaking tour on effective school behavior for younger students in the district. Terrence readily agreed and did an excellent job. Several teachers commented that he was a very effective "behavioral ambassador" for the younger students, especially given that many younger students in the community knew and respected him. When I asked Terrence how this experience affected him, he explained that he felt more responsible and accountable for his actions because he was a teacher now. In Terrence's own words, "I better be good in school because I told these kids to be good. If I mess up they'll be saying I'm all talk and no action. And I'm not a phony."

I have also invited students who have made successful changes to become members of my Consultant Club, a group of former clients who have agreed to let me call on them in the future for ideas and suggestions for other students. Students who join the club are given a framable certificate and wallet-sized card designating them as official members and consultants. The certificate is displayed in Appendix F. As discussed next, certificates and other documents can be used to recognize and empower successful changes.

Using Documents. Letters, certificates, and other documents can be used to reinforce and maintain desired changes in school problems. People of all ages respond favorably to individualized notes and letters. This letter was sent to a fifth-grade student following improvements in her school behavior:

> Dear Denise,
> Congratulations on the changes you have made this week in your school behavior. I know how hard it was to resist the urge to mess around in class, but you did it. I would like to learn more about how you made these changes. I will ask you how you did it the next time we meet.

Appendix F provides other examples of letters and documents that can be used to help students clarify and maintain improvements.

Celebrating Success. It is also helpful to encourage clients to reward themselves for making changes by doing something special to punctuate and celebrate successes. It doesn't matter what it is, just something that adds an exclamation point to the fact that they did something very positive. To further highlight the client's accomplishments, we can suggest a ritual or physical object that symbolizes the change and serves as a reminder and motivator of the client's courage and success. This could be anything from going fishing to making a victory collage, carrying a special coin or picture, reading or writing a poem, reciting a song verse, or inventing a victory slogan, such as "If I did it then, I can do it now." It doesn't matter what it is, as long as it has meaning to the client.

Leaving the Door Open. Another way to empower and maintain progress is by leaving the door open for follow-up visits and booster sessions at the request of the student, parent, or teacher. Although solution-focused counseling conveys confidence in clients' ability to maintain changes, follow-up contacts can help them sustain progress. When goals are reached and counseling ends, we can offer follow-up booster sessions, phone calls, or e-mails to check on progress and encourage people to continue doing what is working and alter what is not working.

The 5-E method, summarized in Box 6.1, is a versatile and systematic way to utilize exceptions to the problem.

Box 6.1
The 5-E Method of Building on Exceptions

Step 1: Eliciting
Listen, ask, assign tasks, use formal and informal rating scales and surveys, and examine school records.

Examples: "In what class is the problem absent or less noticeable?" "Tell me about a time you made it through the whole day without getting kicked out of class," "Pay attention to everything you want to continue happening at school," select or develop solution-focused rating scales and surveys, review records with an eye toward exceptions.

Step 2: Elaborating
Explore related features and circumstances of exceptions.

Examples: "How is your math class different from the classes you are having more problems with?" "During what type of class activities does this student behave better?" "What is different about the times you and your daughter get along better?"

Step 3: Expanding
Encourage clients to expand the exception to a greater frequency or to other situations.

Examples: "What will it take to do this more often at school? You seem to get to school on time when your brother wakes you—is it possible for him to start waking you more often?" "It might be fun to do more of your 'science class behavior' in one of your other classes and observe any differences in the way your teacher treats you," "Since the students behave better during hands-on activities in your class, how could you increase such activities?"

Step 4: Evaluating
Evaluate the effectiveness of counseling using scaling questions, formal and informal rating scales, permanent products, and single-case evaluation designs.

(continued)

Box 6.1 *(Continued)*
The 5-E Method of Building on Exceptions

Examples: "On a scale of 1 to 10, with 1 being the worst it could be and 10 being the best it could be, where would you rate your behavior in math class during the past week?" obtain client feedback on outcomes using the the ORS and self-designed surveys; examine grade reports and discipline records to assess progress on the student's goals of improving grades and behavior; graph and compare repeated measures of goal-related data before and during counseling using simple AB designs, where A is the baseline or precounseling phase and B is the counseling phase.

Step 5: Empowering
Collaborating, giving clients credit, clarifying the impact of change, exploring future plans, preparing for relapse, requesting clients' advice and consultation, using letters and other documents, celebrating, and leaving the door open for future contact.

Examples: "How have you managed to make these changes?" "How do your teachers and parents treat you differently?" "What will it take to continue doing this?" "What will you do when you have a bad day or things slip a bit?" "What would you say to another student/parent/teacher who is struggling with a similar problem?" "What can you do to celebrate your recent victory over the problem?" use letters and documents.

Examples of Building on Exceptions

I have found that the best way to learn and teach counseling strategies is through specific, real-world examples. Therefore, the remainder of the chapter demonstrates how to build on exceptions with a variety of actual clients and school problems. Dialogue and commentary provide an up-close look at the counseling process and the strategy of building on exceptions with students, parents, and teachers.

The Monday Morning Exception

Sam, a 9-year-old third-grade student, was referred by his teachers for noncompliance and oppositional behavior. The referral form noted that Sam was a "bright and academically capable student" who was recently diagnosed with oppositional defiant disorder by a local psychiatrist. The dialogue picks up with the counselor's opening comments in the first session.

> *Counselor:* Sam, the purpose of our meeting is to help make school go more like you want it to go instead of the way it's going now. I need to learn how you want school to be different. I have to ask you some questions to learn

more about what's happening in school and what it's like for you. I will ask you to fill out a couple sheets for me when we meet. These sheets will teach me how things are going for you [referring to the CORS] and how the meetings are working for you [referring to the CSRS]. That's right, Sam, you get to grade me instead of me grading you. These meetings are for you, and I need your help in telling me if things are not working here, so that we can change it and make it better. Is that okay?

Sam: [nods "yes"]

In addition to preparing Sam for the counseling experience, the counselor's orientation statement establishes a feedback culture and conveys respect for Sam's input and participation. Phrases such as "I need to learn" and "I need your help" emphasize the collaborative and client-driven nature of solution-focused counseling. These phrases help to gain the attention and cooperation of struggling students, who may view themselves as passive bystanders versus vital contributors to school solutions.

Counselor: I talked with your mom and teachers yesterday, but I want to hear *your* take on things. This form [showing Sam the CORS] helps me learn how things are going for you at school and other places. So, for this first question that says, "Me (How Am I Doing?)," you need to mark the line anywhere between here [pointing to the left end of the line] and here [pointing to the right end] to show how things are going for you. The closer to this end and the smiley face, the better things are. Marks over here mean that things are not going well. Do you understand?

Sam: Yes.

The counselor walked Sam through the completion of the CORS, which resulted in the following scores: Me (7.7), Family (8.3), School (1.8), Everything (7.6), total (25.4). Sam's mother and language arts teacher, who was the primary referral source, had completed the CORS a few days earlier, with the following results: for the mother, Me (4.9), Family (6.5), School (1.7), Everything (6.3), total (19.4); for the teacher, Me (6.0), Family (7.3), School (1.6), Everything (5.8), total (20.7). These scores verified that school was the primary concern of the major people involved in this case. These scores provide a precounseling baseline and lay the groundwork for evaluating clients' perceptions of progress on an ongoing basis throughout the helping process.

Counselor: So it looks like things are going okay for you in every area except school. Is that right?

Sam: [nods "yes"]

Counselor: Okay. Do you know why your teacher and mother wanted you to meet with me?

Sam: Because I'm bad at school.

Counselor: What do you mean when you say you're bad at school?

Sam: It means I don't mind the teachers. I don't do what they tell me to do, and I'm always getting sent to the principal's office.

Counselor: Being bad and getting sent to the principal's office. [pointing to Sam's mark of 1.8 on the CORS School scale] Does that explain this low mark on the School line?

Sam: Yes.

Counselor: Okay. Thank you. Why do they send you to the principal's office?

Sam: To cool off. The principal talks to me about what I did wrong and tells me to be better.

Counselor: How often do you get sent to the principal's office?

Sam: Just about every day. I told you I was bad.

Counselor: Tell me about a time during the past few days when you went for a pretty long time at school without getting in trouble or getting sent to the principal's office. [This question is designed to elicit exceptions to the problem.]

Sam: [pauses for about 10 seconds] Monday. Yeah, Monday. I didn't get in trouble until after lunch on the playground.

Counselor: Wow. You mean you went the whole morning doing what your teachers asked and staying out of trouble?

Sam: Yes, the whole morning.

Counselor: What did that feel like for you?

Sam: It felt good. I mean, that's pretty good for me.

Counselor: It sure is. I wonder what was different about Monday than most other days.

To elaborate and gather details about the "Monday morning exception," the counselor continued to express curiosity and explore what was different about Monday. It turned out that Sam arrived early for school that day. He walked into his homeroom class and saw Ms. Robinson attempting to move a large bookshelf. He helped her move the shelf across the room and asked whether she needed help with anything else. The teacher put him to work for the next few minutes sorting crayons, watering plants, moving books, and sharpening pencils.

In the following excerpt, the counselor explores the details of the exception and its impact on Sam and his teachers. In addition to clarifying exception-related circumstances, this conversation reinforced a more hopeful story about Sam by inviting him to take credit for the positive turn of events on Monday and connecting these events to his own choices and actions.

Counselor: Let me see if I understand this, Sam. You just decided to help Ms. Robinson on your own.

Sam: That's right.

Counselor: So she didn't even ask you to help, but you helped her anyway?

Sam: Yep.

Counselor: Wow. That's really something. What made you decide to do that? [These comments give Sam credit for the changes.]

Sam: She was trying to push this big old thing across the room all by herself, and it wasn't really moving. I'm pretty strong with pushing and stuff like that, so I thought, "Hey, she needs help and I'm pretty strong," so that was it.

Counselor: And you two pushed it across the room.

Sam: Two other kids helped, too.

Counselor: This is great, Sam. Let me see if I've got this right. You not only helped Ms. Robinson just because you wanted to, but you also rounded up a couple of other kids to help, too. What made you think of getting them to help?

Sam: That thing was heavy. These kids just walked in the room, so I said, "Hey, help us move this," and they did.

Counselor: Not everyone would do what you did. What is it about you that led you to do that instead of letting Ms. Robinson struggle with it herself or find someone else to help?

Sam: I guess I felt sorry for her. I didn't have anything else to do.

Counselor: So you're a caring person. What was it like for you when you helped? How did it feel?

Sam: It felt good.

Counselor: That's good. And the rest of the morning was good, not just in Ms. Robinson's class but in your other morning classes, too. How do you explain that, Sam?

Sam: I don't know. It was just good.

Counselor: I wonder what was different about you and your teachers that made it good.

Sam: I just did my work, and I didn't mess with people as much.

Counselor: So you usually mess with people more, but you didn't do that as much on Monday morning.

Sam: I didn't do it at all.

Counselor: Wow! That must have been hard work, huh?

Sam: Not really. I just did it.

Counselor: You just did it. Like the Nike commercial. Just do it.

Sam: [smiles and nods "yes"]

Counselor: Did your teachers treat you different when you "just did it"?

Sam: Yes.

Counselor: How were they different?

Sam: They were nicer.

Sam described several specific ways that his teachers were nicer, including thanking him for behaving well and picking up after himself in art class, letting him erase the board after math class, and letting him line up in the front spot on the way to the lunchroom.

Counselor: And how was that for you?

Sam: It was good.

Inviting Sam to consider the personal and social impact of his "exception behavior" encouraged him to acknowledge the results of his choices and actions and to take credit for recent improvements rather than viewing them as a fluke. Instead of telling Sam why things were better with his teachers, the school psychologist expressed curiosity and asked questions that allowed Sam to describe things in his own words. In addition to increasing students' ownership of school improvements, "asking versus telling" sustains their attention because it is different from their typical conversations with adults.

When students view positive changes as resulting from their own decisions and choices, they are more likely to take personal responsibility for their actions and to maintain successful behavior after formal counseling has ended. Students like Sam, with a history of ongoing school problems, may resign themselves to viewing school conflicts as an unchangeable matter of fate. Conversations about exceptions create a more hopeful outlook.

The final few minutes of the session took place after a short break, during which the counselor and Sam walked around the playground and tossed a tennis ball for a few minutes. In the next excerpt, which occurred just before the session ended, the counselor appeals to Sam's playful nature by inviting him to try "an experiment" aimed at expanding the exception to other situations.

Counselor: Do you think people at school understand that you're a caring person?
Sam: No. I'm pretty bad at school.
Counselor: I'm not trying to get you to say something that you don't really believe. So it's important for me to know if *you* believe that you're a caring person.
Sam: I think I am. But I can be mean, too.
Counselor: So you're a caring person and you can be mean, too. Do you think people appreciate or understand the caring part of you that likes to help people?
Sam: Not really.
Counselor: Why do you think they don't?
Sam: Because I do bad things.
Counselor: Do these bad things make it hard for people to see the good things about you, like the caring and helping?
Sam: Yes.
Counselor: They don't fully understand you, do they?
Sam: [shakes his head "no," and his eyes tear up]
Counselor: Sam, is it important to you that your teachers and other people understand that you're a caring person?
Sam: Yes.
Counselor: I wonder what it would take for them to understand you're a caring person who likes to help people.
Sam: [shrugs shoulders]
Counselor: Sam, I remember your teachers stating that you liked science. Is that true?

Sam: Yes. [Sam's interest in science was a client factor that was incorporated into the intervention.]

Counselor: Have you ever done a science experiment?

Sam: We do experiments in class sometimes. I think we're going to do one tomorrow.

Counselor: Do you like experiments?

Sam: Yes.

Counselor: Well, you might be able to do a real science experiment starting right now. Do you want to hear more?

Sam: Yes.

Counselor: This is pretty cool, Sam, because you get to be in the experiment and you get to be the scientist who conducts the experiment. I'll need your help designing the experiment, too, but here is what I'm thinking. In order to test out your idea that teachers are nicer to you when you are nicer to them, you could do something caring each day for each teacher, and then pay close attention to how they treat you. You could rate your teachers on how nice they are by giving them a number from 1 to 10. The number 1 means "not nice," 10 means "really nice," and 5 is in between. We can call it the Niceness Scale. Do you understand?

Sam: I think so. This is like a test, and we're testing it out.

Counselor: Exactly. You never know if it's going to work unless you test it out and observe closely to see if it really works.

The counselor and Sam quickly hammered out the details of the experiment. Sam decided to walk up to his teachers as soon as he entered their classroom and offer to help with anything they needed. If they said no, he would say, "Okay. Let me know if you change your mind," then walk back to his seat. Regardless of whether the teacher took him up on his offer, Sam would rate each teacher on the Niceness Scale by writing a number next to the class in an assignment notebook. The session ended with Sam's completion of the CSRS as follows: Listening (9.4), How Important (9.2), What We Did (7.7), Overall (8.5), and total score (34.8).

Counselor: Thanks for filling this out, Sam. So, you felt like I listened to you and we talked about important stuff. These marks [pointing to the What We Did and Overall items on the CSRS) are a little lower than the others. What else could I do, or do differently, to make our visit better for you?

Sam: It was fine. It just took pretty long.

Counselor: I really appreciate you letting me know about this. Wow, this meeting did run pretty long, didn't it? I'll have to keep a better eye on that next time. What else could I do to make it better?

Sam: That's it.

Aside from the benefits of receiving feedback on the counselor's and meeting's goodness of fit for Sam, the counselor's willingness to discuss these issues in a nondefensive manner enhanced the alliance.

The counselor met with Sam 1 week later to review the results of the experiment. After Sam apologized for occasionally forgetting to record the niceness ratings, he said that he had been sent out of class only once the entire week. He described several specific ways his teachers were nicer to him. Sam discussed various chores he had helped his teachers with that week and said that the principal had also asked whether he would be willing to stop in the main office as soon as he arrived at school each morning to sharpen pencils from the previous day and check the copy machine to make sure it had enough paper. Sam willingly agreed to this task and appeared to take great pride in his new responsibilities and behavioral improvements at school.

The remainder of the session focused on empowering desired changes by giving Sam credit ("How did you do this?"), exploring future plans ("What will it take to continue this?"), clarifying the personal and social impact of desired changes ("What has this taught you about yourself?" "How is your life different at school since you've made these improvements?"), and requesting Sam's advice for others ("What advice would you have for other students who are struggling with their behavior in school?"). The counselor also asked Sam about his interest in starring in a short movie about changing school behavior.

Although Sam was committed to sustaining his behavioral progress, the remainder of the year was far from perfect for him. There were several slips along the way, and he eventually lost the opportunity to help in the principal's office. However, he continued to periodically help his teachers and remained in class for the entire day on an average of 4 out of 5 days during the remainder of the school year—a big improvement from the 1 day per week that Sam remained in class all day during the month before counseling began. His grades also improved from an overall average of C to a B following the initiation of counseling services.

Sam and his teachers completed the CORS every other week during the remainder of the school year. Everyone's total score was higher than his or her baseline score on every postcounseling administration. The most dramatic increase in scores occurred on the first postcounseling administration, about 10 days after the first meeting with Sam. Sam's total score increased from a baseline of 25.4 to 34.1. His teacher's score increased from 20.7 to 28.5. His mother's total score also increased, from a baseline of 19.4 to a 26.2. Formal discipline referrals decreased from an average of 3.5 per week to 1 per week following the start of counseling. The following comments from the referring teacher support the social validity of his behavioral improvements: "He seems like a different kid. He's a lot more considerate. There's definitely room for improvement, but we get along much better than we used to. He also gets along better with the other students." In summary, evaluation data and information from multiple sources indicated that Sam made noticeable improvements in school behavior as a result of building on a small but important Monday morning exception.

The Exceptional Quarter

Jeff was referred by his teachers for a psychological evaluation at the end of his fourth-grade year to determine his eligibility for placement in an alternative school for students with behavioral disabilities. Referral concerns included (a) talking out in class loudly, frequently, and without permission; (b) refusal to complete academic assignments; and (c) peer relationship problems. His mother, teacher, and school principal reported that these problems had occurred throughout the school year but were particularly evident during the last 2 months of the year.

The following excerpts are from the first interview with Jeff and his mother (Ms. S) a few weeks after the school year ended. In the start of the interview, Jeff said that he wanted to do better in school, but the teachers and principal "made it impossible." The dialogue picks up with the counselor's attempt to elicit an exception to the problem.

> *Counselor:* What kinds of things help you hang in there in school?
> *Jeff:* Nothing. Well, maybe the after-school program where we get to play basketball in the gym.
> *Counselor:* Mmm. Tell me about that. I'm not familiar with that. [The counselor conveys the ambassador perspective by being curious and requesting Jeff's help in clarifying prior solution attempts and exceptions to the problem.]
> *Jeff:* Once a week, any kids that want to can stay after school and play basketball or volleyball.

Jeff's perception of what has worked or might work is an important consideration in developing interventions that will be acceptable to him. A few minutes later, the counselor explores goals by asking the miracle question.

> *Counselor:* If there was a miracle that happened tonight while you were sleeping, and all these school problems just vanished, what would be different when you went into school or when you woke up in the morning? Ms. S [mother], please jump right in, too.
> *Ms. S:* He won't holler and scream. He won't mistreat his teachers. He won't mistreat the office staff. And I won't be called up there every other day.
> *Counselor:* What else?
> *Ms. S:* He'll start participating in school activities, and his grades will be decent. I'm not saying As or Bs, but not straight Fs.
> *Counselor:* So his grades will be certainly better than . . . ?
> *Ms. S:* At least a C average.
> *Counselor:* Jeff, what else will show you that things are going better in school?
> *Jeff:* I don't know.
> *Counselor:* Ms. S, back to your statement of "he won't mistreat people," can you tell me what that will look like? Give me some examples of that.

The counselor requests a videotalk description to clarify exactly what Jeff's mother means by the phrase "won't mistreat people." The next excerpt picks up a few minutes later, after Jeff said that he spent a large amount of time in the principal's office instead of in class last year.

Counselor: Which did you like better, being in the office or being in class?
Jeff: Class.
Counselor: Why?

Jeff explained the advantages of being in class instead of the office. Most of his comments pertained to what he did not like about the office instead of what he liked about class. The next excerpt occurred about 20 minutes into the interview, following Jeff's comment that "school doesn't really bother me." This statement stood out from Jeff's overall negative description of school. The counselor followed this lead by asking Jeff what he liked about school, as illustrated below.

Counselor: What is it about school that you like?
Jeff: I like math, I like spelling, and I like science.
Counselor: Math, spelling, and science. Of those three, which one do you like the best?
Jeff: Math.
Counselor: What's your favorite thing about it?

The focus of the interview continued to shift from descriptions of the problem and of what Jeff did not like to exceptions and competencies that might be employed to help him reach his goal of staying in class more often.

Counselor: Jeff, can you think of a day this year that you stayed in class all day and weren't sent to the office? [This question is designed to elicit an exception.]
Jeff: Yeah. The whole second quarter, when they gave the special award. I made Cs and Bs.
Counselor: How would you explain that?
Jeff : The teacher gave this special award.
Counselor: What kind of award?

The interview proceeded to elaborate the details of the special award and other aspects of this exception, such as the specific things that Jeff did differently during the second quarter to help himself get better grades and stay in class more often. In addition to exploring this exception, Jeff and his mother were asked to make a written list of anything that would help him reach his goal of improving school behavior. The interview concluded with compliments to Jeff and his mother for their sustained effort and courage in trying to improve things and for making the effort to attend the meeting in the summer.

Examination of school records confirmed Jeff's report of behavioral and academic improvements during the second quarter. Jeff had 43 documented disciplinary infractions during the school year, only 1 of which occurred during the second quarter. He earned an average grade of C for the second quarter, as compared to D for each of the other three quarters.

At the start of the new school year, interventions were developed to encourage Jeff and others to do more of what had already worked during the "second quarter exception." Interventions included adaptations of the special award and Jeff's regular participation in the after-school program. Jeff was also encouraged to do some of the other things that he said had helped him do better in school. For instance, he said it was helpful to remind himself that he did not want to repeat a grade in school. Therefore, it was recommended that he remind himself of this on entering the school building each morning. These interventions were implemented in his regular school instead of an alternative placement, with the agreement that alternatives would be considered if his progress during the first quarter of the year was unsatisfactory.

Jeff's grades and behavior were significantly better during the first quarter of the new year as compared to the previous year. No disciplinary infractions were recorded during the first 2 months of school, and he earned a grade average of B. His teachers and principal commented that he was "doing great" and that he had made "a major turnaround" in school behavior. Two meetings were held with Jeff during the first quarter of the fifth grade for the purpose of empowering and maintaining desired changes, as illustrated in the following excerpt.

> *Counselor:* Things seem to be on track for your goal of passing to the sixth grade. A lot different than last year. What are you doing differently to make this happen? [This question seeks to empower progress by giving Jeff credit for changing and exploring how he did it.]
>
> *Jeff:* Well, I'm doing my work without complaining. I'm listening to the teacher. I'm not smarting off like I used to, because it just gets you in trouble. I'm tired of being in trouble. I was in too much trouble last year.

The counselor and Jeff further explored how he was able to do work without complaining, listen to the teacher, and not smart off like he used to. They also discussed his plans to continue such efforts. Jeff maintained academic and behavioral improvements throughout the entire year and successfully passed to sixth grade. The following letter was sent at the end of the year to recognize and empower his accomplishments:

> Dear Jeff: I want to congratulate you on the improvements you have made in school behavior this year. I know it took hard work to make these improvements. I admire the fact that you hung in there and didn't give up during the tough times this year. That takes courage. Way to go, Jeff!

Jeff was invited to participate in the counselor's Consultant Club to provide suggestions for other students who might experience school difficulties similar to the ones that he overcame. He readily accepted the invitation.

The Test Anxiety Group

This example demonstrates how to build on exceptions in group counseling. A total of five female students in Grades 10 and 11 participated in a six-session test anxiety group. Solution-focused strategies were used in conjunction with educational and skill-building activities, such as study strategies, test-taking tips, and relaxation exercises.

During the first meeting, students completed a few basic information forms and shared what they wanted from the group. Their goals included improved test performance, better study habits, and less worry and tension before important tests.

The following requests were presented at the beginning of the second session to explore what students were already doing toward their stated goals—that is, to identify exceptions to their test-anxiety problems.

- Tell me about a test within the last month or so that you did a little better on. What subject area was the test in? What was different about this test than other tests? What was different about the way you prepared for the test? What did you do differently right before the test? What did you do differently during the test?
- Think of a recent test that you were able to study pretty effectively for. How did you study for the test? What was different about the way you studied?
- Think about a recent test you had that you worried a little less about. How did you manage to do that? What does that tell you about yourself?

The details of these exceptions were explored during the second meeting. The students appreciated the opportunity to discuss things that they were already doing to help themselves. One student commented, "I thought I was doing *everything* wrong." Students were also asked to share strategies that they had thought about doing but had not yet tried and strategies that they thought would help them but were not willing to try at the time. At the end of the second meeting, students were given the following exception-finding task: "Between now and our next meeting in 2 weeks, observe and list those things you are already doing, to prepare for and take tests, that you want to continue doing."

As is often the case when clients are asked to consult on their own problems, the strategies generated by these students were very similar to established interventions in the professional literature, with one main difference—they were in the students' own words. In subsequent meetings, educational materials on test taking, relaxing, and studying were integrated with student-generated language and ideas to enhance the acceptability and relevance of group discussions and skill-building strategies. The last three meetings opened with the following question designed to elicit and explore between-sessions improvements: "What's better since our last meeting?" Students responded favorably to this question, and each meeting got off to a positive, solution-focused start.

Data on the students' test performance and grades indicated that the group was successful. Four of the five students increased their overall grade point average, and all five students reported improvements in test-taking skills on a self-report questionnaire. The comments that students made following the group's termination were also encouraging. Comments relevant to the solution-focused approach included the following:

- I realized that I had good ideas, even if I wasn't using them all the time.
- It was cool when we rattled off all those ideas, and I used some of them.

- It was good to get ideas from other students for a change, instead of the teacher.
- I started doing better on tests when I did the stuff I said I needed to do.

The Student for Whom Nothing Was Going Right

Joel, a 10th-grade student in advanced classes, was referred because his grades, Cs and Ds, were considerably below his ability level. The following conversation took place early in the first meeting.

Joel: Nothing is going right for me.

The perception that nothing is going right is a common one for clients who are dealing with a significant problem. In these cases, it is helpful to validate the client's experience before rushing him or her into questions about exceptions.

Counselor: That stinks.
Joel: I'll say.

Joel went on to say that he had difficulty concentrating in class and was upset by conflicts between him and his father. He was "pretty depressed" about things and wanted to do better in school. He talked about various concerns, including problems with his girlfriend and some of his other friends.

Joel: I don't know what's going on with me. I wish I could just snap out of it.
Counselor: What would you be doing differently if you snapped out of it?
Joel: I don't know. I'd just be happier. I'd be doing my schoolwork like usual.
Counselor: Okay. So you'd be doing your schoolwork, and you'd be happier. That makes sense. If I followed you around with a video camera and filmed you being happier, what other things would I see you doing? [The counselor uses Joel's own language—"snap out of it" and "happy"—to obtain a videotalk description of what he wants to be doing differently in place of the problem.]
Joel: When I'm happy, I kid around more with my friends. I make stupid jokes. Everybody tells me I'm funny.
Counselor: Do you like it when people tell you you're funny?
Joel: Yeah. It makes me feel good because I can cheer them up by cracking jokes.
Counselor: That's a good skill. You know any good jokes you can tell me?
Joel: Not really.
Counselor: They're not all dirty, are they?
Joel: [smiles] Not all of them. In fact, most of them aren't.
Counselor: Wow. That's impressive. It's impressive that you can entertain a group of teenagers with jokes that are mostly clean. You should write a book about that.
Joel: [smiles] Maybe I will.

Several minutes later, as the meeting was winding down, the counselor presented a variation of the formula first session task (de Shazer, 1985).

Counselor: I really appreciate you sharing stuff here. It takes some courage to talk about yourself to someone you just met. I feel like I've got a pretty good handle on the things you're concerned about. I'd like to learn more about the things in your life that are going okay or working for you. I would appreciate it if you could make a list of the things in your life that you want to see continue. When we meet in 2 weeks, we can look at your list and take things from there.

This task invited Joel to consider exceptions to the dominant view that nothing was going right. The formula first session task does not directly challenge people's experience of the problem situation but merely invites them to take another look at things through a solution-focused lens.

Joel returned in 2 weeks with a long list and said that making the list helped him realize that he had a lot of things going for him. Joel's list included several exceptions to the notion that nothing was going right. He said that he appreciated his sense of humor (Exception 1). He also wanted to continue having many friends, especially close friends with whom he could talk about anything (Exception 2). He expressed the desire to continue getting along well with a couple of his teachers (Exception 3) and said that he probably needed to work harder in their classes to "stay in their good graces."

The counselor helped Joel identify additional exceptions by asking him some between-sessions questions regarding what else was better since the previous meeting. Joel said that he had finally confronted his father about several recent promises that his father had made and broken (Exception 4). His father told him that he would be more thoughtful in the future (Exception 5). Joel also reported that he was dating a new girl (Exception 6) and that he was able to concentrate better in class (Exception 7). While reading some stories for English class about different cultures, Joel was impressed by the following message in one of the stories: No matter how hard you try, you can never have complete and total happiness. This helped him relax and enjoy things more, even when he was not as happy as he would have liked to be (Exception 8).

The details of these exceptions were explored, and Joel was encouraged to keep doing them in the future. He chose to work primarily on relating more effectively with his father and doing better in his classes. The conversation ended in the following way.

Counselor: So what can you do to make this stuff keep happening? [Clients sometimes enter counseling blaming others for the problem and waiting for others to change to resolve it. Questions about what they have already done or plan to do to make things better are useful in conveying their own responsibility and personal agency in their life.]

Joel: I guess I can just keep concentrating in school. With my Dad, I guess I'll just talk to him whenever we're having problems.

Counselor: Remind me about what you used to do when the two of you had problems. [Talking about the problem in the past tense empowers desired changes by conveying the notion of "that was then, and this is now."]

Joel's schoolwork improved, and no additional concerns were noted throughout the remainder of the school year. The following excerpt is from a brief meeting with Joel about 1 month before the school year ended.

> *Counselor:* You've really made some heavy duty changes in your life, haven't you? [This question credits Joel for success to enhance his ownership of desired changes.]
>
> *Joel:* Yeah. It seems like it.
>
> *Counselor:* What does making these changes tell you about yourself?
>
> *Joel:* It tells me it was up to me all along. I guess I knew that, but I really didn't believe it.
>
> *Counselor:* Does it change the way you view yourself?
>
> *Joel:* Yes.
>
> *Counselor:* How so?
>
> *Joel:* It makes me feel good. It makes me realize that I can do it. I can change if I want to.
>
> *Counselor:* Have you noticed any differences in the way your parents and teachers treat you since you made these changes?

Sometimes students are unaware of the impact and ripple effects that positive changes can have in their life, including effects on their self-image and on the responses of other people. These questions helped Joel recognize and clarify the overall impact of the changes he had made.

Without directly challenging or discounting Joel's feelings of depression and hopelessness, this exception-finding task invited him to look at his life through a lens of what was working instead of what was not working. Although not all students respond as positively as Joel did, this simple task works well with most people and most problems.

Building on exceptions is conceptually simple and pragmatic: Find something that works, and have people do more of it. However, putting this into practice can be challenging because it requires a shift in the way many of us have been trained to approach problems and the people who experience them. Like diamonds in the rough, exceptions often fall under the radar and will remain unnoticed unless we actively seek them out and integrate them into the counseling process. The theme of discovering and building on what works and what's right with clients is continued in Chapter 7.

Summary and Conclusions

On the basis of the notion that it is easier to move something in the direction that it is already going, building on exceptions capitalizes on actions and events that are already moving in the direction of solutions. The 5-E method, a systematic process of utilizing exceptions to school problems, involves (a) eliciting exceptions to the problem, (b) elaborating on the details and circumstances of the exception, (c) expanding the exception to a greater frequency or to other situations, (d) evaluating the effectiveness of intervention, and (e) empowering desired changes.

The practical strategy of building on exceptions was illustrated by several real-world examples involving students from elementary through high school, including a 3rd-grade student diagnosed with oppositional defiant disorder (*The Monday Morning Exception*), a 4th grader who demonstrated behavior problems (*The Exceptional Quarter*), a group of test-anxious high school students (*The Test Anxiety Group*), and a 10th-grade student who complained of depression (*The Student for Whom Nothing Was Going Right*). Building on exceptions exemplifies the first guideline of solution-focused counseling: If it works, do more of it. The practical utility of this guideline is further illustrated in the next chapter.

Practice Exercises

1. Think of a problem you are currently struggling with. Now think about times or circumstances in which the problem is less noticeable or troublesome. Ask yourself the following questions:
   - What is different about those times?
   - What am I doing differently in these situations in the way I approach, think about, and respond to the situation or people involved in it?
   - What can I do to make this happen more often or in other situations?

2. When discussing a school problem during your next counseling session, ask the client to describe times when the problem doesn't happen or when it is less noticeable.

3. When you meet with students, parents, or teachers for the first time, ask whether they have noticed any slight changes or improvements in the problem since scheduling the meeting. If they indicate that such changes have occurred, explore the details of precounseling exceptions.

4. To practice eliciting exceptions, incorporate at least one of the following strategies in your next meeting with a student, parent, or teacher:
   - scaling questions,
   - miracle questions,
   - exception-finding questions.

5. Select a personal concern or problem in your life, and complete the first three steps of the 5-E method of building on exceptions—eliciting, elaborating, and expanding.

6. During the next week, write a note to a student, parent, or teacher complimenting him or her on something he or she has accomplished in relation to a school problem. Include a question about how he or she managed to do it, and schedule a follow-up meeting to discuss the answer.

7. Have a partner report desired changes in a problem, and practice strategies for empowering progress, including (a) giving credit to the client by using questions and comments that attribute such changes to the client's efforts and actions, (b) exploring plans to continue improving, (c) exploring the personal and social impact of the changes, and (d) asking the client's advice on helping others make similar changes.

8. Describe one small step that you are willing to take in your practice as a result of the information in this chapter.

CHAPTER 7

Building on Other Client Resources

I think we're all heroes if you catch us at the right moment.
—Stephen Frears, *Hero*

Solution-focused counseling is based on the assumption that students, parents, and teachers have the resources to change school problems. Instead of focusing on what clients need to have or do to change, we can build solutions from what they are already doing (exceptions) and already have (resources). This chapter provides strategies for building solutions from a variety of naturally occurring resources in the student's life.

Client resources that can be applied toward resolving school problems include the following:

- Special talents, interests, and hobbies (sports, movies, television shows, music, singing, being a good listener, mechanical skills, bicycling, cooking, etc.)
- Heroes and influential people (parents, grandparents, siblings, friends, actors, athletes, musicians, cartoon characters, and any other real or fictional persons that clients look up to and respect)
- Resilience and coping skills (abilities to withstand and cope with various difficulties in life, including the school problem)
- Community supports (places of worship, social service agencies, Boys and Girls Club, etc.)
- Ideas for solutions (the client's opinions about potential solutions, prior successes with similar problems)

Building on Client Resources

I don't lead musicians, man. They lead me.
I listen to them and learn what they do best.
—Miles Davis

Building on client resources is much like building on exceptions, in that the resources are identified, explored, and applied to the school problem. We can identify naturally occurring resources in the student's life by listening, asking questions, and reviewing the school records. Once resources are discovered, we can work with clients to explore how those resources might be applied toward solutions for the school problem. These tasks are briefly outlined below.

Listen

People often reveal potentially useful resources in the natural course of conversation about school problems. The importance of listening for resources is illustrated in the example of Ben, a fourth grader referred by his teachers because of classroom misbehavior. Behavior problems were especially noticeable during the two classes following lunch. In the midst of discussing the problem, Ben commented that he would do much better in school if he were allowed to play baseball for a few minutes between classes. We spent several minutes discussing his love of baseball, during which he shared his impressive knowledge of major league baseball. I asked him how baseball and school were alike, and we began discussing similarities between the challenges of school and the challenges of playing baseball. We talked about how long the baseball season is and how important it is to not let a few bad games ruin the entire season. Ben agreed to try a baseball approach to school, which involved "stepping up to the plate every day" and doing his best, knowing that he would "strike out" sometimes and have bad days. Ben came back in 2 weeks and told me that things were better in school and that he had shared the baseball metaphor with a friend who also needed help with school behavior.

Ask

Most students do not share information about hobbies, interests, heroes, and other resources unless they are asked. Questions for discovering and clarifying client resources include the following:

- What kinds of things do you enjoy doing outside of school?
- Who do you look up to and respect more than anyone? What does that person do that helps you most?
- Who helps you the most when you have a problem?
- How have you kept things from getting worse?
- Why haven't you given up yet?
- What is more important than anything to you? What do you want your life to stand for?
- What do you think might help turn things around at school?

Look

In addition to listening and asking questions, we can discover resources in school files and documents. For example, vocational interest inventories and teachers' comments on report cards can be useful in identifying potentially useful resources in a student's life. School files might also include information about the student's special interests and talents and his or her participation in extracurricular activities, such as sports and clubs.

Apply

Once a resource is identified, our task is to help clients connect it to the school problem, as illustrated with Ben and his love of baseball. Since every student offers a unique set of resources, the range of resource-based interventions is unlimited. Resource-based conversations and interventions engage the student's attention and energy because they are focused directly on the most important people, ideas, activities, and events in the student's life. This is why counselors and clients find the process of building on resources to be so enjoyable and effective in promoting new ways to respond to school problems.

Another advantage of applying client resources toward school solutions has to do with the maintenance of desired changes. The client's "natural resources" were there before we arrived, and they will be there after we're gone. Therefore, positive changes that are built on the client's resources have a good chance of continuing long after counseling ends.

Examples of Building on Client Resources

The remainder of the chapter illustrates the strategy of building on client resources with a variety of students and school problems, beginning with a provocative situation involving a first grader.

Mrs. T, the Sunday School Teacher

Anthony, age 6, was referred by his first-grade teacher (Ms. Holt) and principal (Mr. Calhoun) for "giving the finger" to students and adults at school. The behavior had steadily increased over the course of 2 or 3 months and had become progressively more disturbing to the teacher, students, and others at the school. Previous interventions included the following:

- Numerous individual meetings between Anthony and his teacher and between him and the school principal aimed at determining why he was doing this and getting through to him about the seriousness of the behavior
- Home–school conferences involving Anthony's mother, teacher, and school principal
- Behavior modification programs involving response cost (e.g., Loss of free time, extra work, after-school detention), restitution (requiring Anthony to apologize to others and say something nice to make up for the impolite gesture), and incentives for the absence of problem behavior (increased computer time and other special privileges)
- Functional behavioral assessment aimed at identifying the purpose or function of the behavior for Anthony (e.g., To obtain attention) and developing interventions accordingly (e.g., Providing extra attention for positive behavior and ignoring problem behavior)

All of these strategies were logical and reasonable. However, none of them was effective in changing Anthony's behavior, and the problem continued to grow at a steady rate. I asked Ms. Holt and other school personnel to keep a tally of the problem behavior every day for 1 week. This resulted in an average rate of 113 gestures per day, with a range of 73 to 134. This had clearly become a strong behavioral habit with a number of unfavorable consequences for Anthony.

Everyone involved was very puzzled and frustrated because the behavior occurred without warning or provocation in the classroom, lunchroom, and other places at school. It was also intriguing that the gesture was not accompanied by any other form of verbal or physical aggression. With the exception of this problem, Anthony's overall school behavior was generally acceptable.

Having listened to Anthony's mother, teacher, and school principal describe their tireless and futile efforts to change the behavior, I was determined to try something different but had no idea what that might be. After some small talk and introductions, here is what happened in our first meeting.

Counselor: Anthony, I know a lot of people have talked to you about the finger stuff. They seem to really care and want you to do well at school. I want to know what you want to be different at school.

Anthony: I told my mom I don't want to get in trouble and lose recess. I try to stop but it just happens. They don't understand.

Counselor: Who doesn't understand?

Anthony: My mom, Ms. Holt [teacher], Mr. Calhoun [principal], all of them.

Counselor: Of all the people at school or home, who understands you better than anyone?

Anthony: Mrs. T.

Counselor: Who is Mrs. T?

Anthony: Her name is Mrs. Thomas, but everyone calls her Mrs. T. She's my Sunday school teacher.

Counselor: That's interesting. Do you like Sunday school?

Anthony: [nods "yes"]

Counselor: How do you know that Mrs. T understands you? What does she do that tells you she understands you?

Anthony: I don't know. She's just real nice.

Counselor: How do you behave in Sunday school with Mrs. T?

Anthony: I'm real good.

Counselor: Do you do the finger thing there?

Anthony: No.

Counselor: That's interesting. How do you resist the urge to do the finger at Sunday school?

[This question credits Anthony for successful behavior at Sunday school, implies that he is capable of controlling the behavior, and invites him to reflect on how he does it.]

Anthony: I don't know, I just do it.

Counselor: Wow. That's really interesting to me. Are you going to Sunday school this weekend?

Anthony: I go every week.

Counselor: Okay. Do you want to try a little experiment this week?

Anthony: [nods "yes"]

Counselor: Okay. When you go to Sunday school this week, pay attention to how you control the finger at Sunday school instead of letting it control you like it does at school. Okay?

Anthony: Yes.

Counselor: Do you have ideas right now about how you are able to do this in Sunday school?

Anthony: [shakes head "no"]

Counselor: Well, I look forward to what you learn as you observe how you do this.

When I met with Anthony 1 week later, the rate of problem behavior at school had not changed. When asked how he controlled finger raising at Sunday school, Anthony shrugged his shoulders and said, "I don't know." I was quickly catching up with the others in my bewilderment about the whole situation. Anthony was a polite, intelligent child who had picked up a habit that was isolating him from others and stigmatizing him as "a strange kid." I felt an urgency to keep plugging away in the hopes of stumbling on something that would make a difference. I met with Anthony later that week to follow up on his earlier comments about Mrs. Thomas.

Counselor: Remember when you told me that Mrs. T is really nice and that she understands you?

Anthony: Yes.

Counselor: It sounds like you really like her and respect her.

Anthony: [nods "yes"]

Counselor: Have you ever talked to her about the finger thing at school?

Anthony: No.

Counselor: Do you know if anyone else has?

Anthony: [shrugs shoulders] I don't know. I don't think so.

Counselor: Would you be willing to talk to her, since she understands you better than anyone?

Anthony: [shrugs shoulders] I don't know.

Counselor: Would it be okay with you if I talked with her about this and asked if she could join our team to help you take control of this problem at school?

Anthony: [nods "yes"]

Counselor: That's good, because she sounds like someone we need on the team right now.

After obtaining parental consent, I contacted Mrs. Thomas by phone and learned that she had known Anthony since he was a baby and had been his Sunday school teacher for the past 3 years. She was shocked on hearing about Anthony's problem behavior at school and vowed to do whatever she could to help him. This delightful older woman spoke about Anthony as if he were one of her own children. It was immediately evident that Mrs. Thomas was a highly influential person in Anthony's life who might serve as a valuable resource in changing the problem. As we concluded our conversation, Mrs. Thomas told me that she would try to see Anthony that evening or the next day.

When I arrived at school a few days later, Anthony's teacher saw me come in the building and practically sprinted down the hallway to tell me how good Anthony had been at school. When asked for details, Ms. Holt said that he had not raised his middle finger one single time for the past 3 days at school. Anthony's dramatic turnaround started the day after my conversation with Mrs. Thomas. I complimented Ms. Holt for her caring and ongoing commitment to Anthony's school success and went straight to my office to call Mrs. Thomas.

It turns out that Mrs. Thomas visited Anthony the very same evening we spoke. She wasted no time getting to the point and telling Anthony, in no uncertain terms, how shocked and saddened she was by his behavior. She explained that his behavior was an unacceptable way to represent himself, his church, and his family. Mrs. Thomas told me that she was holding his face in her hands as she spoke with him and that he was very attentive throughout her short but powerful message. She told Anthony that she expected this behavior to end right now and concluded by asking, "Do you understand what I'm saying to you?" With teary and wide open eyes, Anthony nodded yes and collapsed in her arms.

This was one of the most dramatic behavioral changes that I have ever witnessed. Anthony's problem behavior decreased from an average of 113 per day to 0 and remained there the rest of the year. This was a remarkable accomplishment for Anthony and a testimony to the power of heroes and influential people in the lives of students. I have never seen the "firm but gentle Sunday school teacher intervention" in any counseling and therapy books. Like most resource-based interventions, this one was entirely unique to this client at this point in time. When I took Anthony's lead about an important resource in his life, a problem that had thoroughly stumped several professionals was resolved by the timely input of a grandmotherly Sunday school teacher. Mrs. T is one of many potential "heroes of intervention" who are there for the asking in our work with students and school problems.

The Pillow Brigade

One of my favorite examples of applying the client's ideas toward solutions involves Molly, a precocious 10-year-old student referred to my colleague Barry Duncan. Molly was referred by her mother for nightmares, reluctance to sleep in her own room, and school avoidance. Molly had just finished seeing her second therapist in less than a year. Her prior contacts in the mental health system resulted in a diagnosis of separation anxiety disorder, a prescription for anxiety medication (Imipramine), and twice-weekly therapy aimed at reducing her anxiety and improving her self-esteem and social skills. All involved parties were frustrated with Molly's lack of improvement, and she was being considered for placement in a school program for students with emotional disorders. Despite the frustration of two failed attempts at therapy, Molly's mother scheduled an appointment to see Barry in a desperate attempt to help her daughter. Something very different happened early in the first meeting when Molly was asked for her ideas and opinions.

Counselor: I have read the reports of your other doctors and counselors, so I already know what they think. Before I ask you anything else, I want to know what *you* think might help make things better.

Molly: You're asking me? Now that's a first.

Molly was visibly surprised and pleased that someone had finally asked for her opinion. After some discussion, she suggested that she could barricade herself in her bed with pillows and several stuffed animals to ward off nightmares and fears. Details of the plan were discussed, including what particular animals would be used and how Molly would explain it to her mother.

A meeting was scheduled for the next week to see how the plan worked. The following exchange occurred at the start of the second meeting.

Counselor: How is it going?

Molly: Just fine. I'm sleeping in my own room.

Counselor: That's great.

Molly: Counselors just don't understand that you also have the solutions for yourself, but they say, "Let's try this and let's try that," and they're not helping. You know, you're like, "I don't really want to do that." Your asking me what I wanted to do with my room got me back in my room. So what I'm saying to all psychiatrists is we have the answers, we just need someone to help us bring them to the front of our head. It's like they're locked in an attic or something. It's a lot better when you ask a person what they want to do.

Later in the session, Molly talked about what it was like to implement her own ideas instead of being told what to do by the practitioner.

Molly: I feel a lot better now that I came up with the solution to sleep in my own room, and I did it, and I'm proud of myself. And I couldn't be proud of myself if you told me, "How about if you barricade yourself in with pillows, maybe that'll work." I wouldn't feel like I've done it, so basically what I'm saying is, you don't get as much joy out of doing something when somebody told you to do it, you want to be proud of it. . . . My other counselors never asked me what I wanted to work on. They asked me questions about the subjects that I don't really want to answer. They'd say, "Do this" and "Do that." It didn't help. I didn't want to do it. They weren't my ideas. They didn't seem right. Well, like my other counselor said, "Let's try this for 5 minutes, then go for 10 minutes, then 15, then go for the whole night." I did it once and I decided, "This isn't helping!" I did it for 5 minutes and neglected to do it for 10, and then I didn't do it for 15, and then I didn't do it for half an hour. I didn't want to do that thing, so I basically ignored it. . . . Shouldn't I be telling you what I think about this? I mean you're not here to tell me my life or anything. I should come in and tell the person, "This is what's happening with this situation," and they [the counselors] are saying, "Your mom tells me you're doing such and such a thing," and then there's more stuff and, like, when did I start having problems with that? And you come in there to talk to a person, to get them [problems] out of your system and get them worked on. Instead of she [the counselor] telling or he telling you what he thinks has happened, "Your Dad's doing this, your grandfather's doing this," it's not really helping because you're sitting there going, "Uh-huh, uh-huh," and that's why I usually dreaded going to therapy. It never worked, it never helped. She [the counselor] sat down, and she starts talking. I'm sitting there going [demonstrates her posture, looking down]. She talked the whole hour and I barely got a sentence in!

Counselor: She did not take you seriously.

Molly: No!

Molly felt discounted and ignored by her previous counselors, who focused on self-esteem, social skills, and other goals that they deemed to be more important than Molly's goal of getting out of her mother's room and sleeping without nightmares. The third counselor engaged Molly's interest and involvement by (a) accepting her goal of getting out of her mother's room instead of ignoring or challenging it, (b) requesting her ideas and opinions, (c) collaborating on an intervention based directly on her ideas, (d) acknowledging her ingenuity and contributions, and (e) validating her experience of not being taken seriously.

When provided the opportunity for input, Molly came through in grand style. Although children do not always provide such immediate and dramatic solutions, we have nothing to lose and everything to gain by asking for their opinions. Even when students say, "I don't know," asking for their input enhances outcomes by strengthening the alliance, increasing client involvement, and conveying respect for their wisdom and experience.

Many aspects of this example are unique to Molly and her situation. However, Molly is typical of most students, who simultaneously hold a desire to change and a natural tendency to stand their ground and protect themselves when counseling goals or strategies threaten their dignity or conflict with their opinions and preferences. Eliciting and honoring the ideas of students allows them to maintain their pride, accept help from others, and move gracefully toward improvement.

Sweeping the Sidewalk Twice

Roy, age 13, was referred by the school principal and his parents for having failing grades, refusing to complete schoolwork, cursing, and arguing with teachers. Roy's mother informed the counselor that she and her husband had very little control of him at home. When asked about what Roy did well, his mother said that he worked hard at his lawn-mowing job and managed his money pretty well.

During the opening minutes of the first interview, Roy stated that he hated school, homework, and most of his teachers (especially Ms. Cahill, his math teacher). The counselor shifted the conversation to client resources in the following way.

Counselor: Your mother says you work really hard mowing lawns and that you've made some money at it.

Roy: Yes.

Counselor: What's the same about school and this job?

Roy: They're not the same. You get paid for mowing.

Counselor: What do you have to do to get paid?

Roy: You have to do the job.

Counselor: Do you do the job?

Roy: Yes. One time Mr. Kruger only paid us half. He said we didn't sweep the sidewalk.

Counselor: Do you still mow his grass?

Roy: Yes, and we sweep the walk twice now.

Counselor: Do any of your teachers remind you of Mr. Kruger?

Roy: Ms. Cahill [math teacher]. If you do one little thing wrong, she's on your case.

Counselor: What do you do to help save your money?

Roy: Keep track of it. I know how much I make, and I know how much I can spend. I'm saving to buy a four-wheeler.

Counselor: How well do you keep track of your schoolwork?

Roy: Not very well. I don't get paid for that.

The counselor continued to draw analogies between mowing grass and doing schoolwork. The report card was compared to a paycheck, a crabby lawn-mowing customer to a crabby teacher, and keeping track of money to keeping track of schoolwork. The counselor explored Roy's lawn-mowing success further by asking how he managed to keep at it when things got tough.

Roy stated that he wanted to pass school, and he and the counselor developed a small, specific goal for passing the eighth grade. Roy calculated exactly how many points he needed to get a D in the two classes he was failing. The counselor invited Roy to approach his goal of passing all classes the same way he approached his lawn-mowing job. In Roy's language, the plan was to "do the job" and "sweep Ms. Cahill's sidewalk twice." This translated to studying for tests and not arguing with teachers in class. When they met a week later, Roy reported improved school performance and no discipline referrals. In an effort to empower the changes and give Roy credit, the counselor asked, "How did you do that?" A person of few words, Roy said, "I just did the job like we talked about."

In addition to favorable comments from several of his teachers, Roy's academic and behavioral improvements were verified by his teachers and his grades. The counselor compared Roy's first and second quarter grades to evaluate the effectiveness of the intervention. Roy's first quarter report card included one C, one D, and four Fs. His second quarter grades improved markedly, in the form of two As, one B, two Cs, and one F. The F was in Ms. Cahill's math class. However, Ms. Cahill reported no further discipline problems with Roy, and he passed to the ninth grade.

The case of Roy illustrates how a student's competence in nonschool areas of life can be applied to school problems. Roy's lawn-mowing experience provided a useful metaphor and set of skills that were relevant to his school problems. The counselor's alertness to resources outside of school led to an intervention that accommodated Roy's perceptions, goals, and talents. This was very different from the previous attempts to force him into compliance.

Dorothy's Advice

Bridgette was referred by several ninth-grade teachers for "mouthing off" during class and completing only about half of her school assignments. Her teachers said that she was capable of doing decent work but only applied herself when she felt like it. Bridgette had been suspended for 3 days during the previous month and was very close to being suspended again when I met with her. She had attended several elementary schools and experienced discipline problems at all of them. Previous solution attempts involved trying to find out why she misbehaved and lecturing her about the connection between her misbehavior and after-school detention, suspension, and other undesirable consequences.

Within the opening minutes of the first interview, Bridgette said that she hated school and was tired of schoolwork. We dropped the subject of school and began talking about hobbies. I discovered that Bridgette loved watching old movies with her mother on Sunday afternoons. Her favorite movie was *The Wizard of Oz*. I told her it was one of my favorites as well and asked her what she liked best about it. Bridgette discussed several favorite scenes from the movie. She also commented that Dorothy, the main character, "always looked ahead at how things would be better" instead of "moping around" about being away from home. She added that Dorothy "didn't let anything stop her." Here is what happened next.

Counselor: Do you ever feel like Dorothy, with all these problems happening at school?

Bridgette: All the time. [laughs]

Counselor: You get over one problem in one class, and then something else happens in another class to set you back.

Bridgette: Exactly.

Counselor: This might seem like a weird question, but how do you think Dorothy would handle this school stuff that you're dealing with?

Bridgette: I don't know. I guess she would say, "Don't let it get you down," or something like that.

Counselor: What other words or advice would Dorothy have for you?

Bridgette: She would say, "Don't let them get you down or stop you."

Counselor: Stop you from what?

Bridgette: From getting through school, I guess.

Counselor: Do you want to get through school?

Bridgette: Yes.

Counselor: Why? What's so important about getting through school?

Bridgette: Graduating, because if you don't graduate you'll end up on the street. You don't have any money, no job, stuff like that. Who would want that?

Counselor: Well, some people don't seem to care whether or not they graduate. But you're saying that you do, right?

Bridgette: Yes. I want to graduate and get a decent job so I can have a decent life.

Counselor: So Dorothy would say, "Don't let anybody or anything stop you from your goal of graduating," huh?

Bridgette: Yes. She didn't let anything stop her. She just kept going.

Counselor: What are some things you could do to follow Dorothy's advice about not letting anything stop you from graduating?

Bridgette: Well, I guess I could shut up more in class.

Counselor: I'll bet that's going to be really hard. Especially since you're used to doing it a lot.

Bridgette: Yeah, it will be hard. Especially in some classes.

The conversation continued to explore how Bridgette might apply Dorothy's advice, including asking her mother for help with difficult homework and sitting closer to the front of the room in a couple of classes. We discussed how difficult it would be for Bridgette to ask the teacher about changing her seat, given how important it was for her to be seen as "independent and tough." Toughness and self-reliance were a big part of her familial and cultural environment. I suggested that "perhaps it is actually 'tougher' to have the courage to try and change something than to 'wimp out' and expect others to change things for you." Bridgette agreed to approach one or two of her teachers to request a seating change. Before the session ended, we role-played a few situations in which Bridgette approached the teacher (me) and asked about sitting closer to the front.

Bridgette implemented Dorothy's advice, and her school performance progressed steadily over the next few months. School attendance improved by about 60% during the following 2 months. Bridgette was not suspended during those 2 months and received only 4 days of after-school detention, as compared to 13 days of detention during the 2 months prior to our meeting. She also brought her grades up in two classes, from an F to a D in one class and from a D to a B in the other.

Bridgette had already heard the standard reasons why she should change—to avoid suspension, get better grades, graduate, and so forth. A different approach was needed. Exploring her interest in movies engaged her attention and conveyed the notion that this session was going to be different from previous discussions. If I had told her to change her behavior and ask her teachers about sitting closer, I doubt that she would have cooperated. When it comes to cooperation, I believe that "you get what you give." If we want clients to cooperate with us, then we need to cooperate with them. One way to cooperate is to discuss topics that are important to them, such as their unique interests, hobbies, and talents.

This example illustrates how solutions can evolve from client resources that may initially appear to be remote and unrelated to the problem. These resources remain hidden unless we listen and ask for them. As seen with Bridgette and others in this chapter, client resources often provide the material and direction for customized interventions that are tailored to the unique style and interest of the student. Indeed, "Wizard of Oz" interventions typically are not covered in graduate training programs.

Consulting Camus

Dwayne, an intellectually gifted 12th grader, was referred in early March because he did not complete certain assignments required for graduation. No one questioned his ability to do the work, and his teachers felt that they had exhausted all attempts to reason with Dwayne about the importance of completing the required work. Teachers and administrators were very concerned, as was Dwayne's mother, who thought that Dwayne might need to be referred to a psychiatrist to "find out what was going on with him."

The major theme of attempted solutions was to convince Dwayne that he simply needed to turn in the required papers, even if the quality was mediocre. As logical as these attempts were, they did not work with Dwayne, and something different was required. The following dialogue occurred in the opening moments of the first interview.

> *Counselor:* It would help me to ask you a few quick questions to get a better handle on this thing. You know a lot more about this than I do, so I need your help in filling me in on what's going on with this graduation thing, and required papers, and so forth. Okay?
>
> *Dwayne:* Okay.
>
> *Counselor:* Thanks. First off, do you want to graduate, or is this just something everybody else thinks you should do?
>
> *Dwayne:* I definitely want to graduate.
>
> *Counselor:* Why?
>
> *Dwayne:* I want to go to college.
>
> *Counselor:* And graduation is the ticket to college, right?
>
> *Dwayne:* Right.
>
> *Counselor:* Okay. Thanks. That helps me, because before we start talking about stuff, I want to make sure I know what you want out of this whole thing. So, exactly what do you need to do in order to graduate?
>
> *Dwayne:* There are some required papers. It's not required that you get good grades, just that you turn them in. They're all overdue. The most important one is the 4,000-word essay. My essay is on comparing Camus's *The Stranger* to Hemingway's *The Old Man and the Sea.* I've got an A in that course. I've just got to write it and turn it in.

During the next few minutes, Dwayne shared the idea that he did not want to "just turn it in" for the sake of the grade.

> *Counselor:* Do you think that once you get into this stuff and you get to know these ideas so well, that it's sort of ridiculous to have to write them up for someone else?
>
> *Dwayne:* Exactly. I made a mistake to write about Camus because he's my personal hero. I like existentialism.

As he discussed the writings of philosopher and author Albert Camus, it was obvious that Dwayne had a lot of knowledge and respect for him. Next, Dwayne discussed the essay assignment that had become the focal point of teacher concerns.

Dwayne: I've got plenty of notes on the essay right now.
Counselor: Interesting. And yet you haven't written it.

Next, the counselor explored the possibility of a connection between Dwayne's choice not to complete the essay and his respect for Camus and existentialism. The counselor framed this possibility as a dilemma.

Counselor: I can appreciate the dilemma you have about Camus in that it's easier to write about something you don't care that much about or don't know much about.
Dwayne: That's it. I wouldn't want to cut out things that I thought were important if it came to that, because he's one of my personal heroes.
Counselor: Yeah.
Dwayne: The counselors told me that I'm too perfectionistic. I *want* to do it perfectly. I don't want to turn in something that's not good. I know it just has to be there for me to get credit. It doesn't have to make sense. It just has to be 4,000 words.
Counselor: Now, this question might sound bizarre. Do you actually dialogue with Camus in your own head? Have you had dynamic conversations with Camus, imagining what you would say and what he would say?
Dwayne: Lots of times.
Counselor: Maybe this whole paper issue would be something you could talk with him about and see what emerges. See what kind of feedback he might give you with this dilemma. It seems to me that you would respect his opinion more than anybody else's right now.
Dwayne: [laughs and nods head "yes"]

Clients usually provide various nonverbal indicators of their acceptance or rejection of an idea, including nodding their head, raising their eyebrows, and leaning forward. Dwayne's verbal and nonverbal responses were very positive, and the counselor continued to explore the idea with him.

Counselor: You've already had some experience in dialoguing with Camus. What do you think he might say?
Dwayne: Hmmm [pauses for about 30 seconds]. I think he'd say do it, and that it doesn't have to be a masterpiece.
Counselor: So he would understand your dilemma?
Dwayne: Yes. Camus always talked about how there's a need for discipline in life, but there's also a need to break off from discipline at times. I guess this would be a time to have discipline in my life.

Counselor: Interesting. So he would be okay with you not including every-thing you know about him, as long as you did it for discipline's sake?

Dwayne: Yes. Especially when you weigh all the possible benefits I could get out of it compared to the discomfort it would cause if I didn't do it.

Counselor: Is he pretty pragmatic about some of those benefits?

Dwayne: Yes.

Counselor: What other advice do you think Camus would offer about this di-lemma you're facing?

Dwayne: Just do it.

Counselor: Interesting.

The session ended with the counselor encouraging Dwayne to consider other advice that Camus would offer and decide how to respond. To avoid repeating previous solutions, the counselor made no mention of the essay and other assignments. Given the opportunity to reflect on his dilemma without having to defend himself, Dwayne decided to take Camus's advice and "just do it." He completed the essay within 3 weeks, although he waited on some of the other assignments until a week or so before graduation. The counselor sent Dwayne a letter and award to recognize his completion of graduation requirements (see Exhibits 7.1 and 7.2).

Success Stories: A Schoolwide Program for Recognizing Resilience and Resources

This section describes a schoolwide program designed to recognize and empower the resources, resilience, and positive changes of students in an elementary school. Videotaped interviews were conducted with students who made major academic or behavioral improvements during the school year, and their responses were re-corded in a documentary titled *Success Stories*.

Exhibit 7.1
Congratulatory Letter to Dwayne

Dear Dwayne,

I want to congratulate you on your recent completion of several key tasks associated with completing your school program in order to graduate. I know how difficult this was, and I am impressed with the discipline you showed in dealing with this dilemma. I suspect that Camus would be pleased with the practical strategy you adopted to bite the bullet and "just do it" in order to move on to other life adventures.

Please accept the enclosed Bite the Bullet Award as recognition of your exis-tential accomplishment. Best wishes in the journey ahead.

Sincerely,

Counselor

Exhibit 7.2
Bite the Bullet Award for Dwayne

The Bite the Bullet Award

This is to recognize the existential accomplishment of

Dwayne M.

for a pragmatic display of discipline in "biting the

bullet" and completing the assignments

required for graduation.

The Success Stories program was initiated to

- formally recognize school improvements to help students maintain them,
- implement a schoolwide application of utilizing students as consultants,
- provide a morale boost for school staff by inviting them to focus on hopeful stories of successful students, and
- create a permanent product (videotape) to serve as a source of ideas for other students.

In early May, a note was sent to every kindergarten through sixth-grade teacher in the building to explain the program and obtain the names of two students per class who had made noticeable improvements in behavior or academics during the school year. After formal consent was obtained from the students and their parents, each student was interviewed individually on videotape. Interviews lasted about 10 minutes and involved the following questions:

- How did you improve your grades/behavior?
- How have things been different for you at home and school since you made these changes?
- What helped you keep plugging and hanging in there instead of giving up when things got tough?
- If other students asked for tips on improving their grades/behavior, what would you tell them?

The following excerpt is taken from a portion of the interview with Michelle, a third-grade student who raised her grades from an average of D the first semester to B the second semester. This dialogue explores the personal and social impact of these improvements for Michelle.

Interviewer: Do the teachers treat you any differently now with better grades than they did when your grades were lower?
Michelle: Yes. Better.

155

Interviewer: How?

Michelle: When I had bad grades, they really didn't help me because I really didn't want to do the work, but now they're starting to help me.

Interviewer: So the more they see that you want to do the work, the more willing they are to spend the time to help you?

Michelle: Yes.

Interviewer: Okay. Are there any other changes in the way that you're treated, either at home or school, now that your grades are better?

Michelle: My parents gave me money.

Interviewer: Whoa! They gave you money.

Michelle: Yes. They said I was doing a lot better and getting better grades, so they gave me $5. And they're nicer now.

Interviewer: Wow. Let me see if I understand all this. You made these big changes in school and brought your grades up. Now your teachers treat you better and help you more, your parents gave you money, and you're getting along better with your parents and your teachers. Is that what you're telling me here, Michelle?

Michelle: [smiling] That's right.

Interviewer: Wow. Are there any other changes in the way that you're treated, either at home or school, now that your grades are better?

Michelle: I used to get a lot of detentions, but now that I'm not hanging around my old friends, I haven't gotten a lot of detentions.

Interviewer: Do your old friends still try to get you to hang around with them?

Michelle: Yes.

Interviewer: I imagine it's hard to resist the temptation. Probably hard to say no sometimes, isn't it?

Michelle: Yes.

Interviewer: How do you manage to do that?

Michelle: I just walk away.

Interviewer: Okay. Michelle, what have you learned about yourself in all this? What has this taught you?

Michelle: To be good in school.

Interviewer: What else?

Michelle: You can change yourself if you really want to. You don't have to do what other kids do just because they're doing it. You need to do what you're supposed to do so you don't get in trouble and you can hear what the teacher says and get better grades.

Interviewer: That's a lot of good advice, Michelle. Sounds like you've learned a lot about yourself and about making things better at school. What other advice would you give other students to help them improve their schoolwork like you did?

Michelle: Volunteer more. Answer questions in class.

Interviewer: What else?

Michelle: Don't try be a teacher's pet, because it will probably annoy them.

Interviewer: Sounds like good advice, Michelle. I sure learned a lot from you, and I appreciate you talking with me about it.

All of the students seemed to enjoy and appreciate the opportunity to share their wisdom and resources with others. Several students indicated that the interview gave them a better understanding of how they had changed their schoolwork and behavior and how these improvements made life better in several ways. A few teachers commented that the program improved their attitude by calling their attention to success stories within their classroom—a much-needed shot of encouragement during the waning days of the school year.

The videotape remains on file at the school for use by school staff, parents, and other students as a source of ideas for improving grades and behavior. The tape also serves as a reminder that heroic success stories are occurring at every school in every classroom at any given point in time.

Summary and Conclusions

There are a variety of perspectives or stories that can be considered true of any given client. Therefore, viewing students on the basis of their deficiencies or their resources is a matter of choice, not truth. Building on client resources is based on the practical, strength-based notion that it is easier to develop solutions from what is already available in the lives of students—their natural resources—than it is to start from scratch and try to build brand-new skills, behaviors, and social supports. Every client brings unique strengths and resources to the counseling process, including special interests, hobbies, heroes, resilience, coping skills, community supports, life experiences, and ideas for solutions. Exploring these resources opens up solution possibilities that might otherwise remain hidden and untapped.

Counselors can discover these resources by listening, asking, and looking for them in their work with students, teachers, parents, and others involved in the change process. Once discovered, client resources can be applied toward solutions in a variety of respectful and creative ways. The client's natural resources are present before counseling begins and after it ends. For this reason, positive changes that are built on the client's resources have a good chance of continuing after counseling formally ends.

The strategy of building on client resources was illustrated in this chapter by real-world examples involving a first grader with a provocative problem behavior (*Mrs. T, the Sunday School Teacher*), a precocious 10-year-old who came through in grand style when asked for her opinion (*The Pillow Brigade*), a seventh grader who argued and cursed at teachers (*Sweeping the Sidewalk Twice*), a ninth-grade movie buff who displayed behavioral and academic difficulties (*Dorothy's Advice*), a high school senior who was in jeopardy of not graduating (*Consulting Camus*), and a schoolwide program that showcased the resilience and resources of students (*Success Stories: A Schoolwide Program for Recognizing Resilience and Resources*).

As illustrated by the examples in this chapter, resource-based interventions are uniquely constructed for each client in ways that are relevant, engaging, and motivating to the client. I am continually amazed by students' ability to make remarkable changes in school behavior by capitalizing on the natural resources in their life.

Practice Exercises

1. Select a current concern or difficulty. Now think of a specific difficulty or challenge that you have successfully overcome or coped with in your own life. How did you manage to do this? What kinds of attitudes, beliefs, actions, and other resources contributed to your success? How could these same resources be applied to your current concern? Ask your clients these same questions to help them consider how the resources that helped them handle challenges in other areas of life might be applied to the current school problem.

2. If asked about your special skills and talents, what would your friends and colleagues say? What would you say? How can these talents and skills be utilized in your work as a counselor?

3. Pick one or two clients during the next week, and ask about their special hobbies, interests, and talents. Consider how these resources might be applied to the school problem.

4. Think about a current problem or goal in life. If you could consult with your personal heroes or the one or two people you respect the most in your life, what advice would they offer? Does this seem like good advice for your present situation? If so, list one or two specific ways that you could put part of that advice into practice during the next week.

5. Describe one small step that you are willing to take in your practice as a result of the information in this chapter.

CHAPTER 8

Changing the Doing of the Problem

If you keep doing what you've always done,
you'll keep getting what you always got.
—Moms Mabley

B uilding on exceptions and other resources is a practical way to resolve problems on the basis of the guideline "if it works, do more of it." These strategies are usually attempted first because they build on existing suc cesses and resources in the client's life. In some situations, however, other strategies are required on the basis of the client's circumstances and preferences.

This is the first of two chapters based on the second practical guideline of solution-focused counseling: If it doesn't work, try something different. This principle, derived from the MRI brief therapy model (Fisch et al., 1982), is especially useful in situations in which attempted solutions become part of the problem and need to be replaced by different responses. Consider the example of a student who skips school in protest of what she perceives as rigid and unrealistic parental demands. The skipping prompts stricter and more frequent demands from the parents, and the student responds by skipping even more. This "more of the same" pattern will continue indefinitely until someone does something different to interrupt it.

The discovery that people are stuck in a vicious cycle of ineffective solutions does not imply that there is something wrong with them. As the MRI team observed, there is a natural tendency to reapply the same solution even when it doesn't work. This occurs because we tend to view our solution as the one and only solution—the right and sensible thing to do in response to the problem (recall the Nine-Dot Problem in Appendix B).

When clients are stuck in repeating more of the same well-intentioned yet unproductive solutions, the task of counseling is to interrupt ineffective solutions and encourage different responses. We can do this by altering key interpretations or actions of those involved in the problem pattern—that is, by changing the viewing and doing of the problem. Although "viewing" and "doing" interventions are often used in conjunction in practice, they are addressed separately here for the sake of clarity. Chapter 9 presents strategies for changing the viewing of school problems, and this chapter addresses changing the doing. Like all other strategies in this book, interventions for changing the doing are developed in close collaboration with clients and with careful attention to their preferences, feedback, and theory of change.

From a systems perspective, small changes in any aspect of the problem pattern can ripple into larger and more meaningful solutions. There are as many ways to change the doing as there are clients. Instead of attempting to cover too much and obscuring the basic message of trying something different when stuck in an unproductive problem pattern, this chapter (a) outlines general guidelines and interventions for changing the doing of school problems and (b) provides specific examples involving a variety of clients and problems.

Strategies for Changing the Doing

One of the simplest ways to interrupt the problem cycle is to encourage the client to alter the performance of or response to the problem in some small but significant way. The goal is to simply do the problem differently by trying something else instead of the usual. This can take an unlimited number of forms. It may also include techniques from a wide range of counseling approaches, not to mention the client's own ideas. We can facilitate changes in the doing by (a) acknowledging that things are not working and that something different is required and (b) suggesting the Do Something Different Task or other strategies.

The Do Something Different Task

Students, parents, and teachers can be very creative when given the opportunity to actively contribute toward solutions. The Do Something Different Task unleashes the client's wisdom and creativity by encouraging him or her to try something different during the next week, whatever it might be, in place of his or her usual response to the problem:

> You said you feel like you're going around in circles with this problem. I wonder if we need to try something very unusual and different here in order to shake things up and see what happens. I don't have any great ideas at the moment, so I'm going to suggest that you do something very different during the next week instead of doing what you've been doing. Don't get hung up on finding the "right" thing. Just try *anything* that would be really different from your usual response, then observe what happens to see if anything changes. How does that sound?

I recall the example of Monica and her parents. The parents reported that Monica, age 13, "argued constantly" with them at home. Their usual methods of responding included telling Monica to stop, sending her to her room, and removing privileges. After acknowledging their feeling of being stuck and out of ideas, I suggested that one or both of them try something different instead of more of the same strategies that were not working.

When I saw them the next week and asked how things were going, they looked at each other and smiled. Monica's mother explained that they had decided to stage an argument to better understand the dynamics of their relationship with Monica (the mother was a counselor). They calmly explained this to Monica, informing her that one of them would observe and take notes while the other engaged in an argument with her. Monica looked at them strangely, mumbled something under her breath, and walked into her room. The arguments subsided following the parents' creative response to the Do Something Different Task.

There is nothing about the content of this or other "do something different" interventions that make them effective in some absolute or overall sense. This same strategy may fail with the next client. It was effective for Monica's parents because it interrupted their existing solutions and added a different element to the problem pattern. As illustrated throughout the chapter, sometimes all it takes is a small change to bring about a big solution. I am continually amazed by the clever interventions that emerge from simply asking clients to try something different.

Offering Suggestions for Doing Something Different

There are literally hundreds of interventions that we can offer for changing the doing of a problem. Textbooks are full of such strategies, all of which may be helpful for certain clients in certain circumstances. For the sake of simplicity, this discussion focuses on strategies from brief therapy approaches that are useful for a variety of school problems. Here are a few ideas for starters (adapted from O'Hanlon & Wilk, 1987):

- *Changing the frequency of one's response to the problem.* In a situation in which the parents remind a student about homework completion several times a day, encourage them to alter the frequency of reminders to six randomly selected times per week.
- *Changing the intensity of one's response.* If a teacher typically reprimands the student in a loud voice from across the classroom, encourage her to slowly approach the student's desk and whisper the reprimands.
- *Changing the sequence or order of events.* In a pattern in which the teacher typically confronts the student about his or her misbehavior at the end of each class and the student ends up saying, "I'm sorry, I'll try to do better," encourage the student to apologize on arriving to class each day to "get it over with."
- *Derailing the pattern before it has any momentum.* In a pattern of repetitive conflicts between the student and his or her mother, encourage the parent to say, "Wait a minute, I'll be right back," on the first sign of an argument, then walk out the door and work in the yard, take the dog for a walk, or so forth.
- *Adding or subtracting one element to or from the pattern.* For a student who rarely does homework, encourage the student to turn in something for every homework assignment, if only a piece of paper with his or her name on it.
- *Breaking up any element of the problem into smaller elements.* In a situation in which the teacher has to continually remind the student to bring his or her notebook, pencil, book, and other required materials to class each day, encourage the teacher to walk up to the student, kneel down at eye level, and thoroughly review every single item that he or she should bring to class, perhaps even discussing the specific qualities or history of items, such as the pencil, eraser, and paper.

The next section describes three additional strategies for inviting clients to discontinue ineffective solutions and try something different.

Observe the Problem

This tactic is useful for any problem that is made worse by overattention and overintervention. In these situations, we can suggest that students, parents, and teachers do absolutely nothing about the problem except observe it and record data on it. Observing the problem represents something different and interrupts ineffective solution attempts, especially when people are pressing too hard to control and resolve the problem. This task invites people to stop pressuring themselves or others to change while allowing them to remain involved by observing. Sometimes simply backing off and relieving the pressure improves the situation and prompts clients to adopt a different approach.

Although observation tasks are useful for a broad range of problems, they may be particularly helpful in situations involving anxiety, fears, and bodily functions. Sometimes, when these difficulties occur and people make willful, concerted efforts to fix them, they put themselves in a position of trying to coerce something that can only occur spontaneously. You cannot coerce yourself into not having certain thoughts and feelings. Likewise, you cannot will yourself to sleep or force yourself to be hungry. The trick here is to do something that interrupts these willful solution attempts, which end up making matters worse. Let's look at an example of this intervention in action.

Nick, a 10th grader struggling with a sudden and serious insomnia problem, began arriving at school late and doing poorly on tests. Nick was a dedicated student who earned high grades and was hoping to earn an academic scholarship to college. Nick had a lot to lose if the problem persisted, and he was urgently pressing for a quick solution. He tried a variety of strategies to "make himself" go to sleep, including reading, hot baths, and a variety of relaxation methods. Nothing worked. The harder he tried, the worse it got. As his school performance continued to drop, Nick redoubled his efforts to sleep, to no avail.

Nick acknowleged that his attempts to force himself to sleep were not working, and the counselor suggested that Nick observe the problem for 1 week to learn more about it. The task included recording the time he went to bed, how long it took to fall asleep, and his thoughts while lying in bed. Nick made it until the 3rd night, when his natural sleeping rhythm returned. Observation tasks often free the client up to let nature take its course without the client's well-meaning interference.

Invite What You Dread

This strategy may be useful when clients are trying to solve the problem by avoiding it. It is especially helpful for those struggling with recurring negative feelings or unwanted thoughts. These individuals spend a considerable amount of energy trying to avoid certain feelings or thoughts or to stop them when they occur. Unfortunately, the intrusive thoughts and feelings are made all the more powerful by the effort to control or stop them. In these situations, clients can be encouraged to experience the avoided situation, thoughts, or emotions without any pressure or expectation to change them or master them.

One way to approach avoided thoughts and feelings is to intentionally invite them to happen, thereby turning the tables and putting the client in control. When we are troubled by unwanted thoughts or feelings, they seem to fall completely outside our control and hit us at the most inopportune times. Encouraging clients to invite what they dread makes a dramatic shift by making an involuntary action voluntary. Something that has been perceived as unacceptable and outside the person's control is now acceptable and under his or her control. This interrupts clients' futile attempts at avoidance, allowing them to focus their attention and energy on more productive goals. This can be combined with mindfulness methods, such as breathing steadily, picturing one's thoughts and feelings as unavoidable raindrops or leaves flowing by in a stream, and so forth (Hayes, Follete, & Linehan, 2004).

Cassie, age 16, told the counselor that she felt so depressed that she went to bed as soon as she got home from school. This was scary and confusing because her life was going so well. Cassie had recently moved and found the new school and the exciting new city to be just what she had always wanted. In Cassie's mind, this should have made her happy. Instead, Cassie wound up incessantly trying to convince herself to be happy while simultaneously avoiding all that was negative about her circumstances. This resulted in more and more sleep and increased feelings of hopelessness. The counselor and Cassie discussed her problem (depression and sleeping too much) and her solutions (trying to avoid feelings of depression because she "shouldn't" feel that way). The counselor suggested that Cassie set time aside each day to "give the depression its due" and try to learn what she could from it. This included thinking about her move, the new city, and how much she missed her friends. She started to cry, and instead of quickly drying her tears, she let it go. Cassie did this every day and found that the intensity of the feelings diminished and her tears slowed down. As this occurred, she felt more energetic and slept less.

Go With the Flow

This technique addresses situations in which one person is trying to get another to do something that he or she is not so motivated to do or in which one person sees a problem and the other does not. Such situations start with simply trying to bring the problem to the other person's attention and then escalate to really bringing the problem to the other's attention by confronting, persuading, reasoning, or arguing. Going with the flow fits many relational conflicts because people often respond to any mention of a problem or request for change with natural defensiveness. Although adolescents are famous for this, I've seen it occur across the age spectrum and well into adulthood. The pressure to change may prevent the other person from considering alternatives and possibly changing the problem on his or her own. Going with the flow takes the pressure off and opens up other avenues of change.

Going with the flow requires the person who desires the change to accept and even encourage the other person's actions, thereby avoiding the battle and dropping the other end of the rope. This can take as many different forms as there are situations. Encouraging things to stay the same dramatically alters the problem pattern. Consider Cheryl, a ninth-grade English teacher who requested help in coping with incessant criticism by one of her students. Tim always found something wrong with Cheryl's class and unfailingly reported every perceived shortcoming to Cheryl. Although Cheryl accepted the criticism in a good-natured way at first, it began to really bother her. The situation degenerated into a cycle of criticism, with Cheryl defending her actions to Tim, followed by further criticism of her inability to accept feedback, and so on.

Consider how going with the flow might be applied to this situation. Cheryl could simply find something about the criticism to agree with, or she could ask Tim for his feedback before he had the opportunity to criticize. Both of these options were discussed with Cheryl, but she chose to take it a step further. Instead of simply smiling and nodding in response to critcism, she chose to enthusiastically agree with Tim because she thought that would surprise him even more and have a better chance of changing things. It did.

When Tim criticized Cheryl the next few days at school, she calmly agreed with him and occasionally exaggerated his critcism in the following ways: "Yes, Tim, I'm a terrible lecturer, but I'm working on it. In fact, I can't believe you're hearty enough to stay awake the entire period." "Not only are my tests lousy, but I'm starting to believe that I'm a pretty rotten teacher. I'm amazed you continue to put up with me." If you use this strategy, it is important not to sound sarcastic, as that just creates hostility.

Consider the logic of this intervention as it was presented to Cheryl: If you agree and the criticizer accepts it, you still do whatever you want, the argument is over, and you maintained control and didn't get angry or defensive. So you win. If he or she disagrees with you (remember, you are now accepting criticism), that means he or she is absolving you of blame. So you still win. Cheryl liked this logic, especially the part about not feeling so defensive. She tried it with Tim, who, after a few occurrences and few puzzled looks (but no further discussion), said, "No, I didn't mean it that way. I think you're a great teacher."

Strategies for changing the doing promote solutions by interrupting ineffective solutions and urging clients to experiment with different responses to the problem. As evidenced throughout the chapter, interrupting business as usual by doing something different creates new possibilities for rapid change.

Examples of Changing the Doing

The following examples illustrate the process of changing the doing with a variety of clients and school problems.

A Musical Solution

Billy, age 4, attended a half-day preschool program for students with disabilities. The classroom consisted of six other students, Jan (the teacher), and Carmen (Jan's teaching assistant). According to Jan, Billy had developed the habit of "cursing like a sailor" on exiting the school bus in the morning and periodically throughout the school day.

Jan and Carmen were experienced professionals with an impressive track record of working with the most challenging of situations. By the time they requested assistance, they had tried several reasonable interventions, including the following:

- *Redirection:* Redirecting Billy's attention to a classroom object or activity immediately following his cursing
- *Language substitution:* Responding to curse words with an alternative word (e.g., "Billy, you mean *shoot* or *fudge*")
- *Behavior modification methods:* Rewarding Billy for short periods of non-cursing and establishing a token economy system whereby Billy received buttons for acceptable behavior and lost a button for cursing.

As sensible as these methods were, nothing had any lasting effect on Billy's cursing. When contacted about the problem and ideas for resolving it, Billy's mother said that she was also stumped by the behavior and had no ideas for resolving it. She was very apologetic and embarrassed by the situation and told the counselor and school personnel to do whatever they thought was best to help her son.

Jan and Carmen were at their wits' end by the time they met with the counselor. After discussing the details of the problem and attempted solutions, the counselor commended them on their persistence and encouraged them to try something different in the following way.

Counselor: You've done an incredible job. I can't imagine how frustrating this must be for you. We all seem to agree that something very different is needed. I don't know what that would be, given everything you've already tried, but I have an idea for you. It's obvious that you're both creative people, and I'm going to suggest that you try something very different the next time Billy curses, something entirely different from anything you've tried so far.

Jan: Anything?

Counselor: Anything, as long as it's ethical. It can be *anything,* as long as it's really different.

Carmen: Like what?

Counselor: That's just it. I don't know. As creative as both of you are, I'll bet you'll think of something. Are you willing to try?

Jan: Sure, we can try.

About 1 week later, Jan and Carmen proudly informed the counselor that the cursing had stopped completely on implementation of the new strategy. Drawing on her love of mariachi music, Carmen decided to burst into song and dance as soon as Billy cursed. Carmen was waiting for Billy as his bus arrived the next morning. True to form, Billy greeted her with a few choice words as he exited the bus. When Carmen launched into her spirited song and dance routine, Billy stopped in his tracks and stared at her during the entire episode, which lasted about 20 seconds. He slowly and quietly entered the classroom with Carmen at his side, occasionally glancing up at her with a puzzled look. Carmen's encore performance occurred a few minutes later in the classroom, except this time she hopped up on a small table to enhance the effect. Billy watched in wonder, occasionally glancing at other students as if to make sure that what he was seeing was real. Billy stopped cursing from that day forward, and no additional problems were reported for the rest of the year. Jan and Carmen's willingess to experiment a little and alter their response to the problem turned out to be the difference that made a difference.

How Can You Mend a Broken Heart?

Bruce, an 18-year-old high school senior, was referred by his math teacher, Mr. Howard, because of a sudden change in behavior and attitude. During the week preceding the referral, he left class twice without permission and spoke harshly to the teacher and other students on several occasions. These behaviors were very uncharacteristic of Bruce, who had always displayed a calm demeanor and spoke politely to both teachers and students.

The counselor began the first meeting by asking Bruce whether he knew why Mr. Howard had requested counseling for him. Bruce replied that he had been "feeling and acting strange" and that he understood why Mr. Howard asked him to talk to a counselor. He explained that he had recently broken up with his girlfriend, whom he had gone out with for 2 years. He added that he hadn't slept more than 3 hours at night since the breakup and that he "could not stop thinking about it." Bruce looked very distraught and fatigued throughout the session.

The counselor asked Bruce what he viewed as the most important problem or issue, the breakup itself or worrying and thinking about it. Bruce said that the relationship was definitely over and that his biggest concern was "worrying" and "not being able to get it out of my head." When asked about attempted solutions, Bruce indicated that he tried to avoid unpleasant thoughts and feelings. Whenever he thought about his ex-girlfriend or the breakup, he would immediately try to think of something else. Bruce acknowledged that this strategy was not working well, but he didn't know what else to do. Bruce was getting plenty of advice from others as well. His best friend urged him to "just get over it," and his mother attempted to console him by reminding him that "there are plenty of fish in the sea." Bruce said that he understood what they meant and knew they were right. However, he could not shake these thoughts from his mind. He thought about it "all the time"—at school, at home, and while working at his restaurant job.

Bruce's description suggested a problem pattern in which the harder he tried not to think about it, the more he thought about it. The more he thought about it, the harder he tried not to think about it, and so on. When asked whether it helped to think about it, Bruce said it helped a little because it provided some insight into the breakup. The following dialogue ensued.

Counselor: I don't know how anybody could stop thinking about something that's so important in their lives as this is for you. I'm also not sure it's a good idea to stop thinking about it, since it may help you to figure out some things about the relationship. You know, where things went wrong and stuff like that. In fact, thinking about it might not be what's keeping you up at night. It might be that you're not giving it the proper focus and attention it deserves.

Bruce: [looking puzzled] What do you mean?

Counselor: Well, I'm just wondering whether you can do it justice by trying to think about it in the midst of distractions at school and work. How can you properly clear your head and really think clearly about it if the teacher's talking to you about school stuff, or your boss is telling you to do something at work?

This suggestion invited Bruce to consider something very different from his attempted solution of "trying to forget about it." It also ran counter to his mother's and friend's advice to forget about it. The counselor continued to validate Bruce's perceptions about the importance of the breakup while exploring different ways to "do justice" to this important issue.

Bruce: It's hard to think about anything at work.

Counselor: Would you say your performance at work and school has been better, worse, or about the same since you broke up?

Bruce: A lot worse.

Counselor: A lot worse. So, not only is it hard to think clearly about the breakup, but school and work and sleep are not going as well for you.

Bruce: Right.

Counselor: What time of day would it be the easiest for you to really concentrate on this and give it some thought instead of trying to do it at school and work? You know, a 15- to 20-minute period where you might really be able to focus and perhaps figure something out.

Bruce: I guess after dinner.

Counselor: Would you be willing to try an experiment where you would pick a few days during the coming week to use that time to really focus in and think about the breakup?

Bruce: Yes.

Counselor: Which days do you want to try it?

Bruce's attempted solution of "trying real hard not to think about it" actually intensified the problem. The counselor's suggestion to "invite what you dread" by thinking about the problem instead of avoiding it sought to interrupt previous solutions and replace them with a very different response to the problem. Bruce decided to schedule 20 minutes of "think time" every other evening.

Bruce arrived for the second counseling session looking considerably calmer and more energetic than he had the week before. He reported that things were better and that he was not worrying as much. He said that he spent about 10 minutes of think time the first night and 5 minutes the second night but decided not to do it after that. Bruce's teacher reported that he seemed like his old self again. No additional concerns were reported during the remainder of the year. For Bruce, one answer to the age-old question "How can you mend a broken heart?" is "do something different."

When Less Is More

A sixth grader named Angela was described as a "constant nuisance" to the principal, teachers, counselors, and anyone else who would listen to her lengthy complaints about how other students bothered her. On a typical school day, she talked to three or four staff members for several minutes at a time about these concerns.

After investigating the situation and finding no major support for her accusations, the school counselor and various teachers talked with her numerous times to offer support and understanding in an attempt to discover the "real problem" underlying such behavior. Angela's complaints increased even more. Angela's school counselor, Ms. Rodriguez, requested consultation from another counselor.

In an effort to interrupt existing solutions and alter the problem pattern, the second counselor suggested that Ms. Rodriguez and Angela's teachers present a message to her by way of the following letter:

> Dear Angela,
>
> We've discussed how frustrated we are that we cannot give you and your complaints our closest attention when you talk to us about them during class time and in the hallways. We have an idea that will give you the respect and attention you deserve. Ms. Rodriguez has agreed to reserve 5 minutes a day just for you to talk with her about anything you choose. You can report to her office immediately following fifth period on any day you choose to. We're very pleased that we could arrange this for you.

Every teacher reported an immediate and marked decrease in complaining, and several said that they did not hear another complaint the rest of the year. Angela met with the school counselor 3 days the 1st week and about one time per week after that. Although some meetings included the familiar complaints, they were infrequent and less dramatic than previous complaints.

Instead of repeating the theme of previous solution attempts by trying to uncover the real underlying problem of her complaints, the counselor altered the problem pattern by scheduling daily 5-minute counseling sessions and limiting the number of school staff involved. The intervention also respected Angela's perception of the problem as urgent and serious and her teachers' desire to help her.

To Skip or Not to Skip, That Is the Question

William was an academically talented high school senior in jeopardy of not graduating as a result of high absenteeism from school. In an effort to increase his school attendance and work completion, his teachers and parents frequently lectured him on the importance of being responsible and taking school seriously. Various incentive methods had also been tried, to no avail. For example, his parents had promised to pay for part of his summer vacation if he improved his school attendance. School attendance had become a daily conversation topic between William and his parents. He was referred for counseling in late March of his senior year.

Everyone involved, including William, expressed his or her frustration and desire to improve things. To interrupt attempted solutions, the counselor suggested that the parents and teachers (a) observe the problem without discussing it with William and (b) document what was different about the days that William successfully attended school. The counselor explained that this would help him learn more about the situation as well as provide a chance for everyone to consider other possible solutions.

During the first meeting with William, he expressed a dilemma when asked what he wanted from counseling. It was obvious that he cared about his parents and teachers and did not want to upset them. He also wanted to graduate, yet he greatly enjoyed skipping school with his friends. Instead of arguing with William or challenging his position, the counselor chose to go with the flow. The benefits of skipping were candidly discussed. At one point, the counselor asked William why he attended school at all given how much fun he had skipping. Questions such as, "What are the disadvantages of attending school?" validated his ambivalence and invited him to discuss the problem in a way that was very different from what he was used to.

The counselor explored exceptions to the problem by asking William and his parents and teachers what was different about the days he attended school. For example, the counselor asked William, "How do you manage to get yourself to school on certain days despite the strong urge to skip?" These questions changed the problem pattern by shifting the focus of conversation from what William was not doing to what he was doing to accomplish his goal of graduating and getting along better with his parents and teachers.

Trying something different yielded favorable outcomes for William. His school attendance improved from 40% (January through March) to 80% (April and May) following the initial counseling session. When asked for his explanation of the change, William said he finally realized he was "screwing himself" and that he would not graduate unless he "got his act together" and attended school more often. It is ironic that these were the very points or lessons that his parents and teachers were lecturing him about.

Perhaps backing off the lectures and giving William the chance to freely discuss his ambivalence about school attendance allowed him to shift from defending or justifying his position to examining his attendance choices in light of his bigger goals of graduating and getting along with his parents. In an effort to empower these changes, the counselor asked William how he resisted the urge to skip. William replied, "I remind myself how awful it would be to work at the restaurant I'm working at now for the rest of my life. That helps me make it to school." William graduated with the rest of his class in June.

Let's examine this from the standpoint of interrupting ineffective solutions and doing something different. The parents and teachers discontinued their lectures and observed the problem instead. The counselor's approach was also very different from previous interventions. Instead of lecturing or arguing with William about his choice to skip school, the counselor went with the flow and fully cooperated with William's perspective.

With William and the other clients in this section, suggestions for changing the doing were made with careful attention to each client's frame of reference and goals. Notice also that none of the interventions was overly complex or time consuming. As we have seen throughout the chapter, sometimes all it takes is a willingess to do something different.

Summary and Conclusions

This is the first of two chapters on encouraging students, parents, and teachers to try something different when attempted solutions become part of the problem. Drawn from the brief therapy tradition, several intriguing strategies for changing the doing of school problems were described, including observing the problem, inviting what you dread, and going with the flow. The effectiveness of these interventions is based on interrupting ineffective solutions and replacing them with very different responses to the problem. Encouraging clients to do something different can take on as many forms as the counselor's and client's creativity allows.

Changing the doing of the problem was illustrated by several real-life examples involving a variety of students, parents, and teachers. Examples included a preschooler who "cursed like a sailor" (*A Musical Solution*), a distraught high school student who had recently broken up with his girlfriend (*How Can You Mend a Broken Heart?*), a seventh grader who complained of being harassed by other students (*When Less Is More*), and a high school senior who skipped school (*To Skip or Not to Skip, That Is the Question*).

The strategies in this chapter are not your typical school interventions, which is precisely their strength. Most people have wrestled with a problem for a long time before requesting help and have tried various ways to resolve it. We have seen how easy it is for wise, capable people to get stuck in a pattern of more of the same solution despite its ineffectiveness in changing the problem. Instead of becoming one more voice in the "more of the same" chorus, we can encourage clients to alter the pattern by changing the doing of the problem. Chapter 9 extends the theme of trying something different by describing strategies for changing the viewing of the problem to bring about school solutions.

Practice Exercises

1. Think of a current problem in your own life. What have you or others done to help resolve it? How successful have these efforts been? Do any of these attempted solutions seem to perpetuate the problem instead of improving things? If so, try doing something different—*anything* different—to alter the problem pattern, and observe any differences that result from your new approach.

2. Have your partner describe a school problem in the role of a parent or teacher, and suggest a change in the performance of the problem. Switch roles and repeat the exercise.

3. Think of a school problem you are presently working with. Describe the problem in specific terms (who is saying/doing what to whom, what happens next, etc.). How could the problem be performed differently (at a different time, in a different place, or in a different way)? How could you suggest this to your clients in a way that would be acceptable to them?

4. Describe one small step that you are willing to take in your practice as a result of the information in this chapter.

CHAPTER 9

Changing the Viewing of the Problem

All stories are partial, all meanings incomplete.
—E. Bruner, 1986, p. 153

*I have been interested in how persons organize their lives around
specific meaning and how, in doing so, they inadvertently contribute
to the "survival" of, as well as the "career" of, the problem.*
—White & Epston, 1990, p. 3

C hanging the viewing of the problem, also referred to as reframing, interrupts the problem pattern by inviting different explanations or interpretations. There is an old saying that the optimist sees the bottle as half full,
while the pessimist sees it as half empty. Both are describing the same bottle and
the same amount of liquid. Neither view is more correct than the other. Both views
accurately account for the facts of the situation: a container of liquid holding 50%
of its capacity. The difference lies in their contrasting views of the same reality.

There are multiple views that accurately describe the facts of any given situation or problem. When faced with a problem, we interpret and describe it in a
particular way, and we get locked into whatever solution attempts flow from our
view. Because perception and behavior are interrelated, different views usually
lead to different actions. Changing the viewing is based on the twofold assumption that (a) there are several possible explanations or interpretations for any given
problem and (b) current interpretations may not be as useful as others in resolving
the problem. Solution-focused counseling adopts a very pragmatic approach to
changing the viewing of school problems: If one interpretation is not helping to
change the problem, try a different one.

Choosing a Different View

For a new and different view to be effective, it (a) must fit the facts of the situation as well as or better than existing views, (b) must be sufficiently different from
existing views (different enough to make a difference), and (c) must be acceptable
and sensible to the client. Most school problems can be viewed in many ways.
Depression can be seen as realistic pessimism, classroom misbehavior as a unique
way of communicating, and adolescent rebellion as steps toward independence

and personal responsibility. Reframing often attaches a positive meaning or purpose to actions or people that are typically viewed in negative, unhelpful ways. Box 9.1 provides some examples of this.

Reframing often focuses on the behavior of students, but it can also be used to offer students a different way of viewing their parents or teachers. In parent–adolescent conflicts, for example, the student can be invited to view the parents' behavior as caring and committed instead of controlling and insensitive. Likewise, improvements in classroom behavior may occur when a student changes his or her view of the teacher from mean and bossy to concerned and structured.

In any given situation, there are a variety of options for changing the viewing of a school problem. Different views can be constructed from content provided by (a) theories of counseling and psychology and (b) the client. In many cases, content from both sources can be combined into a new and different meaning or frame for the problem.

Using Content Provided by Theories

When it comes to changing the viewing, solution-focused counseling is an inclusive approach that is not wedded to any one particular theory of counseling or psychology. The content from any theory is fair game, as long as it fits the facts of the situation and makes sense to the client. For example, the theory of self psychology (Kohut, 1980) might suggest that a student's disruptive behavior represents his or her attempt to meet a normal developmental need for affirmation and belonging. If accepted by a parent or teacher who has interpreted such behavior as spiteful and manipulative, this new view may result in different and more effective responses to the student and his behavior.

Let's look at another reframing strategy from narrative therapy, called externalizing the problem (White & Epston, 1990). Externalizing reframes the problem from something that exists inside the student to a seperate and outside entity. For example, an independent-minded adolescent might be invited to view the problem as a dominating "bully" who enjoys pushing the student around at school and watching him or her get into trouble. If this view is accepted, it could lead to different, more productive school behavior.

Box 9.1
Reframing the Problem by Offering Positive Connotations

Controlling = *providing structure and direction*
Defiant = *independent, assertive, committed*
Argumentative = *caring enough to disagree*
Immature = *fun-hearted, playful*
Impulsive = *spontaneous, energetic*
Withdrawn = *introspective, contemplative, observant*
Passive = *has the ability to accept things as they are, laidback*
Rigid = *steadfast and committed to a plan of action*

Using Content Provided by Clients

Like other aspects of solution-focused counseling, changing the viewing includes as much of the client as possible. The case of a 12-year-old student named Maria illustrates how the ideas and comments of clients can be incorporated into new and more productive views of the problem. Maria was referred for counseling because of ongoing classroom behavior problems. She spent a lot of time in after-school detention and was suspended from school twice within a period of 3 months. When asked about possible drawbacks of improving her behavior, she said that her classmates might be disappointed if she did not clown around and make them laugh in class. I offered a different interpretation based on Maria's comments. I asked Maria how much longer she would be willing to sacrifice her own freedom to entertain her classmates, adding that it was very generous of her to do this. She seemed intrigued by this interpretation and commented that she had never thought of her misbehavior as being generous. As we discussed this further, she became determined not to sacrifice her own freedom for the sake of entertaining other students. The session ended with a discussion of other ways that Maria could keep her friends without punishing herself by getting in trouble all the time.

Presenting a Different View

A different view should be presented in a way that conveys the client's freedom to accept or reject it. This allows us the flexibility to present other views if the client rejects the first one. The following phrases are useful in presenting a different view of the problem in a respectful, tentative manner:

- You're the best judge of what might help explain this, so I want to run something by you to see what you think.
- I'm not sure this is on target. See what you think.
- Tell me whether or not you think this is in the ballpark.
- I'm curious what you think of this idea.
- Do you think it's possible that . . .
- Some people would say that . . .

It is important to observe the client's reaction as we are presenting a new view of the problem. People may indicate their interest by leaning forward, raising their eyebrows, and nodding their heads. In addition to observing these nonverbal responses, we can ask the following questions after presenting a different view to assess the client's reaction:

- What do you think of that?
- Does that make sense?
- How does that strike you?
- Is that a possibility?

True to the cooperative spirit of solution-focused counseling, reframing interventions are constructed with careful attention to the client's feedback and theory of change.

Examples of Changing the Viewing

Any story one may tell about anything is better understood
by considering other possible ways in which it could be told.
—J. Bruner, 1987

The following examples illustrate the strategy of changing the viewing with a variety of clients and school problems.

Standing Up to Stealing

Reggie, an energetic and intelligent 7-year-old, was referred for counseling by his parents and second-grade teacher for stealing at school. As far as anyone knew, Reggie had not stolen anything at school prior to the current year. The problem started out sporadically, with small items: a pencil here, a Magic Marker there, and so forth. As the year progressed, the stealing increased and became a greater concern for Reggie's teacher and parents. During the month before the referral, Reggie was caught with several stolen items, such as candy bars from classmates, snacks from the school cafeteria, and, most recently, the teacher's calculator.

The calculator incident was the last straw for the teacher and parents. They contacted me out of desperation, having tried various strategies over the past couple of months to no avail. They were "out of ideas and energy" and hoped that someone new might shed some light on the situation and offer additional suggestions. The most frustrating and baffling aspect of the situation for his teacher and parents was that, aside from the stealing, Reggie was a model student who made good grades, was polite to the teacher, had several friends, and appeared to enjoy school. He loved sports and was particularly good in baseball.

Reggie was the oldest of three boys. His youngest brother was 6 months old, and his other brother was 5. Reggie's parents were baffled by his stealing. They told me that although they did not have a lot of money, Reggie had everything he needed and did not need to be stealing from others. They were caring, attentive parents who rarely missed any of Reggie's baseball games or school functions. They also made sure that Reggie was clean, well dressed, fed, and ready for school when he left the house in the morning.

Reggie's parents were very upset and confused by his behavior. When it was suggested that he might be stealing to get attention, especially in light of the new baby at home, the parents began spending more one-on-one time with Reggie. This included occasional walks in the neighborhood or trips to the ice cream shop in the evening. Reggie's parents and teacher tried on several occasions to "get through to him," find out why he was stealing, and make sure he understood the seriousness of his behavior. As sensible as these strategies were, none of them seemed to help in reducing the stealing.

Working in conjunction with the parents, the teacher and school administrators also tried various strategies to discourage stealing. These attempted solutions included

- requiring Reggie to return stolen items and apologize to the people he had stolen from;

- making sure that Reggie had a sufficient number of pencils, markers, pens, and other supplies at the start of each day;
- witholding certain classroom privileges when he was caught stealing;
- requiring Reggie to call his parents and tell them what he had stolen;
- assigning Reggie to in-school suspension for stealing;
- scheduling periodic meetings between Reggie and the school principal, during which the principal emphasized the seriousness of stealing and the increasingly negative consequences that may result from continued stealing.

Another baffling feature of the situation was that Reggie appeared truly remorseful and ashamed when confronted about stealing. The teacher, principal, and parents verified that Reggie was not the kind of child who plotted and planned against others or stole for malicious purposes. When confronted about his stealing, Reggie typically cried, apologized, and said, "I can't help it."

Having learned what had already been tried without success, I vowed to try something different in approaching Reggie and the problem. During the opening moments of the first meeting with Reggie, I said something that opened the door for suggesting a different view.

Reggie: I can't help it.

Counselor: You can't help it. Help me understand that, Reggie.

Reggie: I can't help it. It just happens. People don't believe me, but . . . I know it's a bad thing. I should stop. I want to stop, but it just happens.

Counselor: That must be hard for you. You want to stop, but . . .

Reggie: I can't stop it. It just happens.

Counselor: What's it like when it happens?

Reggie: I'll be walking along, you know, at school, and I walk by a desk and there's a cool gel pen, and it's like, "Take it, Reggie, nobody's looking." And I take it.

Reggie's last comment opened the door for me to externalize the problem by reframing stealing as an external entity that whispered into Reggie's ear to gain his cooperation and push him into doing things against his better judgment. While continuing to validate Reggie's dilemma of wanting to stop yet feeling powerless to do so, I invited Reggie to view the problem in a way that increased his sense of control and hope.

Counselor: I'll bet that's really hard for you, Reggie, knowing what you want to do but feeling pushed into something that you really don't want to do.

Reggie: It's hard. It happens all the time.

Counselor: You know, you said something that really got my attention and made me think that we might be approaching this whole thing the wrong way.

Reggie: What do you mean?

Counselor: You said it was like someone whispering, "Go ahead and take it, Reggie, nobody's looking," and stuff like that. And then you would take something that didn't belong to you. Is that right?

Reggie: Yes.

Counselor: So, this voice that whispers to you, does it belong to someone who's nice, someone who cares about you, or someone who's mean and doesn't care?

Reggie: Mean.

Counselor: So this mean person somehow gets you to do things that you don't want to do.

Reggie: Yes.

Counselor: Do you know what the word *bully* means?

Reggie: It's like a mean kid who picks on other kids and beats them up on the playground.

Counselor: Exactly. Bullies are not very nice people, are they?

Reggie: No.

Counselor: Well, I think you're dealing with a pretty mean bully that's been pushing you around a lot and talking you into taking things. Does that make any sense?

Reggie: [nods "yes"]

Counselor: Do you think the bully likes to see you get in trouble?

Reggie: Yes.

Counselor: Hmm. Seems like we're dealing with a clever bully here. [Reggie leans forward, all ears.] The weird thing is, the bully never gets in trouble, but you do. It's like the bully likes it when you do what he or she tells you to do. Do you think the bully is a guy or girl?

Reggie: Guy.

Counselor: What do you think his name is?

Reggie: Bruiser.

Reggie enjoyed watching wrestling on TV, and Bruiser was the archenemy of one of Reggie's wrestling heroes. Reggie explained that Bruiser would cheat and break the rules to win a wrestling match. Returning to the problem at hand, I wondered aloud how the stealing problem (aka Bruiser) had recruited Reggie to be on his team and wielded power over him. Without criticizing Reggie for letting Bruiser get the upper hand, I asked additional questions to flesh out the new view:

- "How does Bruiser get you to do what he wants you to do?"
- "How long has he been bullying and pushing you around at school?"
- "Is your life better or worse since Bruiser showed up?"
- "How does he get you to think about yourself? Is this what you want to think about yourself?"
- "How does he get others to think about you? Is this what you want others to think?"
- "Tell me about a time you stood up to Bruiser instead of letting him push you into trouble at school. How did you do it? How did it feel? Is this something you want to do more of? What would it take for that to happen?"

- "You know, some boxers and wrestlers have a team of people in their corner to pump them up and give them tips for beating the opponent. Who do you want on your team to help you stand up to Bruiser?"

At no time did I excuse Reggie's stealing behavior. The externalizing conversation simply added a new and different element to the picture. Reggie accepted it and set out to "put Bruiser in his place." With my help, Reggie decided who he wanted on his team: his parents, teacher, best friend, and former baseball coach (who was also a teacher at his school). We named the team Reggie's Rumblers and held a meeting to discuss ideas for restoring Reggie's power and defeating Bruiser. The externalizing frame was reinforced by wrestling metaphors as we discussed "moves" that Reggie could use to defeat Bruiser, including strategies for body slamming Bruiser, untangling himself from Bruiser's holds, and getting up off the mat instead of giving in and accepting defeat. Other ideas included the following:

- Reminding Reggie to "stand tall" as he left class to go to lunch and recess (two situations involving high rates of previous stealing)
- Taking a photograph of Reggie standing above a fallen opponent (aka bruiser) in a victorious pose and taping the picture to his desk as a reminder of his goal
- Holding weekly pep talks with the school counselor aimed at empowering progress and addressing any problems or concerns

Stealing ceased to be a problem. At the end of the school year, Reggie was proudly admitted into my Consultant Club and given a "Bruiser Basher" certificate in recognition of his victory over a persistent and formidable bully.

Externalizing the stealing problem interrupted ineffective solutions and encouraged new responses. Viewing the problem as an oppressive and dominating bully and naming it accordingly grabbed Reggie's attention and interest. It also encouraged him to redirect his energy from guilt and apprehension about stealing, to a "bring it on" attitude that altered his relationship with the problem and put him in the driver's seat. Whereas the "old Reggie" served at the mercy and request of Bruiser, the "new Reggie," with some help from the Rumblers, stood up to Bruiser and continued to put him in his place.

A Wake-Up Call From the Unconscious

An 11th grader named Jessica was referred because of "concentration problems" and a sudden decline in academic performance. When asked whether anything in her life had recently changed, she said that she had been having recurring nightmares in which she was being chased. She tried to avoid falling asleep so she would not have the dream. Her loss of sleep made it harder to concentrate in school and did not reduce the nightmares. She felt like she was "going crazy." Jessica's view of herself and the situation clearly appeared to be contributing to the problem instead of helping to resolve it.

When asked what she wanted from counseling, Jessica said she wanted to stop having the dreams so she could "start having a normal life again." Jessica had become interested in dreams since reading about them in her psychology course a few months earlier. Intrigued by the notion that the unconscious can express itself through one's dreams, Jessica had a strong desire to understand the meaning of her dreams and fears about them.

When asked about her current interpretation, Jessica explained that she viewed her dreams and fears as signs of weakness, regression, and immaturity. She said that she had grown up a lot in the past couple of years and that the nightmares were a kickback to a younger age, when she was less mature and had similar dreams. Jessica viewed her fears as unjustified and irrational because she knew that she could not really be hurt by someone in a dream. The counselor validated Jessica's fears by explaining that dreams seem very real when they are occuring, and that anyone would be afraid if he or she had the dreams that Jessica was having.

On the basis of the information provided by Jessica, the counselor offered a different interpretation. During the past year, Jessica had become very busy with school and friends. The counselor suggested that she had become so busy that she might have taken her growth and accomplishments for granted and not properly acknowledged them. The counselor wondered aloud whether the dreams might be serving as a reminder or "wake-up call" from the unconscious to take the time to acknowledge her recent accomplishments. Jessica was intrigued, and the counselor continued. Her fears about the dreams were explained by the notion that she presently had much more to lose than she did when she had similar dreams a few years ago. The thought of being chased and killed by someone is much more frightening when you have more to live for. Therefore, as unpleasant as the dreams and fears were, they could be viewed as signs of how much better Jessica's life was now as compared to a few years back.

Not only did Jessica accept this different view, she extended it by stating that she took much better care of herself now than she used to in terms of hygiene and diet. She also said that she rarely gave herself credit for anything good that happened in her life. Jessica did not report any further concerns regarding the dreams, and her grades and concentration improved to their previous level.

This example illustrates how a new view can be constructed completely from content provided by the client. For Jessica, viewing the dreams as unconscious reminders versus signs of craziness and viewing the fears as indications of recent growth and maturity versus signs of weakness and regression provided a whole new way of seeing things.

Giving Them What They Want

Zach, a 17-year-old high school senior, was referred in February by the school principal and his teachers for "oppositional behavior" and "defiance of authority." He frequently refused to do schoolwork and persistently stated his negative opinions about the school, the teachers, and the principal (Mr. Billingsly). After reviewing school records and talking with the principal and teachers, I met with Zach.

Counselor: I've already talked to your teachers and Mr. Billingsly about what they see happening. . .

Zach: Huh! I bet that was great. Did they tell you what an asshole I am?

Counselor: Not exactly.

Zach: I'm surprised. They need to straighten this school out. That's the problem. This school sucks, along with most of the people in it. Now I have to come and talk to you like it's my fault.

Zach resented being referred for counseling and viewed it as yet another way of "blaming him" for everything that went wrong in the classroom or at the school. As illustrated next, I accommodated Zach's position instead of challenging it.

Counselor: What sucks the most for you about the school?

Zach: Almost everything. There are *some* cool teachers, and I've got some friends, but most of the teachers can't teach. You just sit there. Then they go ballistic when you mess around or don't do your work. Now I have to come here like it's my fault.

Counselor: Do you do your work?

Zach: Some of it.

Counselor: Do you do more of it in certain classes?

Zach: It depends. I really don't care about it. I just want to get the hell out of this school.

Counselor: How are you going to do that?

Zach: Just graduate.

Counselor: I mean, as far as credits go, do you have to pass most of your classes to have enough credits to graduate?

Zach: I have to pass every one of my classes this year.

Counselor: Are you going to be able to do that?

Zach: The classes are pretty easy. Well, most of them are. But the last time I got suspended, I missed an English test, and she wouldn't let me retake it. So now I'm failing English.

Counselor: Are you failing anything else?

Zach: I might be failing history. I don't know.

Counselor: What happens if you don't pass these classes? Do you have to wait to graduate or take them in the summer?

Zach: I'm not taking them in the summer. No way.

Counselor: If you failed a class or two, would you just forget it and drop out?

Zach: Probably. For a while, anyway. I really don't want to do that. I mean, I made it this far. I don't know how [laughs].

Counselor: How do you think you made it this far, with all the detentions and suspensions?

Zach: I'm pretty smart. They don't think so. I just don't suck up to the teachers like some kids. I don't raise my hand a lot in class.

Counselor: Who doesn't think you're smart?

Zach: Most of the teachers. And Mr. Billingsly [the principal]. Especially Billingsly. He thinks I'm a waste. He just waits for me to screw up so he can call my parents and give me detention. I don't care. I'm going to do what I want. He doesn't scare me.

After a few more minutes of discussion, it was evident that Zach wanted to graduate, if only to "get the hell out of the school." It was also clear that he viewed the principal and a couple of teachers as "out to get him." Zach's position was "I'm going to do what I want no matter what Mr. Billingsly and the teachers say or do to me."

I asked Zach for a step-by-step video description of the problem, which went like this: (a) Zach was reprimanded for refusing to do his work or for some other infraction and punished, in the form of extra assignments; (b) Zach loudly questioned the fairness of the punishment and refused to comply with it, which resulted in a trip to the principal's office; (c) Mr. Billingsly, the principal, tried to reason with Zach by explaining that he could make it easier on himself if he would take the teacher's punishment without making such a scene; and (d) Zach told Mr. Billingsly to "shove it" or something similar and said that he was going to do what he wanted. These incidents often resulted in Mr. Billingsly calling Zach's parents and assigning additional days of detention. Zach's parents told Mr. Billingsly that they had talked with their son on numerous occasions and withheld car privileges several times in an attempt to improve his school behavior.

This was a classic problem pattern in which everyone was stuck in doing more of the same. The more Zach misbehaved, the more he was punished. The more he was punished, the more convinced he became that the principal and teachers were out to get him. This led to even more misbehavior, on the basis of Zach's view that "they aren't going to break me." In the following excerpt, I offer an alternative view of the situation to interrupt the problem cycle and encourage a different response. The facts of the situation are reframed in a way that accommodates Zach's strong determination to "not give in" and "not let them win."

Counselor: You mentioned that Mr. Billingsly and some of your teachers are out to get you.

Zach: Right.

Counselor: They don't like you, right?

Zach: That's putting it mild.

Counselor: Okay. It seems like you might be giving them what they want. You're playing right into their hands.

Zach: What do you mean?

Counselor: You're doing exactly what they want you to do by giving them an excuse to get rid of you and suspend you for good. You're close to the edge right now of getting suspended, right?

Zach: Yeah.

Counselor: If things keep going like this, and you keep getting sucked into this trap of mouthing off and getting sent to the office, then you'll get suspended soon, and they win. You're gone. They win. [Zach seemed genuinely curious about this, and I continued.] It's like a card game. As long as you keep doing what you're doing, getting sent out of class and getting detention, you're playing right into their hands. They're holding all the cards right now.

Zach: I don't know about that.

Counselor: I don't either, but it's something to think about. You want to graduate, and you won't if you keep giving them a legitimate reason to nail you. Something to think about.

Zach received only two detentions the next week, compared to an average of four per week during the previous month. The next conversation occurred at the end of the week in which Zach received two detentions.

Counselor: So, what's different about this week?

Zach: Nothing, really.

Counselor: Did you think any more about what we talked about?

Zach: Yeah. I guess I kind of see what you mean. But they're not going to stop me from graduating.

Counselor: How are you going to make sure they don't stop you from graduating?

Zach continued receiving occasional detentions, but not nearly as many as he had during the previous month. He received a 3-day suspension a few weeks after the meeting but remained in school and passed all his classes. Zach graduated on time with the rest of his class, thereby meeting his goal of "getting out of this stupid school."

Another noteworthy aspect of this example is that my perceptions of the situation were very different than Zach's. I viewed Mr. Billingsly, the principal, as very kind and compassionate in his dealings with Zach. Mr. Billingsly was one of the most caring and competent administrators I have ever worked with, and I held him in high regard for his willingness to go the extra mile for students. It was not always easy to resist the urge to "correct" Zach's perception of Mr. Billingsly. However, this would have been disastrous for the alliance and would have greatly reduced my effectiveness and influence with Zach. We can accept and accommodate the client's opinion without personally agreeing with it. As illustrated with Zach, the counselor's or anyone else's opinion is always secondary to the client's opinion in solution-focused counseling.

Desperate and Developmental

She sobbed as she described her depression and shame. This was my third meeting with Jane, a 16-year-old student referred by her teachers for her declining academic performance in math and history. The previous two meetings had addressed her academic difficulties and conflicts between Jane and her mother.

Jane said that she had to tell somebody about her problem because she felt like she was "going crazy." She had not slept well for the past 2 weeks, since the problem began. She was falling further behind in her schoolwork and having more trouble concentrating at school. Jane prefaced her description of the problem by saying that she viewed herself as a disgusting person, and that I would view her this way after she told me what she had done.

With great difficulty, Jane told me that she had "talked nasty" on the telephone to a male friend on three separate occasions during the past couple weeks. She was convinced that she was a "sexual deviant" and had a "multiple personality." She said, "I'm going crazy, just like my mother."

Previous meetings revealed that it was not unusual for Jane to be grounded and restricted to her house for 1 or 2 weeks at a time for things such as coming home a few minutes late from school or "talking back" at home. While grounded, Jane was required to be in the house at all times except during school, including weekends. She was also prohibited from talking with friends on the phone. Jane lived at home with her mother, Marilyn, who had been diagnosed with schizophrenia and had been admitted to several psychiatric facilities over the past 5 years. Marilyn had refused two earlier invitations to meet with me to discuss Jane's school performance and conflicts at home.

Aside from the questionable parental practice of marathon groundings, over which Jane and I had very little control, it was obvious that Jane's view of the problem was not helping her in school or elsewhere. After a few minutes of silence, during which she continued to sob and stare at the floor, I offered a different explanation of the phone calls. I suggested to Jane that her behavior, although understandably scary and confusing to her, might actually represent an understandable attempt to meet a normal and typical adolescent need for "lively interaction" with peers and to deal with the normal sexual curiosity that accompanies adolescence. Unlike most of her peers, Jane's access to typical teenage activities and interactions was severely restricted. I explained that these extreme restrictions might have prompted her to resort to extreme measures. In this sense, the phone calls represented Jane's desperate yet understandable attempts to fully experience adolescence in the face of groundings and other restrictions that prevented her from doing so in more conventional ways.

When I asked Jane what she thought of this explanation, she said that it made sense to her. She was visibly relieved to learn that she might not be crazy after all. Within a few minutes, we began discussing how she could improve her grades in English and history. No further mention was made of the telephone problem during our two subsequent meetings, and her teachers reported that she was doing better in class.

Changing the viewing requires flexibility in developing and selecting alternative views that fit the facts and make sense to the client. Jane's behavior could have been interpreted in any number of ways, and there was nothing inherently magical or right about the developmental interpretation. If Jane had rejected it, then it would have been discarded. The developmental view was effective with Jane because it matched the facts, she accepted it, and it introduced something different into the problem pattern.

Pervert or Protector?

A sixth grader named Steve was referred for services after making "obscene remarks and gestures" toward one of his teachers (Ms. Taylor). The counselor met with Steve and his grandparents during the 2nd day of a 1-week suspension from school. Counseling was requested by school personnel to obtain a professional opinion of Steve's mental stability and "sexual problem." School officials also wanted a determination regarding the likelihood that Steve would repeat such incidents in the future.

Steve was living with his grandparents and had been moving back and forth between his father and grandparents for the past year. His grandparents described him as a "nice, polite boy." They proudly added that he occasionally helped out with household chores without even being asked.

Grandfather: He's never used foul language with us or done anything like this. I don't know why he did it.

Counselor: Steve, do you have any theories about why you did it?

Steve: [shrugs shoulders] No.

Counselor: How well do you get along with Ms. Taylor?

Steve: Not real good.

Counselor: On a scale of 1 to 10, 1 being really bad and 10 being great, where would you rate it?

Steve: About a 2 or a 1.

Counselor: Where would you put your other teachers?

Steve: Five or 6.

Counselor: So you definitely clash more with Ms. Taylor than the other teachers.

Steve: Yeah.

Counselor: How important is it to you, again on a scale of 1 to 10, to get along with your teachers at school?

Steve: About 5.

Counselor: How important do you think it is for Ms. Taylor to get along with you?

Steve: Probably a 1. She doesn't like me. She never liked me in the first place. She's got two or three teacher's pets in that room. She always lets them do everything.

After the two discussed Steve's relationship with Ms. Taylor for a few minutes, a different interpretation was offered.

Counselor: You mentioned getting along a lot better with your other teachers than Ms. Taylor. I don't know if this is on target or not, but perhaps it was no accident that you said and did these things in Ms. Taylor's room instead of some other room. Maybe this was your way of trying to draw her attention away from her favorite students, the teacher's pets, and onto you and some other students. Granted, it's not your everyday way of asking for attention, but still, I'm just wondering. What do you think of that?

Steve: I don't care what she thinks of me. She doesn't like me. I don't like her either. It doesn't bother me.

Counselor: [turning to Steve's grandparents] What do you think?

Grandmother: I don't know. Like you said, that's a pretty weird way to get attention. I think he's smarter than that.

This alternative explanation was off target for Steve, and his grandmother's response was lukewarm at best. These reactions prompted the counselor to drop it and move on to something else. The following dialogue occurred later in the meeting, while they were discussing how often Steve saw his father (Don) and how they spent their time together.

Counselor: So, you guys watch TV a lot together.

Steve: Yeah.

Grandfather: You know, I keep telling Donnie to take him places and do things with him, like to the park or ball games, but I can't get through to him. Donnie has had a lot of problems himself. He hasn't held a steady job for a couple years, and he drinks a lot.

While the grandfather continued to describe the difficulties and shortcomings of Steve's father, Steve looked downward and appeared as if he were about to cry.

Counselor: Steve, you really care about your dad, don't you?

Steve: [nods head "yes," still looking downward]

Counselor: Do you help him a lot like you help your grandparents?

Steve: [nods head "yes"]

Counselor: That's impressive. A lot of kids your age don't even think about helping their parents. It wouldn't even cross their mind to think of helping out at home.

Grandfather: Another thing is, Donnie gets these magazines like *Playboy* and leaves them sitting around the house. I keep telling him that Steve doesn't need to be seeing that stuff, but he keeps doing it. That's probably where Steve gets these ideas.

Counselor: What do you think, Steve?

Steve: That stuff doesn't bother me. I can see that stuff anywhere. It's not like I'm a pervert or something.

Counselor: That stuff is available a lot these days. Besides, books or no books, clean house or messy house, you still care a whole lot about your dad, don't you? [Steve nods "yes"; the counselor turns to the grandparents.] Some people would say that Steve is actually trying to protect his father by getting in trouble and drawing attention *to* himself and *away from* Donnie. [Steve looks somewhat interested; the counselor continues to address the grandparents.] If you, your wife, and the school people keep focusing on Steve's problems, then maybe you won't criticize Donnie as much, and Donnie might feel better about himself. Steve might have done this school problem to get everybody to back off and stop criticizing his father. Also, this is one way for Steve to get his dad to pay more attention to him. For example, when this happened, the school called Donnie, and he had to come up to school to get Steve. Steve, what did you do that day after your dad picked you up from school?

Steve: We went back to his house.

Counselor: What did he say about what happened at school?

Steve: He yelled at me some. He told me I better not do it anymore.

Counselor: Do you think he meant it?

Steve: I know he meant it. He was really mad.

Counselor: He was really acting like a dad, wasn't he?

Steve: Yeah. He was acting like my grandpa. [grandparents laugh]

Counselor: What are some other ways you could get his attention and get him to act more like a dad?

Steve: I don't know.

Counselor: I'm just wondering, because it seems like there might be some other ways to do that besides getting yourself suspended from school.

The conversation continued to explore different ways that Steve might support his father and get his father's attention besides misbehaving in school. The grandparents agreed not to criticize Don in Steve's presence and to encourage Don to spend more quality time with his son. Steve returned to school the next week, and no further incidents were reported during the final 2 months of the school year.

The decision to abandon or stay with a new view is based strictly on the client's response. Neither Steve nor his grandparents bought into the idea that Steve's misbehavior represented an attempt to obtain the teacher's attention. Therefore, it was immediately dropped, and the counselor offered a different interpretation later in the session. The notion that a child's problem behavior might serve a specific function in the family—in this case, to protect a parent—is based on the structural theory of family therapy (Minuchin, 1974). This theory, combined with information provided by Steve and his grandparents, provided the content for a reframing intervention that conformed to the facts yet differed markedly from the prevailing notion that there was something perverse and wrong with Steve.

A Nurturing Solution

This example focuses on a parent as the primary client and illustrates the combined use of strategies for changing the viewing and the doing of the problem. Carol, a 34-year-old parent, was referred by the school principal for a conference with the counselor. She had worked her way through the administration at the school, ruffling feathers along the way with her persistent concerns about her 9-year-old daughter Sarina's "depression." The problem was that no one else shared her concerns. Sarina was a hard-working and well-behaved student, according to her teacher. In fact, everyone believed Sarina to be remarkably well adjusted, despite having a mother who was described by school personnel as a "loose cannon."

The counselor met with Carol and Sarina together. Carol was an interesting character, full of extremes. She was charming and impeccably dressed, and she spoke in a boisterous manner, emphasizing her points with sweeping gestures and intense eye contact. Sarina looked like any 9-year-old but, predictably enough, wore an embarrassed expression that said she wanted to be somewhere else. She slumped in the chair and didn't look up as her mother opened the meeting by saying, "Sarina is so depressed."

Pointing to her daughter, Carol continued,

> She complains about being bored and mopes around. I'm depressed, too. I know that I have a chemical imbalance and will need to take antidepressants the rest of my life. I also take antipsychotics, because I had a psychotic break right after Sarina was born. Tried to kill myself and the whole nine yards. My mother is also depressed and takes antidepressants. My doctor told me it was genetic, and I'm sure Sarina is just like my mother and me. She probably needs to be on medication, too.

Sarina's teacher, vice principal, and principal had already attempted to persuade Carol that nothing was wrong with her daughter. The harder they tried, the more persistent Carol became in her efforts to convince them otherwise. Carol perceived these well-intended efforts as belittling her daughter's problems and criticizing her competence as a parent. The counselor met with Carol and Sarina separately to learn more about their perceptions and concerns.

Carol described the problem as Sarina's depression, which was characterized by a general negative attitude, complaining, and boredom. Exploring how such behaviors constituted a problem revealed Carol's personal struggles. When seen alone, Carol let her guard down and discussed her feelings of frustration and helplessness. The more she tried to help her daughter, the more distant and depressed Sarina appeared. Carol's attempted solutions included the following:

- Spending long periods of time observing Sarina to monitor the "depression"
- Frequently asking Sarina whether she was depressed
- Responding to the smallest signs of Sarina's sadness or discomfort by immediately changing the subject or trying to "cheer her up" by "taking her mind off it"
- Entertaining Sarina as much as possible to prevent her from being bored or sad (e.g., Playing board games, watching tv together, inventing word games, insisting that Sarina accompany her on shopping trips when she appeared bored)

Carol cried as she acknowledged that none of these strategies seemed to help. Her biggest fear was that Sarina's "early warning signs" would worsen, damning her to the life of depression that had plagued two generations of women in the family. When asked what she wanted from the counselor and counseling, Carol stated her hope that (a) Sarina would smile more at home and (b) the counselor would verify Sarina's depression and provide suggestions for helping her.

When the counselor met with Sarina, she was quiet and sullen at first but became animated and friendly when the conversation turned to the "mean" boys in her class. She insisted that she was not depressed and that her only problem was that the boys in her class teased her a lot. She added that they teased all the other girls, too. The counselor raised the possibility that the boys might be teasing her because they liked her. Sarina denied this, but the counselor remained skeptical and elaborated on this different view of teasing: "I don't know, Sarina. I used to tease some girls I liked because I was too scared or immature to tell them I liked them. Are you sure they don't really like you?" Sarina giggled and shook her head "no." The counselor relented, "Okay, if you say so, Sarina." Sarina enjoyed the lighthearted banter and left the office with something different to think about. This conversation added several new elements to the problem pattern: the view of teasing as a possible form of socializing or flirting, the view of Sarina as capable of drawing the attention of boys, and the incorporation of playfulness and humor into a situation that had always been viewed as grim and serious. When asked about her goals, Sarina said that she wanted her mother to stop following her around, stop asking whether she was depressed, and stop trying to cheer her up all the time.

The stage was set for encouraging Carol to try something different. By her own admission, Carol's efforts at helping Sarina were ineffective at best and often seemed to make matters worse. For interventions to be successful, they would need to accommodate her depression theory and her strong desire to be helpful to her daughter. It was clear that challenging Carol and her genetic depression theory would have landed the counselor right behind school personnel in the conga line of failed solution attempts.

The counselor suggested that, given the familial predisposition to depression, environmental interventions would be critical in counteracting Sarina's genetic predisposition. Furthermore, to enter adulthood equipped to handle depression and boredom, Sarina would need a lot of support and practice in coping with unpleasant feelings on her own. Perhaps Carol could best help Sarina by permitting her the opportunity to practice coping with depression, instead of trying to cheer Sarina up or fix the problem right away before she had the chance to practice on her own. Introducing a different view of how to help Sarina laid the groundwork for changing the doing by encouraging Carol to go with the flow of Sarina's sadness or boredom.

The counselor accepted Carol's genetic depression theory, validated her worry as appropriate given the family history, and noted her obvious love and concern for her daughter. Surprised and relieved not to have to defend her position, Carol relaxed and appeared ready to consider what she could do differently to help Sarina. Validation of Carol's viewpoint freed her up to consider new ideas and directions. Here is a small sample of the conversation.

Counselor: You may be able to help Sarina cope with her depression by validating her concerns, boredom, and sadness when she expresses it—and then allowing her the space to sort it out herself. For example, if Sarina says,

"I'm bored, there's nothing to do around here; I hate it when no one is around to play with," you could say, "Yes, it must be tough to be all alone in the house with nobody to play with." By validating her concern, she will feel understood, and have the chance to practice coping with the boredom. The hard part for parents is resisting the temptation to cheer up, entertain, or otherwise coerce our kids into feeling better. Besides the fact that it usually doesn't work, as you mentioned with Sarina, it can discount a child's negative feelings. No one wants their kids to experience anything negative. Is this making any sense?

Carol: Yes it is, because I'm a stroker, I'm always upbeat and positive with her . . . always telling her how smart and pretty she is and how school is fun. I guess I sort of discount her feelings and it's not helping. Is that what you are getting at?

Counselor: Exactly, except you are not doing anything wrong. You're doing what any loving parent would do. What I am suggesting is that you "lean into" her depression, invite its expression, and give Sarina a chance to develop coping strategies. Another way of looking at this is to "go with the flow" and respond to Sarina's "gloom and doom" comments with agreement. For example, to the comment, "I hate school," you may respond, "School can certainly be a bummer, and the worst of it is there's so much more to go." In essence, you are teaching her how to cope with it by allowing her the time and space to deal with it.

Carol: I guess you just don't expect kids to have bad feelings, and you want to protect them from any hurt. But that's impossible to do. They suffer just as we do.

Counselor: Exactly. I agree.

Carol: Yeah, I need to allow her to be and support her feelings, even if it's negative.

Carol did just that, which was no small feat given her long-standing habit of trying to fix things for Sarina and cheer her up as soon as she expressed a concern or unpleasant feeling. Soon after implementing her new approach, Carol reported that Sarina was smiling more and complaining less. Carol concluded that her daughter was only mildly predisposed to depression and decided that an antidepressant was not needed.

Counseling sought to interrupt and reverse Carol's ineffective solution attempts by changing the viewing and doing of the problem. The teacher and school administrators repeatedly tried to convince Carol that Sarina was a normal 9-year-old, but Carol didn't buy it and vigorously defended her position. Once it became clear that the counselor was not going to challenge her beliefs, Carol showed greater flexibility and softened her viewpoint about Sarina's genetic depression.

Summary and Conclusions

It is easy to get stuck in sensible yet unproductive ways of thinking about ourselves and our problems. When this happens with school problems, we can invite students, parents, and teachers to view something differently in the hopes of encouraging a different response to the problem. Since perception and behavior are interrelated, changes in the meaning or interpretation of a problem typically lead to behavioral changes as well.

To be effective, a new view of the problem must (a) fit the facts as well as or better than existing views, (b) make sense to the client, and (c) be different enough to make a difference. Theories of psychology and counseling, as well as material supplied by clients themselves, provide useful content for changing the viewing of school problems.

Changing the viewing was illustrated with a variety of clients and problems, including a 7-year-old referred for stealing (*Standing Up to Stealing*), an 11th grader who complained of nightmares (*A Wake-Up Call From the Unconscious*), an angry and strong-willed high school senior (*Giving Them What They Want*), a 16-year-old who thought she was going crazy (*Desperate and Developmental*), a sixth grader who made nasty remarks and gestures (*Pervert or Protector?*), and an outspoken parent concerned about her daughter's "genetic depression" (*A Nurturing Solution*). This is the last of four chapters describing specific solution-focused interventions for school problems. The next chapter presents some suggestions for when and how to end counseling.

Practice Exercises

1. Have your partner present a school problem, and practice changing the viewing by offering an alternative interpretation or explanation of the problem. Switch roles and repeat the exercise.

2. Review a list of common descriptors of school problems (disruptive, impulsive, etc.), and provide a positive connotation for each descriptor. Most behavior rating scales include an ample number of negative descriptors that could be used for this purpose.

3. Think of a problem you are currently experiencing. How do you and other people typically respond to the problem? What actions are being taken in response to the problem, and how effective are they? How do you or others currently view the situation? Think of one or two plausible explanations for the situation. Select one of these views, try it out, and observe the results.

4. Describe one small step that you are willing to take in your practice as a result of the information in this chapter.

CHAPTER 10

When and How to End Counseling

This chapter offers guidelines and strategies for when and how to end counseling. Sometimes the decision to end counseling is made for us. Students move away, the school year ends, we are reassigned, or other duties force us to end counseling more abruptly than we would prefer. These are the realities of school-based counseling, over which practitioners may have little control. When we do have the opportunity to plan for termination, the following considerations are often helpful. Since every counselor and every setting is different, you will probably need to adapt these suggestions to fit your style and circumstances.

Approaching Every Session as the Last

Time constraints and other school-based realities support the recommendation to approach every session as if it were the last. As evidenced throughout this book, every contact with a student, parent, or teacher offers possibilities for change. Solutions can emerge at any point in the counseling process. Approaching each session as if it were the last helps counselors and clients remain focused on specific goals and alert to small signs of success.

Using Goals as Guidelines

Goals are the most useful guidelines for deciding when to end counseling. Termination decisions are most effective when counselors begin with the end in mind by developing specific, manageable goals at the outset of counseling. It is easier to assess improvements in arriving at school on time and turning in homework assignments than it is to assess a vague goal, such as becoming less depressed. In addition to enabling clients and practitioners to detect small improvements throughout the counseling process, specific goals make the task of ending counseling easier.

The purpose of solution-focused counseling in schools is to help people resolve specific problems. Resolving specific problems is hard enough, and it is unrealistic for school practitioners to take on much more than that. Being very clear with ourselves and our clients about the goals and scope of school counseling helps us in making effective termination decisions. These points lead to the next suggestion.

Terminating When Clients Are "On Track"

A complete resolution of the problem is not required for termination. Instead, termination should be considered when clients are on track toward resolving the problem and have a clear understanding of what they are doing successfully. Concrete, measurable indicators of progress are very helpful in this regard. These indicators should be established at the beginning of counseling (e.g., "How will we know when counseling is no longer needed?" "What will be the first small signs of success?" and [pointing to the CORS] "You marked a 4.5 on the School line. What will a 5 or 6 look like?"). Concrete indicators of goal attainment might include specific levels of improvement in school attendance, grades, or number of discipline referrals per week. The more specific the goal is, the easier it is to tell when clients are on track in reaching it.

Collaborating and Leaving the Door Open

Termination in solution-focused counseling is a collaborative decision between the practitioner and client. The following conversation with an 8th grader named Kyle illustrates how to collaborate with clients on termination decisions while leaving the door open for future contacts.

> *Counselor:* I'm really impressed with the changes you've made, Kyle. You seem to have a good sense of what you need to do to keep things moving in the right direction. What do you think?
>
> *Kyle:* I know I've got to keep doing homework to pass and not mouth off as much in class like I used to.
>
> *Counselor:* With these changes you've made, along with your plans to keep doing what's working, what do you think about us scaling back and not meeting each week like we have been?
>
> *Kyle:* That's okay, but if I start messing up, we might need to meet.
>
> *Counselor:* Absolutely, Kyle. In fact, we can plan to meet again in a month or so to visit for a few minutes and check up on things. How does that sound?
>
> *Kyle:* Fine.
>
> *Counselor:* If you want to meet for any reason before then, let me know and we'll set it up. Okay?

Terminating With Students Who Do Not Want to

Some students want to continue meeting even after they have made sufficient improvements and are on track toward continued success. The following ideas may be useful in these situations. First, we can compliment students and validate their desire to continue (e.g., "It takes a lot of courage to discuss problems with someone else and to make the kind of changes you've made. I appreciate the fact that you want to keep meeting, and it shows how committed you are to continuing to improve and do well in school"). Second, we can explain that we are required to help many other students who are experiencing serious problems much like those that the student has experienced and improved. This promotes empathy between the current student and those who are awaiting our services. Third, we can ask students, parents, and other clients whether they are willing for us to call on them in the future for ideas and suggestions to help others with similar problems. Students can be invited to join the Consultant Club for this purpose, as described in Chapter 6. Offering an open door for future contact also seems to reduce students' apprehension about ending counseling.

Termination is the last in a series of interrelated tasks composing the counseling process. Appendix G pulls the process together by outlining each major task of solution-focused counseling in schools. As an additional guide, Appendix H provides a format for conducting first and subsequent counseling sessions.

Summary and Conclusions

The decision to terminate counseling can be a difficult one. Establishing clear goals at the start of counseling lays the groundwork for effective termination decisions. Like every other aspect of solution-focused counseling, the decision to terminate is made in collaboration with clients. This chapter has provided practical suggestions for when and how to end counseling, including viewing every session as the last, terminating when clients are on a solid track for reaching their goals, and leaving the door open for future contact.

Practice Exercises

1. Think of a situation in which counseling was successfully terminated, and consider what you and the client did to make it successful.
2. With a partner serving as the client and you as the counselor, conduct a short counseling session as if it is your first and last session. Make note of any differences between your approach to this session and your usual approach.
3. What are some methods that you have used or thought of using to handle situations in which students do not want to terminate counseling? What else could you do in these situations?
4. Describe one small step that you are willing to take in your practice as a result of the information in this chapter.

PART THREE

Troubleshooting and Getting Started

CHAPTER 11

Troubleshooting When Things Don't Go As Planned

Failure is the opportunity to begin again more intelligently.
—Henry Ford

Most books, including this one, present successful scenarios to demonstrate the intended effect of the counseling approach and strategies. Although the previous examples are real, things do not always work out this way in everyday practice. Despite our best efforts, we occasionally get stuck, and counseling stalls. Strategies that seem perfect for the situation and that are supposed to work, according to some theory or textbook, do not always work. Regardless of expertise and experience, no practitioner is effective with all clients. This book encourages counselors never to give up on clients and to try something different when things aren't working. Chapter 11 rounds out this discussion by offering a series of troubleshooting questions to consider when counseling stalls and nothing seems to be working.

What Does the Client Say?

The first thing to do when counseling stalls is to consult with the client. This book encourages you to consult with clients from the outset of counseling throughout the helping process. At no time is client feedback more crucial than when counseling is not working.

As described in Chapter 4, client feedback can be obtained through informal or formal methods. In addition to simply asking questions (e.g., "What can we do different here to make things better?"), we can follow up on the client's responses to the ORS and SRS. When the ORS indicates no major change or improvement, we might say, "Things are about the same as they were last week. What do you think we should do about it?" We can respond in a similar way to the client's feedback on the SRS (e.g., "You marked this line a little lower than the rest [pointing to Approach or Method scale]. What can I do differently to make these meetings work better for you?"). Appendix D summarizes the process of outcome management using the ORS and SRS, including examples for responding to various kinds of client feedback.

Regardless of what method you use to obtain client feedback, it is crucial to do so at the earliest sign of a problem, be it a lack of progress or problems with the alliance. Research makes it clear that if counseling is not working within the first couple of sessions, it is probably doomed, unless we openly address the issue with clients and collaborate on changing things before it's too late. If we are truly committed to helping our clients change, then we should encourage and welcome negative feedback when they are experiencing our services as ineffective. Accepting and responding to negative feedback in an open, nondefensive manner speaks volumes about our respect for clients, our commitment to being useful to them, and our willingess to adjust ourselves and our services to do so.

Although a counselor might address several of the questions in this chapter in the process of obtaining client feedback, they are listed seperately to highlight their importance in the troubleshooting process.

Is There a Stated Goal?

The fact that three of the questions in this chapter are specifically related to goals speaks to the importance of goal-related issues in the counseling and trouble-shooting process. The most basic of all goal-related considerations is whether you have a goal in the first place. Several years ago, I complained to a colleague about getting nowhere with a particular high school student. Everything I tried was a dead end. After patiently listening to my frustrations (like a good counselor), my colleague asked, "What is the stated goal?" This question stopped me in my tracks because there was no stated goal. No wonder it felt like we were going around in circles. As the saying goes, "If you don't know where you're going, you probably won't get there."

Is the Goal Specific and Reasonable?

Vague and unrealistic goals can impede progress, as can the counselor's or client's expectation that large changes will occur instantly. Although solution-focused counseling is designed to promote change as quickly as possible, some changes occur at a slow pace and in small steps. Counselors and clients may overlook small but important improvements in a chronic problem situation because they are so used to seeing the problem. Specific and reasonable goals help us and our clients notice small but important improvements throughout the counseling process.

Whose Goal Is It?

This question captures one of the most overlooked of all considerations in working with young people and school problems. There is nothing more futile than working with a student on a goal that is important to the teacher or parent but unimportant to the student. Given that most students enter counseling as mandated clients at someone else's request, we need to make sure that we are working on goals that are meaningful to them. Thus, we may need to negotiate different goals with students, parents, and teachers. For example, if the teacher or parent wants the student to take school more seriously but the student does not buy into that goal, we can ask the student whether she is interested in getting her teachers or parents off her case about school. Although they are worded differently, both goals are aimed toward similar outcomes—turning in more homework, arriving at school on time, behaving better in class, and so forth. Accepting the client's frame of reference and negotiating goals accordingly ensures useful goals that are owned by the client.

Is the Client Apprehensive or Ambivalent About Change?

Although people may genuinely want to change, they might also be ambivalent or apprehensive about it. For example, a student may truly want to improve school behavior while being concerned about the possibility of losing friends as a result of the change. Unless this issue is addressed with the student, counseling usually stalls, and both parties become frustrated. Two strategies may be useful in these situations (Fisch et al., 1982): (a) Invite the client to go slowly in making changes (e.g., "Sometimes it's best to take things slow and easy") and (b) explore the disadvantages of change (e.g., "Are there any disadvantages of changing?").

"Go slowly" interventions are particularly effective with apprehensive clients who view change as overwhelming and improbable. The suggestion to take it slowly instead of rushing may relieve people's apprehension, permitting them to pursue change at a pace that is comfortable for them. Asking students about the potential drawbacks or disadvantages of change acknowledges and validates their ambivalence. Consider Kevin, an eighth-grade student who responded to this question by stating that he goofed off in class to make his friends laugh and that he would be letting them down if he stopped. His classroom behavior improved markedly after we candidly discussed this and other possible disadvantages of change, along with other ways he could maintain friendships without getting in trouble at school.

Is Counseling Compatible With the Client's Theory of Change?

Counseling is destined to fail when it is out of sync with the client's theory of change—that is, the client's ideas, experiences, language, preferences, and expectations related to the problem, the solution, and the role of the counselor. Sometimes counselors become overzealous or forceful about their own ideas, forgetting that it's all about the client when it comes to successful outcomes. Solution-focused counselors, like anyone else, may become overzealous in their attempts to be positive, to the point of ignoring important aspects of the problem or invalidating the client's pain and frustration. Given the vital role of client involvement in successful outcomes, examining the extent to which the counseling process is compatible with the client's theory of change is one of the most useful things we can do when counseling is not working. The tools and techniques of outcome management can be very helpful in this regard (see Appendix D).

Is Counseling Seen by the Client as More of the Same or Something Different?

By the time we become involved with a school problem, many interventions might already have been attempted. The last thing we need is to become one more voice in the "more of the same" chorus. Consider a situation in which a student has been lectured extensively by parents and teachers regarding the negative consequences of truancy, to no avail. At this point, it is inadvisable for the counselor to join the chorus by pointing out additional consequences of truancy, such as salaries of high school dropouts or other issues that might not have been adequately covered by the parents or teachers. When counseling is going in circles instead of moving forward, ask yourself and the client whether it is being perceived as more of the same. If so, then it is time to try something different.

Is My View of the Client Helping or Hindering Progress?

The facts of a problem are usually clear-cut (e.g., the student hit another student, cursed the teacher, or skipped school). Interpretations, however, are much more flexible and negotiable. We choose our interpretations, and some are more useful than others when it comes to helping people change. For example, the fact that a client does not implement one of our suggestions can be viewed as a sign of resistance or as useful feedback indicating the client's need for a different intervention. In solution-focused counseling, viewing clients as resourceful and cooperative is more productive than viewing them as resistant or unmotivated.

Is There Someone Else Who Might Provide a Fresh Perspective?

Consulting with colleagues often provides new and fresh ideas when we get stuck. Regardless of one's creativity and problem-solving skills, no one is immune to getting stuck in nonproductive patterns with clients. Sometimes we are simply too close to the trees to see the forest, and one small suggestion or observation from a colleague can turn things around and get counseling back on track.

Is There Someone Else Who Would Be More Effective With the Client?

Sometimes the client would be better off with a different counselor. This does not necessarily imply that we did something wrong. Some clients may insist on working with a counselor of the same gender, race, or religious beliefs. If such options exist, it is best to accommodate the client's request.

Other situations may also prompt us to consider referring the client to someone else. When change has not occurred after several meetings despite our best efforts to adjust services on the basis of client feedback, we can talk with the client about seeing another counselor if that is possible. In one study of 6,000 clients, therapist effectiveness ranged from 20% to 70% (Hansen & Lambert, 2003). This study suggests that even the best therapists may not be effective with one out of every four clients. These figures, along with the other points in this discussion, indicate that we should maintain the option of referring clients to a different counselor when it appears to be in their best interest.

Summary and Conclusions

This chapter has presented several troubleshooting questions and strategies to consider when things do not go as planned in counseling. I hope these ideas will assist you with the inevitable glitches that occur in the real world of school-based counseling. The next and final chapter offers recommendations and encouragement for putting solution-focused counseling into practice where you work.

Practice Exercises

1. Make a list of current clients who are progressing very slowly or not at all, and ask yourself the following goal-related questions for each case:
   * Is there a stated goal?
   * If so, is the goal clear and reasonable?
   * Whose goal is it? Does the client own the goal?
   * Is the goal worded in a way that fits the client's position?
2. Think of a current situation in which you feel stuck. Who could you talk to about ideas and suggestions for getting unstuck? You may want to make an offer to similarly assist one of your colleagues. Perhaps you and some colleagues could schedule a monthly brainstorming meeting to discuss ideas and strategies for dealing with difficult counseling situations.
3. The next time you encounter a roadblock in counseling, ask for the client's opinion on getting unstuck.
4. Describe one small step that you are willing to take in your practice as a result of the information in this chapter.

Putting Solution-Focused Counseling Into Practice

Small opportunities are often the beginning of great enterprises.
—Demosthenes

This book is not intended to cast solution-focused counseling as a cure-all magic bullet for every school problem or to suggest that other counseling strategies be abandoned. To be effective, counseling techniques must be flexibly applied and tailored to the unique circumstances of the people involved. This is easier said than done, and it takes practice.

Chapter 12 offers ideas for integrating the principles and practices of solution-focused counseling into everyday life on the job. These suggestions are based on my own experiences and those of colleagues, supervisees, and workshop participants. You know yourself and your job better than I do, so I encourage you to adapt these ideas accordingly.

Start Where You Are, and Take It Slowly

1. Take a moment to think about why it is important for you to implement ideas and strategies from this book. What motivates you to do this? Remember these values, as they provide needed energy and motivation for staying with it and persisting in the face of obstacles.

2. Think about what you are currently doing to address client, relationship, and hope factors in your work with students and others. This includes thoughts and attitudes as well as actions. Make a list titled "What I Am Already Doing," and add to it as needed in the future.

3. Pick one item from your "What I Am Already Doing" list and make a practical plan for acting on it during the next week. Think small. If that means devoting 5 minutes to the plan during the upcoming week, then so be it. That's 5 minutes more than the week before, and that's progress.

4. Continue to do this with other items from the list at a pace that works for you. Think small and go slowly, because going slowly is better than not going at all.

5. Remind yourself that it takes hard work to refine and expand your counseling skills. If you feel burdened by trying to do too much, slow down and give yourself a break. Practice being solution focused with yourself by taking the time to acknowledge and celebrate how far you have already come.

6. In addition to building on what you are already doing, adapt the above steps to some new ideas and strategies from the book. Pick a specific skill or technique, such as giving clients credit for small changes or using the SRS, and try it out during your next meeting with a student, parent, or teacher.

7. If it is possible to collaborate with others who have a similar interest, do so in whatever form possible, including monthly meetings, phone calls, e-mails, and listservs. These connections spawn new ideas and energize us to continue learning and growing.

8. Have fun! This is not your typical textbook recommendation, but bear with me here. I am honored to be invited into people's lives to help them change, and I take it very seriously. The work we do is vitally important, but that does not mean that it cannot or should not be enjoyable and, yes, downright fun at times. Not Disney World fun, but fun nonetheless. Helping people resolve school problems can be painful, frustrating, gratifying, and enjoyable. The fun and adventure of this work have been seriously underrated. Clients can tell whether we approach our work as a burden or a joy, and I ask you—if you were a client, which of these would you prefer? In my experience, the counselors who are most effective tend to approach their work with a childlike sense of curiosity and adventure. I recommend doing the same in your efforts to apply the ideas and strategies of this book.

Learn More About It

Reading this book can go on your list of what you are already doing to increase your knowledge of solution-focused counseling. You can also consult other books and articles from the reference list. Training in solution-focused counseling and other collaborative approaches is more available now than it has ever been. These opportunities are regularly listed on Internet search engines. Workshops may be available through professional organizations in your discipline, national and regional training agencies, and individuals who specialize in this kind of work.

More and more school districts are offering in-service training on positive approaches to counseling and schooling. Many times, these workshops result from the enthusiasm and efforts of one person who convinced the district to sponsor a particular training session. The advantage of working with a group from a local school district or agency is that the training can be tailored to the needs and circumstances of the setting and trainees. As you can see, there are many opportunities to learn more about solution-focused counseling.

Practice Thinking "Solution Focused"

Solution-focused counseling, as described in this book, is much more than a set of techniques. It is an entirely new way of thinking about problems, people, and change. Schools tend to notice and respond to undesired behavior more than desired behavior. This tendency pervades much of our society, including the media and the helping professions. As a result, we know a lot more about problems than we do about solutions.

Solution-focused practice and the outcome research that supports it (e.g., the change pie in Chapter 2) hold great promise for schools. Whereas this book focuses on counseling per se, applications of solution-focused thinking in schools are unlimited. Whatever your job is, I recommend that you practice thinking solution focused and look for opportunities to integrate it into your everyday life on the job. This means thinking about how you can tap into client, relationship, and hope factors in your work with students, teachers, parents, and others. Remember that every contact is an opportunity for change and growth. As you begin to do this, you will notice more and more ways solution-focused thinking can benefit you and the people you serve. The remainder of the chapter provides a glimpse of the promise and possibilities of solution-focused thinking in schools.

Working With Diverse Populations

The solution-focused emphasis on respecting the client's beliefs and perceptions is helpful in working with people from a variety of cultures and belief systems. This is a vital consideration in light of the world's increasingly diverse population and multiculturalism. Respect and validation, which I believe to be the heart and soul of solution-focused counseling, are effective with all people in all circumstances—preschoolers and grandparents, people of different races and beliefs, parent conferences, organizational change, crisis situations, team meetings, teacher and parent education, and classroom management, to name a few. Several of these areas are addressed below.

Parent–School Relationships

Parent–school relationships have received considerable attention in recent years, in part because of a growing body of research linking students' school success to parent involvement. Parent conferences have been an integral part of school life for many years, and for good reason. As the primary caregivers in the student's life, parents and guardians often hold a wealth of information and influence that is very useful in addressing student-related problems. Parent–school conferences and relationships are enhanced when approached in a solution-focused manner.

Parents are typically contacted by the school personnel only when their child is in trouble or struggling. Some parents avoid schools because most or all of their interactions with school personnel are negative. This is especially true for parents of students with school problems. The solution-focused emphasis on recognizing student resources and small successes provides opportunities to contact parents in other circumstances as well, such as when the student has a better day or to ask about the student's hobbies and interests. Imagine your reaction, as the parent of a struggling student, if you were called by the teacher or counselor to inform you that your child had a great week at school. You might even be asked your opinion of how such improvements occurred and what you and your child did to bring about these changes.

A solution-focused mind-set encourages school personnel to interact with parents in respectful ways. When meeting with parents or guardians, we can set a collaborative tone by acknowledging their unique expertise and intimate relationship with the child: "You know your child better than anyone else, and we really need your help here." Opening a meeting in this way lets parents know that we respect their perspective and that we want to work with them on behalf of their child. We can also ask parents to identify exceptions and other potentially useful resources at home: "Pay attention to what is different about the times that you and Paula get along better at home" or "Who in the family has the most influence with Paula?" This is just one of many ways we can approach parents from a solution-focused perspective that casts them as essential partners in problem solving and other school-related goals.

Classroom Teaching

A solution-focused perspective is also helpful in classroom teaching. Several researchers (Freiberg, 1999; Pianta, 1999; Zins, Weissberg, Wang, & Wahlberg, 2004) have linked positive student outcomes to teaching styles that (a) respect the integrity and individuality of students; (b) demonstrate confidence in their ability to learn and act responsibly; (c) encourage students to examine and resolve their own problems; (d) involve students in classroom discussions, activities, and decisions; and (e) facilitate positive teacher–student relationships.

Just as effective counseling requires the client's participation, the success of teaching rests largely on a solid student–teacher relationship that encourages the student's active involvement in learning (Pianta, 1999; Zins et al., 2004). Effective teachers manage the process and structure of the classroom while encouraging student input and participation, providing ample opportunity for students to share their opinions, experiences, and successes and connecting instructional topics and activities to the experiences and interests of students (Doll, Zucker, & Brehm, 2004). For example, in presenting a geography lesson, the teacher might encourage students to read and write about a place they have actually visited.

Solution-focused practices can also assist teachers in preventing and resolving classroom behavior problems. Effective teachers explicitly recognize and amplify students' strengths, resources, and successes instead of attending only to their mistakes and problems (S. Goldstein & Brooks, 2007). For example, a teacher might ask a student who is displaying behavior problems to present a class report on his or her favorite hobby. This may improve the teacher–student relationship as well as showcasing the student's unique talents and resources. Similarly, a teacher could ask the student's opinion of what might help turn things around for the better. As illustrated throughout this book, we have nothing to lose and everything to gain by enlisting students as consultants on their own problems and goals. Students, like the rest of us, appreciate being asked for their opinions and ideas. Even if the student has no specific ideas for improving things, the question itself conveys respect and enhances the teacher–student relationship—which is a benefit in teaching and behavior management. Additional ideas for applying solution-focused principles to teaching and establishing resilient, effective classroom environments can be found in Berg and Shilts (2004), S. Goldstein and Brooks (2007), and Doll et al. (2004).

Parent and Teacher Training

Parent and teacher training can also be approached from a solution-focused perspective. Several years ago, I was asked to present parents of children with developmental difficulties. My plans to work on the presentation were blocked on several occasions, and I was less prepared than I wanted to be as I stood before the 50 or so parents who attended. After stumbling around a bit without really saying anything, I asked the parents about their biggest concerns, along with strategies for handling these challenges.

For the remainder of the hour, parents eagerly described various challenges and related coping strategies. I simply recorded their ideas on the board and occasionally asked questions to clarify their comments. Feedback from the parents who attended this session was very favorable and included comments such as "It was great to have a chance to talk instead of being talked to," "I had no idea how many good ideas other parents had," and "We need a local support group so we can do this more often."

Teachers can be given similar opportunities to share effective teaching ideas and strategies as part of staff development programs. The best in-service program that I participated in as a high school teacher was one in which my social studies colleagues and I spent 2 hours sharing instructional strategies that worked particularly well for us. I was amazed at the number and quality of teaching ideas that I learned during this session—from colleagues in the same building who taught the same students. This experience continues to serve as a reminder to look within and utilize existing resources, whether I am counseling an individual student or training teachers and parents. Just as it is important to ask an individual client what is already working in addressing the problem, training groups can be asked about what they are already doing effectively in the area for which they are being trained. Likewise, teachers can be included in planning in-service programs, given that they are on the front line and know their needs better than anyone else.

Peer-Mediated Interventions

Peer-mediated interventions utilize one of the school's most valuable resources—the students themselves—to address a wide range of school-related problems and goals. Individual and classwide peer tutoring programs have repeatedly been shown to improve the school performance of both tutors and tutees in a variety of areas, including reading skills (Kourea, Cartledge, & Musti-Rao, 2007), classroom attention and work completion (DuPaul & Henningson, 1993), social skills (Trapani & Gettinger, 1989), and anger management (Presley & Hughes, 2000).

Peer mediation and mentoring programs have also been very successful in schools. In peer mediation, students typically work with same-age peers to understand and resolve school-related conflicts. Peer mediation, a popular component of violence prevention programs, has been shown to reduce in-class fighting (Bell, Coleman, Anderson, Whelan, & Wilder, 2000) and out-of-school suspensions (Schellenberg, Parks-Savage, & Rehfuss, 2007). Peer mentoring programs link older students with younger students to provide support and assistance as needed. In a study examining the impact of mentoring on students' transition from middle to high school, mentoring led to a more favorable connection to the high school, fewer discipline infractions, and fewer unexcused absences (Stoltz, 2006).

Among the many advantages of peer-mediated intervention programs is the fact that these programs have proven beneficial to both the recipients and the providers of the intervention (Franca, Kerr, Reitz, & Lambert, 1990). Studies in which students with behavioral difficulties have served as tutors have reported behavioral improvements for the tutors (Tournaki & Criscitiello, 2003). Enlisting "difficult students" as peer tutors demonstrates faith in their ability to help others and to contribute to the mission of the school. This increases their sense of belonging and reduces the likelihood of problem behavior.

Peer-mediated interventions are based on the empowering, solution-focused belief that we can resolve many problems by identifying and utilizing valuable resources within the system. Peer-based programs use the most valuable of all school resources—the students themselves—in addressing a variety of problems and goals. Refer to Ginsburg-Block, Rohrbeck, and Fantuzzo (2006) for more information about peer-mediated programs in schools.

Group Counseling

Of the many advantages of group counseling in schools, perhaps the greatest is the ability to serve several students at the same time. Every idea in this book is applicable to group as well as individual counseling. As evidenced in the group counseling example involving students with test anxiety (Chapter 6), groups can be asked to identify exceptions and other resources that may help them reach their goals. Group members can also be asked to regularly rate their progress toward goals and to provide feedback on the usefulness of each session. As with individual counseling, a strong alliance between the group leader and members will improve the outcomes of any group. Additional examples of solution-focused groups in schools can be found in Tollison and Synatschk (2007).

Parent and Teacher Consultation

As illustrated in various examples throughout the book, consulting with parents and teachers is often useful in building solutions. It is impossible and unneccessary to provide direct services to every student who experiences a school problem. We can indirectly serve more students by consulting with teachers, guardians, parents, and other caregivers in their life.

It is easy to see how the principles and practices of solution-focused counseling can be applied to consultation services. We can validate teachers' or parents' struggles, explore their ideas, acknowledge their resilience, involve them in important ways, and request their feedback throughout the duration of consultation. Teachers, parents, and other adults respond very favorably to respect, validation, collaboration, and other key elements of solution-focused practice described in this book. The positive impact of validation in consultation with adults was illustrated in Chapter 9 with Carol, who was convinced that her daughter was predisposed to genetic depression. The practitioner respected Carol's position and collaborated with her on developing interventions to counteract the predisposition.

Consultation is included as a separate category in this chapter for two main reasons. First, students and workshop participants often ask how solution-focused ideas can be applied in their work with teachers and parents. Second, many practitioners who work primarily with young people find it more difficult to apply these ideas with adults. For example, instead of validating and going with the flow as a teacher or parent describes the situation, the practitioner may have difficulty being patient and resisting the urge to tell him or her what to do. It is not surprising that parent and teacher consultation is more effective when we (a) work on goals that are important to the parent or teacher, (b) collaborate with him or her in developing interventions instead of imposing our ideas and interventions, and (c) provide ongoing opportunities for his or her active involvement and contributions. In other words, much of what works in counseling students seems to work in consulting with parents and teachers.

Organizational Change

Although school reform has always been a hot topic in American education, discussions over the past 2 decades have conveyed an unparalleled level of urgency. The call for schools to adopt system-level changes to effectively serve an increasingly diverse student population in an ever-changing world has never been louder.

Researchers and experts have identified the following features of successful organizational change in schools (Schmuck & Runkel, 1994): (a) identification of the goals and concerns of the people who are expected to implement the change; (b) analysis of organizational strengths and barriers related to the goal; (c) collaborative development, planning, and implementation of change strategies; (d) collaborative evaluation of outcomes and related adjustments. If these strategies sound familiar, it is because they are almost identical to the tasks of solution-focused counseling in schools.

For meaningful change to occur, the strategies of change must be presented in a way that is compatible with the goals and values of the people within the system. As with interventions in counseling, the success of organizational interventions depends largely on the input and approval of those who are expected to implement them (Hersey, Blanchard, & Johnson, 2005). In discussing organizational change in schools, Curtis and Stollar (1996) emphasized "the importance of acknowledging and building upon the existing strengths, resources, and successes of the organization" (p. 412). In addition to capitalizing on strengths and resources within the school, the goal-driven focus of organizational change helps teachers and other school personnel shift their attention from past problems to future possibilities. All of these features speak to the relevance and promise of a solution-focused approach to organizational change in schools.

Referral Forms

In most schools, the first step in requesting counseling services is to complete a referral form. Although forms vary from school to school, most require a description of the problem, relevant background information, and attempts to resolve the problem. Forms can be very helpful in orienting the practitioner to the problem and providing related information.

Some practitioners have revised the referral forms at their school to reflect a solution-focused emphasis on strengths, exceptions, and other resources. Many times, solution-focused items are simply added to existing forms to supplement problem-related information and prompt ideas for exception- or resource-based interventions. Appendix I provides sample items from a referral form that I have used with teachers, parents, and students in a behavior intervention project. This form has been helpful in alerting me to a variety of resources and solution opportunities before I ever meet with the child, parent, or teacher.

Video Self-Modeling

Video self-modeling is a unique application of building on exceptions in which a student learns productive behavior by observing himself or herself engaged in positive behavior on edited videotapes. Self-modeling is based on the well-established principle of modeling, which states that people are more likely to perform a desired target behavior if they have previously observed someone else performing that behavior (Bandura, 1977). Modeling effects are most powerful when the observer and model share similar characteristics. Self-modeling makes optimal use of this principle by employing the most powerful model of all—oneself.

Self-modeling typically involves the following steps: (a) Videotape the student; (b) edit out all problem behavior to create a self-modeling video, a 2- to 5-minute seamless display of positive behaviors ("video exceptions"); and (c) have the student watch the tape four or five separate times over a 2-week period. Allowing students to see themselves behaving well is a unique and empowering way to help them improve school behavior. Video self-modeling has been effective in improving communication skills (Murphy & Davis, 2005), classroom conduct (Kehle, Clark, Jenson, & Wampold, 1986), social skills (Savina & Murphy, 2007), and many other school-related behaviors (Hitchcock, Dowrick, & Prater, 2003). Students who are referred for services generally do not receive a lot of positive feedback about their school behavior. Some may wonder whether they are doing anything right at school. Self-modeling provides indisputable, empowering evidence of their ability to behave productively at school.

The technological requirements of self-modeling make it impractical for some practitioners and some settings. However, as video technology and equipment become more user friendly and accessible, self-modeling holds great promise as a positive intervention for a variety of school problems from preschool through high school. Appendix J provides a practical handout on self-modeling for school personnel, including basic instructions for creating self-modeling videotapes.

These are just a few examples of how change-focused research and principles can be applied in schools beyond counseling for individual problems. This book is more than a set of techniques for changing school problems—it is a whole new way of thinking about people, problems, and schools. As people become more familiar with the research on what works in helping people change, I believe that this way of thinking will become even more prevalent in schools of the 21st century.

Above Anything Else, It's All About the Client

People are generally better persuaded by the reasons which they have them-selves discovered than by those which have come into the minds of others.
—Blaise Pascal

A summary of this book in one phrase is, It's all about the client. Everything we do in counseling should be driven by the client's goals, perceptions, resources, and feedback. Counseling models and techniques can be very seductive, reaching cultlike status among their followers. Certain methods may work well with most clients. However, we should never become so attached to a technique that we fail to see the person in front of us. The techniques in this book are no exception. Although they are logically derived from research findings, they should never take precedence over the perceptions and feedback of the client.

Students, teachers, and parents know themselves and their circumstances better than we ever will. However, it is easy to lose sight of this in the midst of an overwhelming school problem. As illustrated in this book, creative and effective solutions emerge when clients are cast as the heroes of change and occupy center stage throughout the counseling process.

There is much to be optimistic about. We know more now than we ever have about what works in helping people change. I encourage you to put clients first in all your efforts to help them change.

References

American Psychiatric Association. (1952). *Diagnostic and statistical manual of mental disorders.* Washington, DC: Author.

American Psychiatric Association. (2000). *Diagnostic and statistical manual of mental disorders* (4th ed., text rev.). Washington, DC: Author.

Anderson, H., & Goolishian, H. (1992). The client is the expert: A not-knowing approach to therapy. In S. McNamee & K. J. Gergen (Eds.), *Therapy as a social construction* (pp. 25–39). London: Sage.

Asay, T. P., & Lambert, M. J. (1999). The empirical case for the common factors in therapy: Quantitative findings. In M. A. Hubble, B. L. Duncan, & S. D. Miller (Eds.), *The heart and soul of change: What works in therapy* (pp. 33–56). Washington, DC: American Psychological Association.

Bachelor, A., & Horvath, A. (1999). The therapeutic relationship. In M. A. Hubble, B. L. Duncan, & S. D. Miller (Eds.), *The heart and soul of change: What works in therapy* (pp. 133–178). Washington, DC: American Psychological Association.

Bandura, A. (1977). *Social learning theory.* New York: General Learning Press.

Bandura, A. (2006). Toward a psychology of human agency. *Perspectives on Psychological Science, 1,* 164–180.

Barlow, D. H., Hayes, S. C., & Nelson, R. O. (1999). *The scientist-practitioner: Research and accountability in the age of managed care* (2nd ed.). Boston: Allyn & Bacon.

Bedi, R. P., Davis, M. D., & Williams, M. (2005). Critical incidents in the formation of the therapeutic alliance from the clients' perspective. *Psychotherapy: Theory, Research, Practice, Training, 42,* 311–323.

Bell, S., Coleman, J., Anderson, A., Whelan, J., & Wilder, C. (2000). The effectiveness of peer mediation in a low-SES rural elementary school. *Psychology in the Schools, 37,* 505–516.

Berg, I. K. (1991). *Family preservation: A brief therapy workbook.* London: Brief Therapy Press.

Berg, I. K., & de Shazer, S. (1993). Making numbers talk: Language in therapy. In S. Friedman (Ed.), *The new language of change* (pp. 5–24). New York: Guilford Press.

Berg, I. K., & Shilts, L. (2004). *Classroom solutions: WOWW approach.* Milwaukee, WI: Brief Family Therapy Center.

Berg, I. K., & Steiner, T. (2003). *Children's solution work.* New York: Norton.

Blatt, S. J., Zuroff, D. C., Quinlan, D. M., & Pilkonis, P. (1996). Interpersonal factors in brief treatment of depression: Further analyses of the NIMH Treatment of Depression Collaborative Research Program. *Journal of Consulting and Clinical Psychology, 64,* 162–171.

Bohart, A. C. (2006). The active client. In J. C. Norcross, L. E. Beutler, & R. Levant (Eds.), *Evidence-based practices in mental health: Debate and dialogue on the fundamental questions* (pp. 218–226). Washington, DC: American Psychological Association.

Bohart, A. C., & Tallman, K. (1999). *How clients make therapy work: The process of active self-healing.* Washington, DC: American Psychological Association.

Boyd-Franklin, N. (2003). *Black families in therapy: Understanding the African-American experience.* New York: Guilford Press.

Brown, J., Dreis, S., & Nace, D. K. (1999). What really makes a difference in psychotherapy outcome? Why does managed care want to know? In M. A. Hubble, B. L. Duncan, & S. D. Miller (Eds.), *The heart and soul of change: What works in therapy* (pp. 389–406). Washington, DC: American Psychological Association.

Bruner, E. (1986). Ethnograpy as narrative. In V. Turner & E. Bruner (Eds.), *The anthropology of experience* (pp. 139–155). Chicago: University of Illinois Press.

Bruner, J. (1987). Life as narrative. *Social Research, 54,* 11–32.

Castonguay, L. G., Goldfried, M. R., Wiser, S., Raue, P. J., & Hayes, A. M. (1996). Predicting the effect of cognitive therapy for depression: A study of unique and common factors. *Journal of Consulting and Clinical Psychology, 64,* 497–504.

Curtis, M. J., & Stollar, S. (1996). Applying principles and practices of organizational change to school reform. *School Psychology Review, 23,* 409–417.

Dempsey, I., & Dunst, C. J. (2004). Help-giving styles as a function of parent empowerment in families with a young child with a disability. *Journal of Intellectual and Developmental Disability, 29,* 50–61.

de Shazer, S. (1985). *Keys to solution in brief therapy.* New York: Norton.

de Shazer, S. (1988). *Clues: Investigating solutions in brief therapy.* New York: Norton.

de Shazer, S. (1991). *Putting difference to work.* New York: Norton.

de Shazer, S., Berg, I., Lipchik, E., Nunnally, E., Molnar, A., Gingerick, W., & Weiner-Davis, M. (1986). Brief therapy: Focused solution development. *Family Process, 25,* 207–222.

de Shazer, S., Dolan, Y., Korman, H., Trepper, T., McCollum, E., & Berg, I. K. (2007). *More than miracles: The state of the art of solution-focused brief therapy.* New York: Haworth Press.

Doll, B., Zucker, S., & Brehm, K. (2004). *Resilient classrooms: Creating healthy environments for learning.* New York: Guilford Press.

Duncan, B., Miller, S., Huggins, A., & Sparks, J. (2003a). *Young Child Outcome Rating Scale.* Chicago: Author.

Duncan, B., Miller, S., Huggins, A., & Sparks, J. (2003b). *Young Child Session Rating Scale*. Chicago: Author.

Duncan, B., Miller, S., & Sparks, J. (2003). *Child Outcome Rating Scale*. Chicago: Author.

Duncan, B., Miller, S., & Sparks, J. (2004). *The heroic client: A radical way to improve effectiveness through client-directed, outcome-informed therapy*. San Francisco: Jossey-Bass.

Duncan, B. L., Miller, S. D., Sparks, J. A., Claud, D. A., Reynolds, L. R., Brown, J., & Johnson, L. D. (2003). The Session Rating Scale: Psychometric properties of a "working" alliance. *Journal of Brief Therapy, 3,* 3–12.

Duncan, B. L., Miller, S. D., Sparks, J. A., & Johnson, L. D. (2003). *Child Session Rating Scale*. Ft. Lauderdale, FL: Author.

Duncan, B. L., Sparks, J. A., Miller, S. D., Bohanske, R., & Claud, D. A. (in press). Giving youth a voice: A preliminary study of the reliability and validity of a brief outcome measure for children, adolescents, and caretakers. *Journal of Brief Therapy*.

Dunst, C. J., Boyd, K., Trivette, C. M., & Hamby, D. W. (2002). Family-oriented program models and professional helpgiving practices. *Family Relations, 51,* 221–229.

DuPaul, G. J., & Henningson, P. N. (1993). Peer tutoring effects on the classroom performance of children with attention deficit and hyperactivity disorder. *School Psychology Review, 22,* 134–143.

Durrant, M. (1995). *Creative strategies for school problems*. New York: Norton.

Dweck, C. S., & Leggett, E. L. (1988). A social–cognitive approach to motivation and personality. *Psychological Review, 95,* 256–273.

Egan, G. (2007). *The skilled helper: A problem-management and opportunity-development approach to helping* (8th ed.). Pacific Grove, CA: Brooks/Cole.

Epstein, M. H. (2004). *The Behavioral and Emotional Rating Scale-2: A strength-based approach to assessment*. Austin, TX: PRO-ED.

Erickson, M. H. (1954). Pseudo-orientation in time as a hypnotic procedure. *Journal of Clinical and Experimental Hypnosis, 2,* 161–283.

Erickson, M., & Rossi, E. (1979). *Hypnotherapy: An exploratory casebook*. New York: Irvington.

Evans, D. R., Hearn, M. T., Uhlemann, M. R., & Ivey, A. E. (2008). *Essential interviewing* (7th ed.). Belmont, CA: Brooks/Cole.

Fisch, R., & Schlanger, K. (1999). *Brief therapy with intimidating cases: Changing the unchangeable*. San Francisco: Jossey-Bass.

Fisch, R., Weakland, J. H., & Segal, L. (1982). *The tactics of change: Doing therapy briefly*. San Francisco: Jossey-Bass.

Franca, V. M., Kerr, M. M., Reitz, A. L., & Lambert, D. (1990). Peer tutoring among behaviorally disordered students: Academic and social benefits to tutor and tutee. *Education and Treatment of Children, 13,* 109–128.

Frank, J. D., & Frank, J. B. (1991). *Persuasion and healing* (3rd ed.). Baltimore: Johns Hopkins University Press.

Frankl, V. E. (1959). *Man's search for meaning.* New York: Beacon Press.

Freiberg, H. J. (Ed.). (1999). *School climate: Measuring, improving, and sustaining learning environments.* Philadelphia: Falmer Press.

Friedman, E. H. (1990). *Friedman's fables.* New York: Guilford Press.

Gelso, C. J., & Hayes, J. A. (1998). *The psychotherapy relationship: Theory, research, and practice.* New York: Wiley.

Gergen, K., & Gergen, M. (Eds.). (2003). *Social construction: A reader.* London: Sage.

Ginsburg-Block, M., Rohrbeck, C., & Fantuzzo, J. (2006). Peer-assisted learning strategies. In G. G. Bear & K. M. Minke (Eds.), *Children's needs: Vol. 3. Development, prevention, and intervention* (pp. 631–645). Bethesda, MD: National Association of School Psychologists.

Goldstein, A. P., & Martens, B. K. (2000). *Lasting change: Methods for enhancing generalization of gain.* Champaign, IL: Research Press.

Goldstein, S., & Brooks, R. B. (2007). *Understanding and managing children's classroom behavior: Creating sustainable, resilient classrooms.* New York: Wiley.

Greenberg, R. P., Bornstein, R. F., Greenberg, M. D., & Fisher, S. (1992). A meta-analysis of antidepressant outcome under "blinder" conditions. *Journal of Consulting and Clinical Psychology, 60,* 664–669.

Haas, E., Hill, R. D., Lambert, M. J., & Morrell, B. (2002). Do early responders to psychotherapy maintain treatment gains? *Journal of Clinical Psychology, 58,* 1157–1172.

Haley, J. (1973). *Uncommon therapy: The psychiatric techniques of Milton H. Erickson, M.D.* New York: Norton.

Haley, J. (Ed.). (1985). *Conversations with Milton H. Erickson, M.D.: Vol. 3. Changing children and families.* New York: Triangle Press.

Hansen, N. B., & Lambert, M. J. (2003). An evaluation of the dose-response relationship in naturalistic treatment settings using survival analysis. *Mental Health Services Research, 5,* 1–12.

Harris, A. H. S., Thoresen, C. E., & Lopez, S. J. (2007). Integrating positive psychology into counseling: Why and (when appropriate) how. *Journal of Counseling & Development, 85,* 3–13.

Hayes, S. C., Follette, V. M., & Linehan, M. M. (2004). *Mindfulness and acceptance.* New York: Guilford Press.

Hersey, P., Blanchard, K. H., & Johnson, D. E. (2005). *Management of organizational behavior* (8th ed.). Upper Saddle River, NJ: Prentice-Hall.

Hitchcock, C. H., Dowrick, P. W., & Prater, M. A. (2003). Video self-modeling intervention in school-based settings. *Remedial and Special Education, 24,* 36–45.

Johnson, L. D., Miller, S. D., & Duncan, B. L. (2000). *Session Rating Scale 3.0.* Chicago: Author.

Karver, M. S., Handelsman, J. B., Fields, S., & Bickman, L. (2006). Meta-analysis of therapeutic relationship variables in youth and family therapy: The evidence for different relationship variables in the child and adolescent treatment outcome literature. *Clinical Psychology Review, 26,* 50–65.

Kazdin, A. E. (1980). Acceptability of alternative treatments for deviant child behavior. *Journal of Applied Behavior Analysis, 13,* 259–273.

Kazdin, A. E. (2004). Psychotherapy for children and adolescents. In M. J. Lambert (Ed.), *Bergin and Garfield's handbook of psychotherapy and behavior change* (5th ed., pp. 543–589). New York: Wiley.

Kazdin, A. E., Marciano, P. L., & Whitley, M. K. (2005). The therapeutic alliance in cognitive–behavioral treatment of children referred for oppositional, aggressive, and antisocial behavior. *Journal of Consulting and Clinical Psychology, 73,* 726–730.

Kazdin, A. E., & Weisz, J. R. (Eds.). (2003). *Evidence-based psychotherapies for children and adolescents.* New York: Guilford Press.

Kehle, T. J., Clark, E., Jenson, W. R., & Wampold, B. E. (1986). Effectiveness of self-observation with behavior disordered elementary school children. *School Psychology Review, 15,* 298–295.

Khan, A., Kolts, R. L., Rapaport, M. H., Krishnan, K. R., Brodhead, A. E., & Brown, W. A. (2005). Magnitude of placebo response and drug-placebo differences across psychiatric disorders. *Psychological Medicine, 35,* 743–749.

Kohut, H. (1980). Reflections. In A. Goldberg (Ed.), *Advances in self psychology* (pp. 473–554). New York: International Universities Press.

Kourea, L., Cartledge, G., & Musti-Rao, S. (2007). Improving the reading skills of urban elementary students through total class peer tutoring. *Remedial and Special Education, 28,* 95–107.

Kral, R. (1988). *Solution Identification Scale.* Milwaukee, WI: Brief Family Therapy Center.

Krupnick, J. L., Sotsky, S., Moyer, J., Elkin, I., Watkins, J. T., & Pilkonis, P. A. (1996). The role of the therapeutic alliance in psychotherapy and pharmacotherapy outcome: Findings in the National Institute of Mental Health Treatment of Depression Collaborative Research Program. *Journal of Consulting and Clinical Psychology, 64,* 532–539.

Lambert, M. J., Burlingame, G. M., Umphress, V., Hansen, N. B., Vermeersch, D. A., Clouse, G. C., & Yanchar, S. C. (1996). The reliability and validity of the Outcome Questionnaire. *Clinical Psychology and Psychotherapy, 3,* 249–258.

Lambert, M. J., & Ogles, B. (2004). The efficacy and effectiveness of psychotherapy. In M. J. Lambert (Ed.), *Bergin and Garfield's handbook of psychotherapy and behavior change* (5th ed., pp. 39–193). New York: Wiley.

Lambert, M. J., Whipple, J. L., Hawkins, E. J., Vermeersch, D. A., Nielsen, S. L., & Smart, D. W. (2003). Is it time for clinicians routinely to track patient outcome? A meta-analysis. *Clinical Psychology, 10,* 288–301.

Lambert, M. J., Whipple, J., Smart, D., Vermeersch, D., Nielsen, S., & Hawkins, E. (2001). The effects of providing therapists with feedback on patient progress during psychotherapy: Are outcomes enhanced? *Psychotherapy Research, 11,* 49–68.

Lawson, D. (1994). Identifying pretreatment change. *Journal of Counseling & Development, 72,* 244–248.

Lewis, B. A., & Pucelik, F. (1982). *Magic demystified: Pragmatic guide to communication and change.* Portland, OR: Metamorphous Press.

Linssen, F., & Kerzbeck, U. (2002, September). *Does solution-focused therapy work?* Paper presented at the meeting of the European Brief Therapy Association, Cardiff, Wales.

Locke, E. A., & Latham, G. P. (1990). *A theory of goal setting and task performance.* Englewood Cliffs, NJ: Prentice-Hall.

Luthar, S. S. (Ed.). (2003). *Resilience and vulnerability: Adaptation in the context of childhood adversities.* New York: Cambridge University Press.

Martin, D. J., Garske, J. P., & Davis, M. K. (2000). Relation of the therapeutic alliance with outcome and other variables: A meta-analytic review. *Journal of Consulting and Clinical Psychology, 68,* 438–450.

Mautone, J. (2005). The relationship between treatment integrity and treatment acceptability across two consultation models. *Dissertation Abstracts International, 66B,* 1704.

Mayall, B. (1999). Children and childhood. In S. Hood, B. Mayall, & S. Oliver (Eds.), *Critical issues in social research: Power and prejudice* (pp. 10–24). Philadelphia: Open University Press.

Mayall, B. (2002). *The sociology of childhood.* Philadelphia: Open University Press.

McDonald, A. (2007). *Solution-focused therapy: Theory, research, and practice.* London: Sage.

Metcalf, L. (1995). *Counseling toward solutions.* New York: Center for Applied Research in Education.

Miller, S., & Duncan, B. (2000). *Outcome Rating Scale.* Chicago: Author.

Miller, S. D., Duncan, B. L., Brown, J., Sorrell, R., & Chalk, M. B. (2006). Using outcome to inform and improve treatment outcomes. *Journal of Brief Therapy, 5,* 26–36.

Miller, S. D., Duncan, B. L., Brown, J., Sparks, J., & Claud, D. (2003). The Outcome Rating Scale: A preliminary study of the reliability, validity, and feasibility of a brief visual analog measure. *Journal of Brief Therapy, 2,* 91–100.

Miller, W. R., & Rollnick, S. (2002). *Motivational interviewing: Preparing people for change.* New York: Guilford Press.

Minuchin, S. (1974). *Families and family therapy.* Cambridge, MA: Harvard University Press.

Moerman, D. E. (2002). *Meaning, medicine, and the placebo effect.* Cambridge, England: Cambridge University Press.

Molden, D. C., & Dweck, C. S. (2006). Finding "meaning" in psychology: A lay theories approach to self-regulation, social perception, and social development. *American Psychologist, 61,* 192–203.

Murphy, J. J. (1994). Working with what works: A solution-focused approach to school behavior problems. *School Counselor, 42,* 59–65.

Murphy, J. J. (1997). *Solution-focused counseling in middle and high schools.* Alexandria, VA: American Counseling Association.

Murphy, J. J. (in press). Best practices in conducting brief counseling with students. In A. Thomas & J. Grimes (Eds.), *Best practices in school psychology* (5th ed.). Bethesda, MD: National Association of School Psychologists.

Murphy, J. J., & Davis, M. W. (2005). Video exceptions: An empirical case study of self-modeling with a developmentally disabled child. *Journal of Systemic Therapies, 24,* 66–79.

Murphy, J. J., & Duncan, B. L. (1997). *Brief intervention for school problems: Collaborating for practical solutions.* New York: Guilford Press.

Murphy, J. J., & Duncan, B. L. (2007). *Brief intervention for school problems: Outcome-informed strategies* (2nd ed.). New York: Guilford Press.

Nelson, T. S., & Thomas, F. N. (Eds.). (2007). *The handbook of solution-focused brief therapy: Clinical applications.* New York: Haworth Press.

Ness, M. E., & Murphy, J. J. (2001). The effect of inquiry technique on reports of pretreatment change by clients in a university counseling center. *Journal of College Counseling, 4,* 20–31.

Newman, B. M., & Newman, P. R. (1991). *Development through life: A psychological approach.* Pacific Grove, CA: Brooks/Cole.

O'Connell, B. (2005). *Solution-focused therapy* (2nd ed.). London: Sage.

O'Hanlon, W. H., & Weiner-Davis, M. (1989). *In search of solutions: A new direction in psychotherapy.* New York: Norton.

O'Hanlon, W. H., & Wilk, J. (1987). *Shifting contexts: The generation of effective psychotherapy.* New York: Guilford Press.

Orlinsky, D. E., Rønnestad, M. H., & Willutzki, U. (2004). Fifty years of psychotherapy process-outcome research: Continuity and change. In M. J. Lambert (Ed.), *Bergin and Garfield's handbook of psychotherapy and behavior change* (5th ed., pp. 307–389). New York: Wiley.

Parsons, R. D., & Kahn, W. J. (2005). *The school counselor as consultant.* Belmont, CA: Brooks/Cole.

Pedersen, P. B. (2000). *Hidden messages in culture-centered counseling: A triad training model.* Thousand Oaks, CA: Sage.

Pianta, R. C. (1999). *Enhancing relationships between children and teachers.* Washington, DC: American Psychological Association.

Presley, J. A., & Hughes, C. (2000). Peers as teachers of anger management to high school students with behavioral disorders. *Behavioral Disorders, 25,* 114–130.

Ridley, C. R. (2005). *Overcoming unintentional racism in counseling and therapy: A practitioner's guide to intentional intervention* (2nd ed.). Thousand Oaks, CA: Sage.

Rossi, E. L. (Ed). (1980). *The collected papers of Milton Erickson.* New York: Irvington.

Rowan, T., & O'Hanlon, W. H. (1999). *Solution-oriented therapy for chronic and severe mental illness.* New York: Wiley.

Savina, E., & Murphy, J. J. (2007, March). *Effects of a self-modeling intervention on self-initiated social behaviors in a child with Down syndrome and autism.* Paper presented at the annual meeting of the National Association of School Psychologists, New York.

Schave, D., & Schave, B. (1989). *Early adolescence and the search for self: A developmental perspective.* New York: Praeger.

Schellenberg, R. C., Parks-Savage, A., & Rehfuss, M. (2007). Reducing levels of elementary school violence with peer mediation. *Professional School Counseling, 10,* 475–481.

Schmuck, R. A., & Runkel, P. J. (1994). *The handbook of organization development in schools and colleges.* Long Grove, IL: Waveland Press.

Seligman, M. E. P. (1998, January). Building human strength: Psychology's forgotten mission. *APA Monitor,* pp. 175–189. Retrieved February 13, 2003, from http://www.apa.org/monitor/jan98/pres.html

Seligman, M. E. P., Rashid, T., & Parks, A. C. (2006). Positive psychotherapy. *American Psychologist, 61,* 774–788.

Shapiro, J. P., Friedberg, R. D., & Bardenstein, K. K. (2006). *Child and adolescent therapy: Science and art.* New York: Wiley.

Shelef, K., Diamond, G. M., Diamond, G. S., & Liddle, H. A. (2005). Adolescent and parent alliance and treatment outcome in multidimensional family therapy. *Journal of Consulting and Clinical Psychology, 73,* 689–698.

Shirk, S. R., & Karver, M. (2003). Prediction of treatment outcome from relationship variables in child and adolescent therapy: A meta-analytic review. *Journal of Consulting and Clinical Psychology, 71,* 452–464.

Short, D., Erickson, B. A., & Klein, R. E. (2005). *Hope and resiliency: Understanding the psychotherapeutic strategies of Milton H. Erickson, M.D.* Norwalk, CT: Crown House.

Sigelman, C. K., & Rider, E. A. (2003). *Life-span human development* (4th ed.). Belmont, CA: Wadsworth/Thomson.

Simon, J. B., Murphy, J. J., & Smith, S. M. (2005). Understanding and fostering family resilience. *Family Journal: Counseling and Therapy for Couples and Families, 13,* 427–436.

Sleek, S. (1998, December). Psychology's cultural competence, once "simplistic," now broadening. *APA Monitor,* pp. 1, 27.

Snyder, C. R. (1995). Conceptualizing, measuring, and nurturing hope. *Journal of Counseling & Development, 73,* 355–360.

Snyder, C. R. (2002). Hope theory: Rainbows of the mind. *Psychological Inquiry, 13,* 249–275.

Snyder, C. R., Ilardi, S., Michael, S. T., & Cheavens, J. (2000). Hope theory: Updating a common process for psychological change. In C. R. Snyder & R. E. Ingram (Eds.), *Handbook of psychological change: Psychotherapy processes and practices for the 21st century* (pp. 128–153). New York: Wiley.

Snyder, C. R., & Lopez, S. J. (2007). *Positive psychology: The scientific and practical exploration of human strengths.* Thousand Oaks, CA: Sage.

Snyder, C. R., & Taylor, J. D. (2000). Hope as a common factor across psychotherapy approaches: A lesson from the dodo's verdict. In C. R. Snyder (Ed.), *Handbook of hope: Theory, measures, and applications* (pp. 89–108). San Diego, CA: Academic Press.

Stepansky, P., & Goldberg, A. (1984). *Kohut's legacy: Contributions to self psychology.* Chicago: University of Chicago Press.

Stoltz, A. D. (2006). The relationship between peer mentoring program participation and successful transition to high school. *Dissertation Abstracts International, 66A,* 2494.

Sue, D. W., & Sue, D. (2007). *Counseling the culturally diverse: Theory and practice* (5th ed.). New York: Wiley.

Tallman, K., & Bohart, A. (1999). The client as a common factor: Clients as self-healers. In M. Hubble, B. Duncan, & S. Miller (Eds.), *The heart and soul of change: What works in therapy* (pp. 91–131). Washington, DC: American Psychological Association.

Teyber, E. (2000). *Interpersonal process in psychotherapy: A relational approach* (4th ed.). Belmont, CA: Brooks/Cole.

Tollison, P. K., & Synatschk, K. O. (2007). *SOS: A practical guide for leading solution-focused groups with kids K-12.* Austin, TX: PRO-ED.

Tournaki, N., & Criscitiello, E. (2003). Using peer tutoring as a successful part of behavior management. *Teaching Exceptional Children, 36,* 22–29.

Trapani, C., & Gettinger, M. (1989). Effects of social skills training and cross-age tutoring on academic achievement and social behaviors of boys with learning disabilities. *Journal of Research and Development in Education, 22,* 1–9.

Vernon, A., & Al-Mabuk, R. H. (1995). *What growing up is all about: A parent's guide to child and adolescent development.* Champaign, IL: Research Press.

Wampold, B. E. (2001). *The great psychotherapy debate: Models, methods, and findings.* Mahwah, NJ: Erlbaum.

Wampold, B. E. (2006). Not a scintilla of evidence to support empirically supported treatments as more effective than other treatments. In J. C. Norcross, L. E. Beutler, & R. Levant (Eds.), *Evidence-based practices in mental health: Debate and dialogue on the fundamental questions* (pp. 299–308). Washington, DC: American Psychological Association.

Watzlawick, P., Weakland, J., & Fisch, R. (1974). *Change: Principles of problem formation and problem resolution.* New York: Norton.

Weiner-Davis, M., de Shazer, S., & Gingerich, W. (1987). Using pretreatment change to construct a therapeutic solution: An exploratory study. *Journal of Marital and Family Therapy, 13,* 359–363.

Whipple, J. L., Lambert, M. J., Vermeersch, D. A., Smart, D. W., Nielsen, S. L., & Hawkins, E. J. (2003). Improving the effects of psychotherapy: The use of early identification of treatment and problem-solving strategies in routine practice. *Journal of Counseling Psychology, 50,* 59–68.

White, M., & Epston, D. (1990). *Narrative means to therapeutic ends.* New York: Norton.

References

Witt, J. C., & Elliot, S. N. (1985). Acceptability of classroom management strategies. In T. R. Kratochwill (Ed.), *Advances in school psychology* (Vol. 4, pp. 251–288). Hillsdale, NJ: Erlbaum.

Wolin, S., Desetta, A., & Hefner, K. (2000). *A leader's guide to the struggle to be strong: How to foster resilience in teens.* Minneapolis, MN: Free Spirit.

Zins, J. E., Weissberg, R. P., Wang, M. C., & Wahlberg, H. J. (Eds.). (2004). *Building academic success on social and emotional learning.* New York: Teachers College Press.

Client Index

Although some clients are discussed in several places, this lists the page where they first appear with a brief description.

Alia (*Alia: An Example of Accommodating the Client's Theory of Change*), p. 74
    Ninth grader referred for disruptive classroom behavior; said counselor "couldn't make her talk"; counselor agreed and worked within Alia's theory of change to develop new strategies for approaching school
Andre, p. 61
    Seventh grader referred for truancy; counselor used the language of presupposition to explore small changes; attendance increased
Andrew, p. 93
    Middle school student; wanted to be a better student; the counselor asked for a videotalk description of being a better student to develop a more specific and measurable goal
Angela (*When Less Is More*), p. 168
    Seventh-grade student; complained to teachers, counselor, and principal about other students bothering her; the counselor acknowledged her concerns and scheduled discussion times with her
Anthony (*Mrs. T, the Sunday School Teacher*), p. 143
    Six-year-old referred for "giving the finger" to other students and adults; the couselor enlisted the involvement of a highly respected, influential person in Anthony's life
Billy (*A Musical Solution*), p. 164
    Four-year-old preschool student referred for cursing at school; teacher (Jan) and assistant (Carmen) attempted many unsuccessful solutions before trying something very different and unconventional
Bridgette (*Dorothy's Advice*), p. 150
    Ninth grader referred for "mouthing off" and minimal work completion; the counselor utilized Bridgette's interest in old movies to encourage a different approach to school challenges
Brittany (*Brittany: The Benefits of Listening and "Not Knowing"*), p. 52
    Twelfth-grade student; prior sexual abuse; practitioner listened from a position of not knowing rather than telling Brittany what to do

Bruce (*How Can You Mend a Broken Heart?*), p. 166

Eighteen-year-old; agitated about recent breakup with girlfriend; "couldn't stop" thinking about it; scheduled "think times" to give the problem its due

Carol and Sarina (*A Nurturing Solution*), p. 187

Nine-year-old student (Sarina) and parent (Carol); parent insisted that daughter was prone to genetic depression; the counselor accepted Carol's theory and framed suggestions accordingly

Cassie, p. 163

Sixteen-year-old; had recently moved to a new city; concerned about depression and sleeping too much; agreed to give depression its due instead of trying to avoid it

Cheryl, p. 164

Ninth-grade teacher bothered by student's incessant criticism; changed from defending herself to agreeing with and exaggerating the student's criticism

Christina, p. 99

Twelve-year-old; counselor used scaling strategies to explore what it would look like when things were a little better for Christina at school

Claire (*Client and Relationship Factors in Action: Claire*), p. 12

Fifteen-year-old complaining of "constant bickering" with her father; counselor enlisted Claire as active collaborator and utilized exceptions to the problem to build a solution

Clint, p. 64

Twelve-year-old; practitioner listened to Clint's exact words to learn about his theory of change

Daniel, p. 102

Fifth-grade student; counselor followed up on the miracle question to encourage effective goals consistent with the 5-S guideline of goal development

David, p. 100

Six-year-old; the counselor used wooden blocks as a scaling technique to help David describe what needed to happen for him to move up to the next block

Diora (*Example of Solution-Focused Therapy: Growing Solutions From Small Seeds of Success*), p. 39

Ninth grader referred by parents for arguing; the counselor utilized student's and mother's common interest in gardening to improve their relationship and decrease arguments

Dwayne (*Consulting Camus*), p. 152

Twelfth-grade student; had not completed graduation requirements; the counselor encouraged the student to consider what his hero would advise him to do

Elise, p. 51

Fourth-grade teacher with a track record of success with difficult students; embarrassed about "losing it" with a student; practitioner validated her frustration

Emma, p. 22

Preschool student with classroom behavior problems; teacher utilized Emma's interests in singing and dinosaurs to develop a simple intervention

Gary (*Keeping It Simple*), p. 95

Fifth grader referred by mother (Brenda) for peer problems and classroom misbehavior; Brenda suggested small changes (combing hair, tucking in shirt), which led to bigger changes (fewer discipline problems)

Group application (*The Test Anxiety Group*), p. 134

Five high school students complaining of test anxiety; integrated solution-focused techniques with skill-building activities

Jane (*Desperate and Developmental*), p. 183

Tenth-grade student; declining grades, shame, and depression about "nasty" phone behavior; scared of going crazy; the counselor offered a normalizing, developmental perspective

Jason, p. 34

Second-grade student; everyone was stuck in a vicious cycle of more of the same; the practitioner suggested that the teacher and parents "try something different" to break up the problem pattern

Jeff (*The Exceptional Quarter*), p. 131

Fourth grader referred for "behavior disability" assessment because of talking out, oppositional behavior, and peer difficulties; the counselor encouraged Jeff to do more of what worked during the second quarter of school year

Jessica (*A Wake-Up Call From the Unconscious*), p. 179

Eleventh-grade student; was having nightmares, loss of concentration; the counselor suggested that nightmares might be an unconscious reminder to acknowledge her personal growth and progress

Joe (*Example of Brief Strategic Therapy: Tripping the Responsibility Trap*), p. 36

Third-grade student; low grades and minimal homework completion; parents' attempted solutions were perpetuating the problem; parents stopped nagging and held Joe responsible for schoolwork

Joel (*The Student For Whom Nothing Was Going Right*), p. 136

Tenth-grade student in advanced classes who complained of depression, declining grades, family conflicts; the counselor invited Joel to list aspects of his life that he wanted to continue

Jolene (*Jolene: An Introduction to Solution-Focused Counseling*), p. 3

High school student with academic and behavior problems; the first counselor tried "more of the same" lectures to no avail; the second counselor accepted Jolene's position and encouraged her to build on previously successful strategies

Kristy, p. 94

Ninth-grade student; hoped to raise her math grade from an F to a B; the counselor encouraged her to focus on small steps to promote a smaller and more manageable initial goal

Kyle, p. 194

Eighth-grade student; the counselor collaborated with Kyle to end counseling while leaving the door open for future contact

Maria, p. 175

Twelve-year-old student referred for classroom behavior problems; the counselor changed the viewing of the problem by asking Maria how long she was willing to sacrifice her freedom to entertain peers

Mario (*Mario and the Meaningful Goal*), p. 91
 Tenth-grade student; thought principal and teachers were "out to get him"; the counselor renegotiated a goal that was relevant and meaningful to Mario

Molly (*The Pillow Brigade*), p. 146
 Ten-year-old; referred by mother for nightmares, anxiety, and school avoidance; contributed useful intervention ideas; urged helping professionals to ask clients for their ideas and opinions

Monica, p. 160
 Thirteen-year-old; referred by parents for frequent arguments; assigned the Do Something Different Task

Ms. Brock, p. 65
 Third-grade teacher requesting help with difficult student; the first counselor criticized Ms. Brock and tried to talk her out of her perceptions; the second counselor validated and accommodated her perceptions

Nick, p. 162
 Tenth-grade student who complained of insomnia; tried various ways to fall asleep at night; the counselor recommended that he observe the problem without trying to change it

Paul (*Example of Erickson's Approach: The Student Who Refused to Read*), p. 33
 Twelve-year-old who refused to read; practitioner (Erickson) accepted Paul's choice not to read, and they "looked at" maps instead of "reading" them

Reggie (*Standing Up to Stealing*), p. 176
 Seven-year-old referred for stealing; renamed the problem as an oppressive bully (Bruiser) who pushed Reggie into trouble at school; encouraged Reggie to take a stand against Bruiser and reclaim control of his behavior

Rosa (*Rosa: Why Haven't You Given Up?*), p. 109
 Seventeen-year-old; failing two classes, erratic attendance, challenging home life; the counselor explored Rosa's resilience and coping skills by asking how she managed to "hang in there" and not give up

Roy (*Sweeping the Sidewalk Twice*), p. 148
 Eighth-grade student; failing grades, cursing, and minimal homework completion; encouraged to apply effective lawn-mowing skills and attitudes to schoolwork

Sam (*The Monday Morning Exception*), p. 125
 Nine-year-old referred for noncompliance and diagnosed with oppositional defiant disorder; had a better day after helping his teacher in the morning; the teacher allowed Sam to help out more at school

Schoolwide application (*Success Stories: A Schoolwide Program for Recognizing Resilience and Resources*); *Michelle*, p. 154
 Third-grade student; improved her grade average from D to B; the counselor explored how she did it and what advice she had for other students

Sharon, p. 96
 High school student; did not get along with teachers; the practitioner helped Sharon focus on a self-manageable goal that was within her control

Stacy, p. 59

High school student; said school needed new teachers; the counselor used the language of empowerment to shift Stacy's focus to personal goals and related actions

Steve (*Pervert or Protector?*), p. 185

Sixth-grade student; made obscene remarks and gestures to a teacher; the counselor invited student and grandparents to consider a more positive function of the problem behavior

Ted, p. 117

Sixth-grade science teacher; requested help in managing classroom behavior; identified and expanded exceptions to problem behavior

Terrence, p. 123

Fifth-grade student; made steady behavioral improvements at school; assisted counselor in planning and conducting discussions with younger students about school behavior

William (*To Skip or Not to Skip, That Is the Question*), p. 168

Twelfth-grade student; skipped school, in jeopardy of not graduating; the counselor explored the "disadvantages" of attending school

Zach (*Giving Them What They Want*), p. 180

Seventeen-year-old referred for defiant school behavior; the counselor asked whether defiant behavior represented giving in to the teachers and principal

The Nine-Dot Problem and Solution

Part One: The Nine-Dot Problem

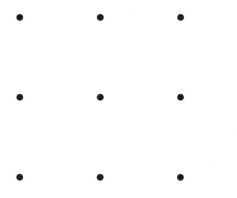

Instructions: The nine dots in this puzzle can be connected using only four straight lines, drawn without lifting your pencil off the paper. After trying to solve it for a few minutes, turn to the next page for the solution.

Part 2: The Nine-Dot Solution

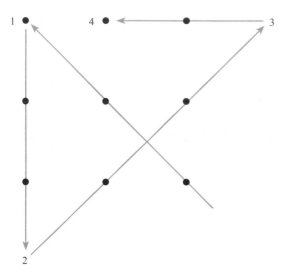

Very few people think of extending the straight lines beyond the dots, even though nothing about the task or the instructions prohibits doing so. Most people super-impose an imaginary square on the dots. The arbitrary assumption that the lines cannot extend beyond the dots leads to "more of the same" solution attempts, despite their ineffectivness in solving the problem. The belief that this is the only reasonable or sensible way to approach the problem inevitably leads to failure and frustration, the same two outcomes that befall students, teachers, parents, and counselors who are stuck in a pattern of applying more of the same ineffective strategies to a school problem.

You might have quickly recognized after just one or two tries that a solution to the puzzle was impossible yet continued to apply the same solution over and over again. You probably varied specific aspects of your solution attempt, such as the speed or intensity in which you applied it. However, the general theme of the solution remained the same on the basis of the assumption that you needed to stay within the square. In situations in which people's attempts to resolve a school problem actually perpetuate it, effective solutions often emerge when counselors and clients step outside the box and try something different.

Note. From *Change: Principles of Problem Formation and Problem Resolution* by Paul Watzlawick, John Weakland, and Richard Fisch, New York: W. W. Norton. Copyright © 1974 by W. W. Norton & Company, Inc. Used by permission of W. W. Norton & Company, Inc.

Outcome and Session Rating Scales

This appendix displays the outcome and session rating scales used to monitor client perceptions of outcome and alliance throughout the counseling process. These scales are for illustration purposes only. The actual scales, which include 10-centimeter lines for each item, are free for individual use and may be downloaded from www.talkingcure.com.

Outcome Rating Scale

Name: _____ Age: _____ Session #: _____ Date: _____

Looking back over the last week, including today, help us understand how you have been feeling by rating how well you have been doing in the following areas of your life, where marks to the left represent low levels and marks to the right indicate high levels.

Examination Copy

Individually
(Personal well-being)

|———————————————————————————————|

Interpersonally
(Family, close relationships)

|———————————————————————————————|

Socially
(Work, school, friendships)

|———————————————————————————————|

Overall
(General well-being)

|———————————————————————————————|

Child Outcome Rating Scale

Name: _____ Age: _____ Session #: _____ Date: _____

How are you doing? How are things going in your life? Please make a mark on the scale to let us know. The closer the smiley face, the better things are. The closer the frowny face, things are not so good.

Examination Copy

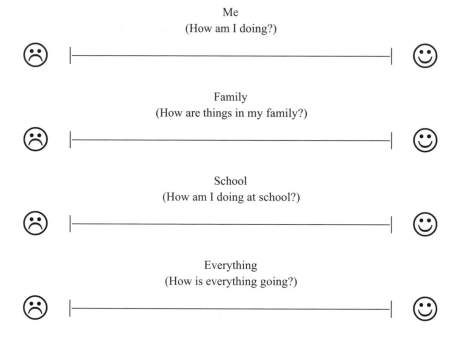

Me
(How am I doing?)

Family
(How are things in my family?)

School
(How am I doing at school?)

Everything
(How is everything going?)

Young Child Outcome Rating Scale

Name: _____ Age: _____ Session #: _____ Date: _____

Choose one of the faces that show how things are going for you. Or, you can draw one below that is just right for you.

Examination Copy

Session Rating Scale (Version 3.0)

Name: _____ Age: _____ Session #: _____ Date: _____

Please rate today's session by placing a hash mark on the line nearest to the description that best fits your experience.

Examination Copy

Relationship

| I did not feel heard, understood, and respected. | |———————————————————| | I felt heard, understood, and respected. |

Goals and Topics

We did not work on or talk about what I wanted to work on or talk about. |———————————————————| We worked on and talked about what I wanted to work on and talk about.

Approach or Method

The therapist's approach is not a good fit for me. |———————————————————| The therapist's approach is a good fit for me.

Overall

There was something missing in the session today. |———————————————————| Overall, today's session was right for me.

Child Session Rating Scale

Name: _____ Age: _____ Session #: _____ Date: _____

How was our time together today? Please put a mark on the lines below to let us know how you feel.

Examination Copy

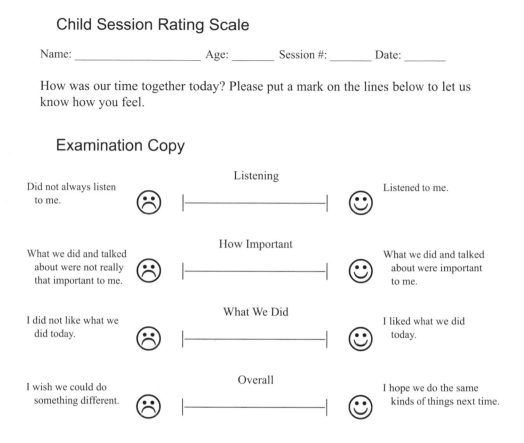

Young Child Session Rating Scale

Name: _____ Age: _____ Session #: _____ Date: _____

Choose one of the faces that shows how it was for you to be here today. Or, you can draw one below that is just right for you.

Examination Copy

Note. All measures are used by permission of the Institute for the Study of Therapeutic Change (www.talkingcure.com).

Outcome Management in Schools: Guidelines and Examples

Client involvement is the centerpiece of successful counseling. One of the surest ways to give students, parents, and teachers an ongoing voice in the change process is to integrate outcome management into everyday practice. Outcome management requires counselors to (a) obtain client feedback on outcome and alliance and (b) use client feedback to guide the counseling process—that is, to continue to do what is working and change what is not working. Outcome management ensures accountable, consumer-driven services as well as legitimizing services to clients, supervisors, regulatory agencies, insurance companies, and other interested parties. Other reasons to do this include the following:

- Given that most change occurs early in counseling, we need to assess the client's perception of change (outcome) from the very beginning of counseling and make adjustments when they report no progress.
- Given that the clients' perception of the alliance is the best predictor of success, we need to know how they view us and our services and make adjustments on the basis of their feedback.

Partnering with clients to monitor alliance and outcomes begins with an attitude that values the client's perceptions and shows faith in his or her ability to improve.

Monitoring Outcome and Alliance Using the Outcome Rating Scale (ORS) and Session Rating Scale (SRS)

Two quick and reliable instruments are used to formally monitor the client's perceptions of outcome and alliance—the ORS and SRS. Each scale takes about 1 minute to administer in most situations. Child versions of each measure are available for children 12 years and younger (see Appendix C for all measures). All of these instruments are free for individual use from www.talkingcure.com.

ORS

The ORS is administered at the beginning of (or just before) every session to assess the client's perception of (a) individual (personal) well-being; (b) interpersonal well-being (family, intimate relationships); (c) social satisfaction with work, school, and peers; and (d) overall well-being—all valid indicators of successful outcomes (Lambert et al., 1996). Clients rate each dimension by making a mark along a 10-centimeter line, and the total score is the sum of the client's four marks to the nearest millimeter, measured by a centimeter ruler or 10-centimeter template. The highest possible score is 40, and most people who enter scores in the 20s or below are experiencing noticeable distress.

SRS

The SRS is completed at the end of every session to assess the client's perception of the counselor and the meeting in regard to (a) relationship and respect, (b) goals and topics, (c) approach or method, and (d) overall effectiveness—all valid predictors of successful outcomes. As with the ORS, one scores the SRS by adding the total of the client's marks on the four 10-centimeter lines (0–34 = poor alliance, 35–38 = fair alliance, 39–40 = strong alliance). The major reason for using the SRS is not to "score high" but to detect any emerging alliance problems and correct them as soon as possible. Low scores should be welcomed and discussed with clients in a candid, nondefensive way.

Introducing the ORS (or Child Outcome Rating Scale/ Young Child Outcome Rating Scale) at the First Meeting

To an older client, parent, or teacher:

> As I mentioned when we spoke on the phone last week, I will be asking you to complete two forms about how you think things are going out there and in our meetings. To make the most of our time together and get the best outcome, we need to make sure we're on the same page about how you are doing and how our meetings are working. Your answers will help us stay on track. Will that be ok with you?

To a younger client:

> Here is that paper with the smiley and frowny faces that I was talking about earlier. This form tells me how you're doing, and it only takes about a minute. Can you give it a try?

Discussing ORS Results

In discussing results with a student, you could say, "From your ORS, it looks like you're experiencing some real problems," "Your total score is 15. Things must be pretty tough for you. What's going on?" or "From your score, it looks like you're doing okay. Why do you think you were referred for counseling?"

In discussing a particular scale, you could say, "This mark on the Individual Scale tells me that you're really having a tough time. Would you like to tell me about it?" Alternatively, if all the marks are to the far right, you could say, "When people make their marks so far to the right like you did, it usually means things are going well for them. Is that true for you?"

In discussions with a teacher, an example is "Your rating of this client tells me you're quite concerned about her, especially in school and personal well-being.

Does this make sense with what you are thinking?" Another example is "Your rating on the CORS is 34, which indicates that this child is doing well overall but that you have some concern with the client's school performance or behavior. Is that true?"

In many cases, counselors need to help clients (a) connect their experience with their ORS marks and (b) consider what needs to happen to make things better.

To a Student:

I need your help to understand what this mark [pointing to a mark on one of the ORS scales] means in your life. Does the stress from missing your older brother [or from your relationship with your father, from anxiety about taking tests, etc.] explain your mark on this Individual [or other] scale? What needs to happen for that mark to move just a little to the right?

To a teacher:

It sounds like talking out in class and then talking back to you when you correct him are your biggest concerns about William. Are those the things that explain your mark of 2.4 on the School scale? Is there anything else that accounts for your mark on the School scale? What would need to happen for your mark to move 1 or 2 centimeters to the right?

Introducing the SRS (or Child Session Rating Scale/Young Child Session Rating Scale) at the First Meeting

To a parent, teacher, or older client:

Let's take a minute here and fill out a form that asks your opinion about our work together. It's like taking the temperature of our meeting today. Your feedback will help me stay on track and be useful to you. Will you help me by filling out the form?

To a younger client:

Before we wrap up, I want to ask you to fill out another form that has faces on it. This one deals with how you think I am doing. That's right—you get to grade me! Can you help me out with this?

Discussing SRS Results

When SRS results are uniformly high (9 or above in each category), the practitioner can simply acknowledge this and invite any other comments or suggestions from the client. Since people tend to rate alliance measures highly, the practitioner should address any hint of a problem on the SRS. Anything less than a total score of 36 (or under 9 in any area) may signal a concern and warrant discussion.

Okay, these marks are way over here to the right, which suggests that we're on the same page, that we are talking about things that are important to you, and that today's meeting was right for you. Please let me know if I get off track at any point during our work together, okay?

Let me see how you think we are doing. Okay, it seems like I am missing the boat somewhere here. Thanks for being honest and giving me a chance to change things to make it work better for you. Was there something else I should have asked about or done to make this meeting better for you? What was missing here?

The counselor's nondefensive acceptance of alliance problems and willingness to make adjustments speak volumes to the client and usually turn things around quickly. The best practitioners are those who elicit and candidly discuss alliance problems when warranted. The SRS provides a practical and systematic way to address alliance problems right when they occur instead of waiting until things reach the point of no return—when the client shuts down or drops out.

Later Meetings

Each meeting compares the current ORS with previous ratings. ORS scores serve as discussion prompts to engage clients in discussing their progress and future plans. When scores increase even just a little, practitioners should give clients credit for the change and explore their role in it, as well as using other methods to empower progress.

To a student:

Wow, your marks on the personal well-being and overall lines moved about 4 centimeters to the right! Your total increased by 8 points. That's quite a jump! How did you pull that off?

To a teacher:

Okay, your rating of Maria improved to a 24, which is 4 points higher than it was at our last meeting. What have you done differently to make things better with Maria? Did you learn anything new about yourself or Maria during this? Where do you think we should go from here?

When scores take a big dive or lower scores remain unchanged, we need to discuss what to do differently to improve the situation.

Okay, so things haven't changed since the last time we talked. What do you make of that? Should we be doing something different here, or should we just hang in there and see if things change next week?

When ORS or SRS ratings remain low across two or more consecutive counseling sessions, we can initiate a discussion along the following lines:

[Responding to consecutively low ORS scores] These scores suggest that we need to try something pretty different to make things better. What could you do that might be different enough to make a difference?

[Responding to consecutively low SRS scores] These scores haven't changed for the past 3 weeks. If our meetings aren't helping, I wonder what we can do to shake things up and try something different, even if that means switching to another counselor who might be more effective with you. What do you think?

Closing Comments and Reminders

Integrating the ORS and SRS into everyday practice has been shown to double the effectiveness of practitioners in some settings. Partnering with clients gives them an active voice in counseling and ensures more accountable services. Since clients often drop out before discussing alliance problems, the SRS provides opportunities to remedy problems before it's too late. Given these benefits, outcome management may be the most effective and accountable way to conduct and evaluate counseling services in schools.

No counselor is effective with every student, parent, or teacher. Outcome management is most beneficial with clients who are not benefiting from our services, because it prompts us to make adjustments instead of plowing forward in our ineffectiveness. The best thing we can do for our clients is to be useful and effective. Outcome management helps us do just that. Refer to Murphy and Duncan (2007) for additional information about outcome management in schools.

Solution Identification Scale and Quick Survey

This appendix consists of two instruments: (a) Solution Identification Scale (Kral, 1988) and (b) Quick Survey.

Solution Identification Scale

Name: _____ Date: _____ Rated by:_____

Please answer all questions. Beside each item, indicate the degree to which it occurs.

		Not at all	*Just a little*	*Pretty much*	*Very much*
1	Respectful to grown ups				
2	Able to make/keep friends				
3	Controls excitement				
4	Cooperates with ideas of others				
5	Demonstrates ability to learn				
6	Adapts to new situations				
7	Tells the truth				
8	Comfortable in new situations				
9	Well behaved for age				
10	Shows honesty				
11	Obeys adults				
12	Handles stress well				
13	Completes what is started				
14	Considerate to others				
15	Shows maturity for age				

(Continued on next page)

Solution Identification Scale *(Continued)*

		Not at all	Just a little	Pretty much	Very much
16	Maintains attention				
17	Reacts with proper mood				
18	Follows basic rules				
19	Settles disagreements peacefully				
20	Gets along with brothers/sisters				
21	Copes with frustration				
22	Respects rights of others				
23	Basically is happy				
24	Shows good appetite				
25	Sleeps OK for age				
26	Feels part of the family				
27	Stands up for self				
28	Is physically healthy				
29	Can wait for attention/rewards				
30	Tolerates criticism well				
31	Can share the attention of adults				
32	Is accepted by peers				
33	Shows leadership				
34	Demonstrates a sense of fair play				
35	Copes with distractions				
36	Accepts blame for own mistakes				
37	Cooperates with adults				
38	Accepts praise well				
39	Able to "think" before acting				

40 COMMENTS:

Quick Survey

Student: _____ Grade: _____ Date: _____

Teacher: _____

The following questions will help me learn more about situations in which the student does better in your class. This information might help us improve things by building on something that the student is already doing successfully.

1. Please list *anything* the student is currently doing, or has done, to succeed in your class. List it even if it rarely occurs.

    _____
    _____
    _____
    _____

2. Describe specific times and situations when the student has done a little (or a lot) better than usual in your class.

    _____
    _____
    _____
    _____

3. Based on the above information, what can we build on to improve the student's success in your class?

    _____
    _____
    _____
    _____

4. What else is important for me to consider in helping you and the student?

    _____
    _____
    _____
    _____

Thank You For Your Cooperation.

Note. Reproduced with permission of the Brief Family Therapy Center.

Documents to Help Students Clarify and Maintain Improvements

Document 1

The Consultant Club

This is to recognize

[Student's Name]

as an Official Member of the Consultant Club.

The Consultant Club consists of heroic students who have made important changes in school performance, and who are willing to serve as a consultant to [School Counselor's name] for advice on helping other students make changes.

_____, Consultant
Student's Name

_____, Club President
School Counselor

Document 2

The Behavior Change Award

This award goes to

[Student's Name]

for making important, difficult changes in school behavior.

_____, School Principal

_____, School Counselor

Document 3

The Courage Award

In recognition of

[Student's Name]

for having the courage to make difficult, important changes in
order to reach future career and life goals, and for remembering
that any change worth making involves some bumps and
slips along the way.

_____, School Counselor

Document 4

<u>Letter One</u>

Dear _____,

Congratulations on the recent changes you have made in your school work and behavior. I know that changes like this are hard work. It takes courage to keep on plugging instead of giving up when things get tough.

I'm glad to hear that your teachers are treating you better. I guess it's hard to get on someone's case when they are polite in class and earning Bs and Cs instead of Ds and Fs.

I am very curious about what you have done to bring your grades up, and what it will take to continue. The best ideas and suggestions that I have heard for helping students have come from students themselves— people like you who have made important and difficult improvements. Your ideas and advice will help me to help other students who are struggling in school like you used to do before you changed. It is cool that you can be a hero for them by sharing your ideas with me.

Congratulations again on your victory over this problem. I look forward to meeting next week, and I can't wait to hear your ideas for other students.

Sincerely,

School Counselor

Document 5

Letter Two

Dear _____,

Wow! You did it. You really stood up to this problem and showed it who's the boss. As you know, I get real interested in how people make the kind of changes that you have made during the past couple weeks. It inspires me, and it gives me ideas for helping other students.

I would like to meet with you to celebrate your success and to learn more about how you did it. Please be thinking about what you have done to make things better, and what you are planning to do to keep things moving in the right direction. I will contact you next week to set up a time when we can meet to discuss this.

Congratulations!

Sincerely,

School Counselor

Document 6

Letter Three

Dear _____,

Thank you for having the courage to discuss things at school. I was impressed by your honesty and your ability to talk about things that are important to you.

I know you value your freedom and want to protect it. This will take some hard work, because other people will say and do things that "push your buttons" and tempt you to act in ways that get you in trouble and steal your freedom. It was very interesting to hear how you were able to hold your freedom and resist the urge to go off on that girl who bumped your shoulder a couple weeks ago at school. I wonder what it would take to do that more often?

In the coming weeks, maybe you could keep track of your other victories over urges that push you into trouble and rob your freedom. I look forward to working together on helping you act in ways that move you closer to the life of freedom that you want.

Sincerely,

School Counselor

Tasks of Solution-Focused Counseling

1. *Establish Cooperative, Change-Focused Relationships*
   - Adopt the ambassador mind-set, and approach clients with humility and respect.
   - Look, listen, learn, and validate clients.
   - Compliment clients to boost their self-efficacy and hope.
   - Use change-focused language of empowerment, qualification, and presupposition.
   - Accomodate the client's theory of change by exploring prior solutions, client beliefs, and client preferences. Accommodate interventions to the client's theory.
   - Obtain client feedback on outcome and alliance, and adjust services accordingly.
2. *Clarify the Problem and Related Details*
   - Define a specific, changeable problem.
   - Explore related details, including how the situation is a problem, prior solution attempts, the client's theory, and how counseling can help.
3. *Develop Goals*
   - Use scaling or miracle questions to invite clients to focus on a better future and to describe the small steps in that direction.
   - Formulate goals that are significant, specific, small, start based, and self-manageable.
4. *Build on Exceptions and Other Resources*
   - Identify and build on exceptions to the problem.
   - Identify and build on other resources in the client's life.
5. *Invite Clients to Change the Doing or Viewing of the Problem*
   - In changing the doing, encourage clients to do something differently in their performance of or response to the problem.
   - In changing the viewing, suggest different interpretations of the problem.
   - Evaluate progress by using client-based scaling, paper-and-pencil measures, permanent products, and single-case evaluation designs.
   - Empower progress by giving clients credit, clarifying the personal and social impact of changes, asking their advice for others, preparing for relapses, and using documents.

6. *Terminate Counseling*
   - Approach every session as the last.
   - Use goals as guidelines, and terminate when clients are on track.
   - Leave the door open for follow-up contacts.

Format for First and Later Sessions

Format for First Session

Note. These steps should be flexibly applied and may vary depending on the client and the circumstances.

Orient Client: Use small talk to set client at ease; explain desire to be useful and importance of client feedback.

Problem and Related Details: Define client concerns in videotalk using Outcome Rating Scale (ORS) or other questions; explore related details ("How is it a problem?" "What is your theory about the problem/solution?" "What's been tried, and was it helpful?" "How can I help?").

Goals (5-S Guideline): Use scaling (ORS or other scaling strategies) or miracle question to develop goals that are significant, specific, small, start based, and self-manageable.

Exceptions and Other Resources: Exceptions ("When doesn't the problem happen?" "What's different about those times?" "What will it take to do more of it?"); other resources (explore client's ideas about solutions, resilience, hobbies, heroes, and social supports; how can resources help client with current concern?).

Can Intervention Be Developed From Exceptions or Other Resources?
_____ Yes _____ No
If yes, collaborate with client on intervention that utilizes exceptions and/or other resources. If no, move to next step.

(As Needed) Change the Doing/Viewing of the Problem: Change the doing by suggesting the Do Something Different Task and anything else that alters the problem pattern; change the viewing by offering a different interpretation of the problem.

Wrap-Up: Compliment client on positive attributes/actions, attempts to make things better, and other relevant assets; review interventions and future plans; address any questions or comments from client; administer and discuss the Session Rating Scale; thank client for cooperation and input; schedule next meeting.

Format for Second (and Later) Sessions

Note. These steps should be flexibly applied and may vary depending on the client and the circumstances.

Review Progress: Use scaling (ORS or other scaling strategies) to assess the client's perception of progress and compare it to previous reports.

When Client Reports Improvement: Ask for client's theory ("How do you explain this?"), compliment and credit the client ("Very impressive. How did you figure out what to do?"); explore exceptions ("What was different about this week that made things better?"); empower progress ("How is life different at school since making these changes?" "What's different about the 'new you' compared to the 'old you'"?).

When Client Reports No Change (or Slip): Ask for client's theory ("What do you make of that? Should we try something different or hang in there and see if things change next week?"); normalize and validate ("Sometimes things get worse before they get better"); ask coping questions ("How have you kept things from getting worse? Where do you find the strength to keep trying?"), explore exceptions/other resources ("As bad as it was, was there anything that went well at school this week? What have you thought about doing but haven't done yet? How can we rally your support team to help turn things around?" "Is there anything you've learned from all this that might help you in the future?").

Can Intervention Be Developed From Exceptions or Other Resources?
_____ Yes _____ No

If yes, collaborate with client on intervention that utilizes exceptions and/or other resources. If no, move to next step.

(As Needed) Change the Doing/Viewing of the Problem: Change the doing by suggesting the Do Something Different Task and anything else that alters the problem pattern; change the viewing by offering a different interpretation of the problem.

Wrap-Up: Compliment client on positive attributes/actions, attempts to make things better, and other relevant assets; review interventions and future plans; address any questions or comments from client; administer and discuss the Session Rating Scale; thank client for cooperation and input; schedule next meeting or terminate services on the basis of client progress and input ("How will we know when to quit?")

Solution-Focused Items for Referral Forms

Items From Teacher Referral Form

What does the student do that you would like to see continue?
What is the student good at?
What does the student like to do in his or her free time?
Who helps the student most when he or she has a problem?
Of all the people in the student's life, whom does he or she respect the most?
What special interests, talents, or hobbies does the student have?
Describe a recent situation in which the problem usually occurs but was absent or less intense.
What was different about that situation? What did you or the student do differently? What will it take for that to happen more often in the future?
What do you think would improve things at school?

Items From Parent Referral Form

What is your child good at?
What does your child like to do in his or her free time?
Who helps your child most when he or she has a problem?
Of all the people in your child's life, whom does he or she respect the most?
What are your child's biggest interests and talents?
What does your child have trouble with?
What do you do when your child misbehaves at home, and how does it work?
What do you do when your child behaves well at home, and how does it work?
What needs to change at your child's school that would help with his or her behavior?
What else do you want us to know to help us work with your child at school?

Items From Student Referral Form

These are based on student interview or completed independently by the student.

What do you want to continue happening at school?
Who helps you most when you have a problem at school?
Of all the people in your life, whom do you admire and respect the most? What do they do that is helpful to you?

What do you like to do when you're not at school?

When does the problem not happen? What is different about those times? What will it take to do more of that?

What could we do to make school better for you?

Is there anything else we need to know in order to help you?

Instructions for Self-Modeling

1. *Videotape the student (S) performing desired behavior.* You may need to videotape a few different times to get enough behavior. You can also prompt S to perform the targeted behaviors if they are not occurring enough on their own. The purpose is to get the appropriate behaviors on tape, prompted or otherwise.

2. *Edit out inappropriate behaviors to create one or two videotapes of positive-only behavior (2–3 minutes per tape).* The editing does not have to be perfect. Small gaps between different episodes of positive behavior are no problem.

3. *View the tape with S four or five times over a 2-week period.* There are two ways to do this: (a) You can simply sit with S and watch the tape, redirecting S's attention to the tape as needed, or (b) you can make occasional comments during the viewing session (e.g., "Wow, you're really working hard there"), as well as briefly following up on the session with a few comments or questions aimed at empowering desired behavior (e.g., "How did you manage to pay attention so well and keep working?").

4. *Measure changes in desired behavior.* Pick selected times at school to observe and measure the desired behavior. Compare levels of behavior before and after beginning the self-modeling viewing sessions. Ask for S's perceptions of change (e.g., "How is school different for you now?").

Index

Boxes, figures, and tables are indicated by "b," "f," and "t" following the page number.